THE CANADIAN GENERAL ELECTION OF 1993

A CARLETON CONTEMPORARY

THE CANADIAN GENERAL ELECTION OF 1993

By

ALAN FRIZZELL

JON H. PAMMETT

ANTHONY WESTELL

CARLETON UNIVERSITY PRESS
OTTAWA
1994

Printed and bound in Canada
A Carleton Contemporary

Canadian Cataloguing in Publication Data
The Canadian general election of 1993
(A Carleton Contemporary ; 13)
ISBN 0-88629-228-X

1. Canada. Parliament — Elections, 1993.
2. Canada — Politics and government — 1993 - .
3. Mass media — Political aspects — Canada.
I. Frizzell, Alan, 1947- . II. Pammett, Jon H.,
1944- . III. Westell, Anthony, 1926- .
IV. Series.

FC630.C367 1994 324.971'0648 C94-900186-4
F1034.2.C36 1994

Carleton University Press
160 Paterson Hall
Carleton University
1125 Colonel By Drive
Ottawa, Ontario
K1S 5B6
(613) 788-3740

Distributed in Canada by:

Oxford University Press Canada
70 Wynford Drive
Don Mills, Ontario
M3C 1J9
(416) 441-2941

Cover Design: Aerographics

Interior: Xpressive Designs – typset in 10/13 Stone Serif and Stone Sans

Acknowledgements

Carleton University Press acknowledges the support extended to its publishing programme by the Canada Council and the Ontario Arts Council.

The Press would also like to thank the Department of Communications, Government of Canada, and the Government of Ontario through the Ministry of Culture, Tourism and Recreation, for their assistance.

TABLE OF CONTENTS

THE CONTRIBUTORS

KEITH ARCHER is Associate Professor of Political Science at the University of Calgary. He has written extensively on voting and political parties, and is completing a book on the New Democratic Party with Alan Whitehorn.

ANDRÉ BERNARD is Professor of Political Science at l'Université du Québec à Montreal. He is author of many books, including *What Does Quebec Want?, Option Quebec, 1968-1988, Politique et gestion des finances publiques: Quebec et Canada,* and *Problemes politiques: Quebec et Canada.*

STEPHEN CLARKSON is Professor of Political Science at the University of Toronto, author of *Canada and the Reagan Challenge* and co-author of *Trudeau and Our Times.*

FARON ELLIS is a doctoral candidate at the University of Calgary, and is working on a dissertation involving the Reform Party. He has published in the *Canadian Journal of Political Science.*

LAWRENCE LEDUC is Professor of Political Science at the University of Toronto. He is co-author of *Political Choice in Canada* and *Absent Mandate,* and has written numerous articles on Canadian and comparative voting behaviour.

LIONEL LUMB is Associate Professor of Journalism at Carleton University. He wrote for the Calcutta *Statesman,* Reuters in London, and *The Scotsman,* Edinburgh. He has worked in television since 1968, with BBC Television News in London, and in Canada as a news and documentary producer for CTV, Global, and CBC.

ALAN WHITEHORN is Professor of Political Science at the Royal Military College in Kingston, Ontario. He is author of *Canadian Socialism* and the forthcoming *Canadian Trade Unions and the NDP* and *The NDP in Convention.*

PETER WOOLSTENCROFT is Associate Professor of Political Science at the University of Waterloo. He has published articles on the selection of party leaders in Canada, the politics of education, electoral geography, and the spatial bases of urban politics.

PREFACE

This is the third in a series of Canadian election studies, and we plan to publish a volume after each federal election. The goal is to provide a concise, readable, and yet analytical account of the election, and the method is to blend journalism and social science.

The editors for this study are Alan Frizzell and Anthony Westell, both from the School of Journalism at Carleton University, and Jon Pammett from the Department of Political Science. In addition, other political scientists have contributed chapters on the parties' campaign organizations and strategies, and on the leaders' debates. The editors wish to thank Stephen Clarkson, Peter Woolstencroft, Alan Whitehorn, Keith Archer, Faron Ellis, André Bernard and Lawrence LeDuc. On the journalistic side, Lionel Lumb contributes an analysis of the television coverage of the 1993 campaign. Biographies of all the contributors appear at the end of the book. For research assistance, we wish to thank Jason Young, Lise Ballantyne and especially Heather Pyman, Senior Researcher at the Carleton University Survey Centre. Finally, our thanks to the Chief Electoral Officer Jean-Pierre Kingsley and his staff, for providing the data in the appendix to this volume.

Ottawa
April, 1994.

Alan Frizzell
Jon H. Pammett
Anthony Westell

CHAPTER 1

INTRODUCTION

BY THE EDITORS

The 1993 election can in one sense be interpreted as a revolution in Canadian politics. Of those who had voted in the previous election, over half switched to a different party, a massive swing. More important, many of the volatile voters switched from traditional parties to new parties. The Progressive Conservative party, with a history going back to Confederation and before, was not merely thrown out of office, but almost out of the House of Commons. The New Democratic Party, sometimes called the conscience of Canada, was so badly mauled that it may never recover. The Liberal victors now face many of the same problems that destroyed the Conservative government, plus new Opposition parties in the Commons armed with the enthusiasm of the young, the confidence of the inexperienced, and the credibility of those who have not been tested by responsibility.

On closer examination, the election of 1993 appears less revolutionary. The Liberals are back in power, with a majority government, as they have been for much of this century. The newly emergent parties represent the old realities of Western protest and Quebec nationalism. Regional consciousness and perceptions of the unequal distributions of the costs and benefits of federalism have been perennial findings of studies of Canadian public opinion.[1] The same studies have demonstrated the negativism shown by many Canadians toward politicians of all stripes. All of these components of public opinion have been present for a long time, but they have not always been prime motivators of behaviour in federal elections. In 1993, voters took advantage of the new alternative parties to express some of these attitudes.

The degree to which the public turned away from the previous Conservative government was unprecedented. In part, this was due to the ill-advised campaign waged by the party. However, bad election campaigns run by governing parties are not unknown in Canada. In some ways the Conservative campaign of 1993 resembled the Liberal campaign of 1984. In both cases, the party had changed the leader shortly before calling the election, in an attempt to put a new face on the party. Both went into campaigns based on images of novelty without substantive policy programmes. Both ran into organizational difficulties through the lack of experience of their headstrong leaders. Both lost badly.

The extent of Conservative losses was a function of several factors. The party was faced with three strong opponents, each with support in particular regions of the country. The Liberals were the natural party for the electorate to turn to in Ontario and the Maritimes. Reform joined the Liberals as an anti-government voice in the West. The Tories' Quebec support crumbled before the Bloc Québécois. The issue agenda was set by these other parties, not by the Conservatives; the Liberals achieved credibility on job creation, Reform on budget cutting, and the Bloc on both economic issues and Quebec representation. The party leader stumbled badly during the campaign. In the end, most voters just did not see any good reasons to vote Conservative.

In some countries, a party on the ropes can be saved from disaster by the residual loyalties of its supporters, who will back it in unfavourable circumstances out of ideological conviction or traditional feelings of identification. Canada does not display this general pattern of public attachment to parties. While there are certainly some people who stick with 'their party' through thick and thin, the majority of the electorate is quite *flexible* in its link to the party it feels closest to at the moment. Attitudes toward parties are changeable, partly because of the amount of cynicism which exists toward politicians, and partly because Canadian political parties do not have distinguishable social bases of support. Rather than representing particular classes, religions, languages, or other interests, they act like brokers, trying to put together new electoral coalitions each time the country goes to the polls. As a result, most Canadian voters make up their minds according to their evaluations of the short term factors operative at election time, or in the recent past. In 1993, these factors centred around the sputtering economy and recent experiments with constitutional reform. In neither case could Canadians find much reason to go on voting for the Conseratives.

THE ECONOMY

The single most important factor in the election, without doubt, was the state of the economy. Growth slowed in 1989, and the economy shrank for four quarters in 1990-91. Unemployment rose as corporations went bankrupt, "downsized" to cut costs, or moved to the United States. The recovery in 1991-2 was so hesitant as to be barely noticeable, and by the election of 1993 was not widely felt. The U.S. and other developed countries had similar problems, and a recession caused by a turn down in the business cycle was compounded by fundamental restructuring of the global economy in which Canada is a cog turned by larger cogs. The informed debate in Canada was about whether the government's policy initiatives had made a bad situation worse or bravely set the country on the road to a brighter future. The popular view was that free trade with the US, the replacement of a hidden tax at the manufacturing level with a highly visible and irritating tax on goods and services (the GST), and the

Bank of Canada's relentless pursuit of zero inflation were responsible for the recession. The Tory government was therefore the villain for all sorts of reasons, and the solution to economic problems was to remove it from power as soon as possible, or sooner.

It is worth noting that economic difficulties – causing real hardship for some and a loss of confidence for most – unsettled governments in many democracies. For example, Prime Minister Margaret Thatcher was dumped by her own party seeking a kinder and gentler leader, and President George Bush's defeat ended Republican rule in the United States. In Canada, NDP governments won power in three provinces – Ontario, Saskatchewan and British Columbia – but quickly disillusioned their followers when social democrats proved to have no better solutions than their liberal democratic predecessors. This failure was one reason why voters who supported the NDP in the 1988 federal election switched heavily to other parties in 1993, including to Reform and its right-wing populism.

Free trade with the US was the dominant issue in 1988 and continued to be highly controversial after that election. Liberals, social democrats, trade unions, nationalist groups and others blamed this policy for the sharp decline in manufacturing which wiped out thousands of skilled and semi-skilled jobs – the kind of jobs which had raised many blue-collar families into the middle class. Free trade was again on the agenda in 1993, this time in the form of a treaty negotiated by the Conservative government to join Canada, the US and Mexico in a North American free trade area. It was opposed by the Liberal and New Democratic parties in the Commons, and a new party – the National Party of Canada – was formed in part to fight it in the election. The founding leader of the National Party, Mel Hurtig, was for years a leading spokesman for nationalist causes, and he raised large sums of money and recruited candidates across the country. However, he was excluded from the televised leaders' debates because of the party's lack of any Commons representation and its poor standing in the opinion polls, thus denying this party a chance to establish its legitimacy by appearing before a vast audience on an equal footing with leaders of the traditional parties. In 1993 the free trade issue never caught fire during the campaign, and the National Party sank almost without trace, obtaining only a tiny percentage of the vote. Soon after the election, the Liberal government accepted NAFTA with only cosmetic changes.

The 1993 economic issues focussed on jobs and the reduction of the deficit. On neither of these did the Conservatives have a lot of credibility. Employment had supposedly been a priority for the Government ever since Mulroney proclaimed "jobs, jobs, jobs" as the sole issue of the 1984 election which brought them to power. The public saw little evidence that Conservative policies, whether the Free Trade Agreement or anything else, had improved or even held steady the job situation. Similarly, Finance Ministers Wilson and Mazankowski had identified the reduction of the budget deficit as a goal for the last nine years, and had introduced a series of spending cuts and tax increases designed to bring this about. The result was a higher deficit. When Prime Minister Campbell claimed lack of knowledge of this during the election campaign, the field on this issue was yielded to the other parties.

From Accord to Discord

A second major factor undermining the Conservative government was the failure of its constitutional initiatives, which had enormous and unforseen consequences in federal politics. Prime Minister Mulroney seemed to have triumphed in 1987 when he persuaded the provincial premiers, meeting at Meech Lake near Ottawa, to agree on a package of reforms which met Quebec's minimum requirements for a settlement of its problems with Confederation. But by 1990 the controversial deal had unravelled, and along with it went a sag in Conservative support in Quebec, a keystone in the national coalition which had elected Conservative governments in 1984 and 1988.

Mulroney tried again and this time brought all governments, including the Liberal government in Quebec, to approve a new and more extensive set of constitutional changes. This was submitted to the people in a referendum in 1992, supported by the Liberal and New Democratic parties, most of the major news media, and the leaders of business and labour – in other words, by the Canadian Establishment. It was opposed by the Bloc and the Reform party – and, as it turned out, by a majority of the people voting in the referendum. Analyses of referendum voting show that no single factor determined the outcome, and that the important influences varied from region to region.[2] However, key to the defeat was negative public reaction outside Quebec to two proposed clauses involving that province, its designation as a "distinct society" and its guarantee of a quarter of the membership of the House of Commons in perpetuity. Going along with the substance of the Charlottetown Agreement as reasons for its defeat was the electorate's negative verdict on Mulroney himself. The electorate used the constitutional referendum as an opportunity to express its displeasure with Mulroney's personality as well as his policies.

The referendum was widely interpreted as a populist rising against elites, as well as another blow to the Conservative government. It was a blow also to the NDP which, by supporting the deal, had placed itself on the side of the Establishment, leaving Reform as the voice of protest in the West. The news media were shocked to discover that they were out of touch with readers and viewers, and this caused them to rethink the way they would cover the coming election.

The economy and the constitutional failures were two obvious causes of the Conservatives' problems, but there were others. The government was accused by the political left of slashing spending in a neo-conservative fashion, and by the right of running enormous budget deficits. Prime Minister Mulroney came to lack the credibility to reply effectively. His style and personality seemed increasingly to grate on Canadian nerves, and getting rid of him became almost an obsession with large numbers of voters. There was a general sigh of relief, shared by many of his own party, when he announced in February 1993 that he would retire when another leader had been chosen. The Conservative party now saw a chance to win a third election in a row if it could just find an attractive new leader with new ideas who cause voters to forget the past.

The leader they came up with was certainly different, and initially attractive, a relatively young and politically inexperienced woman from Vancouver. But the results suggest that Kim Campbell was in fact the wrong choice, too inexperienced (and too arrogant to take instruction) to fight and win what was bound to be a difficult election against a veteran opponent. Some Conservatives complain that she was unfairly treated by the news media, and our analysis of newspaper coverage lends that idea some support. But the truth was that the government's unpopularity was so widespread and deep-seated, and the election campaign so inept, that not even the most favourable coverage could have changed the result.

IMPLICATIONS OF THE ELECTION RESULTS

Before the election was called, there were notions that this would be a different kind of electoral contest. Party strategists, the media, and even some politicians felt that in the post-Meech, post-Charlottetown era, a new type of campaign would emerge. Politicians and ordinary citizens would be brought closer together through technology; the media would incorporate ordinary Canadians into their coverage to an unprecedented extent. The focus would be taken off the leaders' tours, and the parties would not be able to unilaterally set the agenda. The need to represent change, so visibly desired by voters, would permeate all aspects of the campaign. Some experiments in 'inclusive coverage' were tried, primarily by the television networks with their ' town hall meetings', but by and large the media covered the campaign as they had before. It seems doubtful if the 1993 experience will lead to any variation in the ways future elections are presented to the people.

The implications for the party system of the existence of two new parties is a major question for the future. New parties have sprung up in Canada before, and withered almost as quickly, but the situation now may be different. The Bloc Québécois is not really new at all, in one sense. The sovereigntist movement has taken shape and substance in Quebec over the past quarter-century, but for tactical reasons has not been officially represented in the federal parliament. The Bloc is that overdue representation. Its future depends on the outcome of the struggle between federalists and sovereigntists in Quebec. But its immediate task is to help its parent, the Parti Québecois, win the 1994 provincial election by opposing the federal government and exposing the flaws it can find in the federal system. If the PQ wins power, a referendum on sovereignty will quickly follow, and the Bloc will be in the eye of the storm, the advocate in the Commons of Quebec's case for independence. In the event of the defeat of a referendum on independence, however, the party may disappear, leaving the way open for a potential Conservative revival under a new Quebec leader.

Whether the Reform party will expand to become more than a Western-based protest party remains to be seen. Reform picked up more than half its vote from former Conservative supporters, many of whom were unhappy with the Conservative leadership and its economic and constitutional policies. But Reform also won support because, as a party, it projected an attractive image to voters unhappy with the "old politics." Now is that it has replaced the Conservative party in the Commons, it has the potential to replace it as well as the voice of neo-conservative opinion. It won about 20% of the vote in Ontario, and a seat in the House of Commons from that province, which provides it with a potential take-off point. The fact that it has no presence in Quebec is both a strength and a weakness. It is a strength among those Canadians who are opposed to any constitutional concessions to Quebec. It is a weakness in Quebec itself where the future of federalism is likely to be the focus of politics for the upcoming period.

The future of the Liberal party could follow at least two scenarios. If there is no comeback by the Conservatives, and no breakthrough by Reform, the Liberals will be left as the only national party in Canada. Under this possibility, the party may establish itself in a hegemonic governmental position well into the next century. However, it may be a mistake to imagine that the election of a Liberal majority government will return the country to such stability. If the Liberals fall victim to the same forces which destroyed the Conservative government, the future may hold a splintered party system and a series of coalition governments. Forecasting at this point is pure alchemy, not an ability possessed by the editors. But we can say that the remaining years of the twentieth century will be momentous and uncertain ones for Canada.

NOTES

1 See, for example, Chapters 1-3 of Harold D. Clarke, Jane Jenson, Lawrence LeDuc and Jon H. Pammett, *Political Choice in Canada* (Toronto: McGraw-Hill Ryerson, 1979).

2 Lawrence LeDuc and Jon H. Pammett, "Referendum Voting: Attitudes and Behaviour in the 1992 Constitutional Referendum," *Canadian Journal of Political Science*, forthcoming.

CHAPTER 2

"*Doing Politics Differently*": *The Conservative Party and the Campaign of 1993*

PETER WOOLSTENCROFT

INTRODUCTION

The election of October 25 1993 produced the greatest defeat for any political party in Canadian history, both in terms of the number of seats lost and decline in popular vote. The vote for the Progressive Conservative party dropped from 43 percent in 1988 to 16 percent, and the number of seats from 169 to two. This debacle reflected the interplay between two factors. The first was the campaign waged by the PC party. Inept and incompetent were the commonplace judgments made by just about anybody who felt moved to comment on the campaign strategy and tactics. At the outset, the party was in a difficult but nonetheless competitive position, to the extent that the likely result of the election – majority or minority government, Liberal or Conservative – was far from settled. Toward the end, the party might have salvaged perhaps 20 to 40 seats, far fewer than had been hoped, but a result that would have given the Tories official party status in parliament, continued media presence, and a base on which to rebuild. But decisions made by party strategists almost eliminated even that hope.[1]

The second factor is the judgments made by Canadians about the kind of government they had been given by Prime Minister Brian Mulroney and the Progressive Conservative government from 1984 to 1993. Mulroney's government had introduced a number of far-reaching economic policies and constitutional initiatives: free trade with the United States; the pending North American Free Trade Agreement with the United States and Mexico; the Goods and Services Tax; and the failed Meech Lake and Charlottetown accords. Their effect in sum was intense public hostility. The protracted and deep economic recession which began in 1990 had contradicted the Tory promises during the 1984 and 1988 elections that their policies would produce economic prosperity. The effect on the party's electoral standing is simply stated. Throughout 1992, the Gallup Poll found that the Tory share of the committed vote ranged between 11 and 22 percent whereas the potential Liberal vote ranged between 36 and 49 percent, and seemed to be strengthening as the year closed. Even in

Quebec, Mulroney's home province, his party trailed both the Liberals and the Bloc Québécois throughout 1992. And the Prime Minister himself recorded low positive evaluations in polls.

Dismal poll figures were only part of the story. From 1984 to 1993, the Tory party had seen two components of its electoral coalition challenged by the emergence of two regionally oriented parties. The Reform Party, with its base and leadership in western Canada, and the Bloc Québécois, committed to sovereignty association for Quebec and running candidates only in that province, had very different agendas, but they shared the fact that much of their energy and many of their members came from the Tory party.[2] And the viability of Reform and the Bloc in different parts of the country also meant one other thing: Ontario, always pivotal because of its large number of parliamentary seats, would determine even more than usual the fate of the PC party, and it had been more ravaged by the economic contractions of the 1990s than by any other postwar recession. In the free trade election of 1988, Ontario had surprisingly given 46 of its 99 seats to the Conservatives, but the party would be hard-pressed to do as well in 1993.

THE LEADERSHIP CONVENTION

Tory activists' hearts beat a little faster on February 24, 1993 when Prime Minister Mulroney unexpectedly announced that he was not going to lead the Conservative party in the forthcoming election. Although there had been considerable speculation following the defeat of the Charlottetown Accord in October, 1992 that Mulroney might resign, as the New Year unfolded it appeared that he had decided to stay. Activists knew that the polls, public and private, had the Tories mired in the 'teens, far behind the Liberals, and there was little to suggest that fortunes would improve before the election. The announcement, then, that Mulroney would step down both surprised and heartened party members, who now could envisage a leadership convention and a new leader who could redefine the party and its image sufficiently to make it competitive, perhaps even strong enough to form a majority government.[3] The question was whether the Tories would emulate the Liberals' brilliant selection of Pierre Elliott Trudeau in 1968 or their disastrous choice of John Turner in 1984. The leadership campaign, to be capped by the selection of the new leader on June 13 in Ottawa, soon developed a surrealistic aura. Almost immediately after Mulroney's announcement, media interest and insider talk focused on Kim Campbell, who had been a prominent Minister of Justice and had recently been appointed Minister of Defence and Minister of Veterans Affairs. For many, Campbell was more than an attractive personality. Holding an urban riding in British Columbia meant that she represented a very different element of the party than did Mulroney. As a relatively young woman, purportedly bilingual, well-educated, highly intelligent, and verbally expressive, she seemed to represent the new kind of political leadership that Canadians were looking for, a "generation shift," as the trendy phrase of the day put it. Many in the Tory party were conscious of the fact that since 1968 Quebec had produced two long-serving prime ministers and thought it was in both the party's and the country's interest to have a prime minister with different roots and geographical identification. At the same time, since she had been a prominent supporter of the Charlottetown Accord, her credentials as one sympathetic to French Canada were well-established. Indicative of the burgeoning interest in Campbell was the occasion of an otherwise ordinary speaking appearance before a Conservative audience in Kitchener, Ont., shortly after Mulroney's announcement. Although the declaration of her candidacy was more than a week away, she attracted not just an unusually large contingent of Canadian media but international reporters as well. Highly credible putative contenders – most notably cabinet ministers Perrin Beatty, Michael Wilson, and Barbara McDougall from Ontario, Don Mazankowski from Alberta, and Bernard Valcourt from New Brunswick – surprised observers by announcing that they would not seek the leadership. MPs, cabinet ministers (including Beatty and Wilson), party organizers and workers were joining the surging support for Campbell so quickly and eagerly that talk of a coronation was pervasive. Some wondered about the necessity of having a convention at all. Joe Clark, a former party leader and prime minister, who had announced his retirement from politics in January, judged that the weight of support had moved so much in Campbell's direction that his candidacy would be ill-advised. Hugh Segal, long-term Tory activist and media commentator, found widespread interest in the party in electing a leader who would be Canada's first female prime minister, and decided not to be a candidate.

In the end, Campbell was challenged in the race by one cabinet colleague, Jean Charest, a young Quebec MP and Minister of the Environment. But it was widely reported that, given the apparent stampede to Campbell, he had been so reluctant to enter the fray that even Mulroney had to urge him to run. Three backbench MPs, Jim Edwards from Alberta, and Garth Turner and Patrick Boyer from Ontario, rounded out the field. The early assumption that Campbell would have an overwhelming victory was soon belied by her uncertain performances in the policy forums organized by the party across the country. Controversy about some of her comments in a *Vancouver Magazine* interview with journalist Peter Newman raised doubts about the sensitivity of her political antennae. Fears that her otherwise attractive expressiveness had a down side arose when she had to explain in detail the context of derogatory comments about apathetic Canadians, and also her remark that she had been confirmed as an Anglican at the age of 12 because of a "desire to ward off the demons of the papacy." Would she create political problems for herself and eventually the party by her spontaneous and apparently ill-considered comments?

Charest, adopting the motif of the tortoise, received excellent reviews for polished, apparently effortless appearances, and increasingly attracted delegates. Polls published before the convention indicated that Campbell's early popularity had shrunk, Charest now being the candidate most favoured by voters. But Campbell's supporters for the most part did not waver, reflecting the fact that many had been chosen as delegates and had made commitments to Campbell well before the ascension of Charest. Her convention organization, far superior to that of the other candidates, took advantage of slips by the Charest campaign in the last week of the race to firm up her support, despite her indifferent speech to the convention on the night prior to the voting. Nonetheless, what had been billed as a cake-walk for Campbell turned out to be a much more uncertain event, with Campbell securing victory over Charest on the second ballot of the convention by a margin of 1817 to 1630.

The convention contained two hints of future trouble, one public, one not so. The first was exemplified by Campbell's acceptance speech, which curiously contained only a perfunctory reference to the impact of Charest's campaign.[4] The second was that little thought had been given to the post-convention period. The focus of the Campbell organizers, understandably enough, had been on winning the convention, not on what would be required for an immediate run-up to an election. There was no transition team in place and this meant that the electoral strategy of the new prime minister and her government had to start at ground zero.[5]

The Conservative party, however, had been preparing, and even though attention had been distracted by its involvement in the Charlottetown Accord referendum, the election organization, for the most part, was in place by the time of Mulroney's retirement announcement. In November 1991, Mulroney appointed as campaign co-managers John Tory, a Toronto lawyer and long-term Conservative activist who had been involved in more than 20 national and provincial campaigns, and Pierre Blais, a cabinet minister from Quebec. They headed a National Campaign Preparedness Committee of 134 members, many of whom belonged to provincial and territorial campaign committees. A budget had been struck, many campaign managers had been recruited and trained, and most of the key personnel had been slotted into the campaign's organization chart. But many pre-election preparations were put on hold once the leadership race began, as the party had to devote its resources, including its head office staff, to mounting the convention. A number of party activists who had been placed in key positions joined campaigns of the leadership candidates. Therefore, election preparations, above and beyond such technical things as the development of the party's riding polling and direct mail programs, were at a standstill until after the convention.

The party was especially unprepared on policy. An elaborate national policy convention had been held in Toronto in 1991, and in 1992 a National Platform Planning Committee, the first in the party's history, had been established. Led by Marcel Côté, who had been a senior official in the Prime Minister's Office, it comprised a wide cross-section of parliamentarians and elected and appointed party officials. The committee's charge was to develop recommendations to the prime minister on an election platform, but it did not meet in the period between Mulroney's retirement announcement and the leadership convention. Prior to the election of the new leader, no significant work on policy had been done, other than summarizing the resolutions passed at the conference. Contrary to the impression given in an article by William Thorsell in *The Globe and Mail* there was no detailed policy platform awaiting Campbell.[6] The effect of this policy vacuum was ambiguous. Negatively, the party shortly would be fighting an election in which it would be challenged to defend the government's record and to specify its agenda for a number of pressing issues. Positively, Campbell, now prime minister, was not encumbered with a campaign platform built by others, and had latitude to define new policy directions. The force of her candidacy, above and beyond her personality, geographical base, gender, and generation, was the promise of "doing politics differently." But was there anything substantial driving this rhetoric?

PRE-ELECTION PREPARATIONS

Within two days of the convention, Campbell invited John Tory to serve as national campaign manager, and Allen Gregg, president of Decima Research and long-time pollster for the party, to serve as chief campaign strategist. Both accepted, with Tory stipulating that he must have full access to her as he had with Mulroney, and freedom to choose the best people for the campaign organization. Blais retained his title as national co-campaign manager but essentially was involved in the Quebec campaign preparations. Patrick Kinsella, an old friend of Campbell's from British Columbia, joined the senior team in June to travel with her on the campaign bus throughout the campaign. Tom Trbovich and Harry Near, senior party operatives, also served on the national team.

In her first two weeks as prime minister, Campbell was pre-occupied with restructuring the cabinet (a Mulroney suggestion) and appointing ministers. In early July there was a meeting of the G-7 countries in Japan. Except for one meeting of the cabinet, she paid little attention to election planning. Some soothing of convention bruises was apparent in Campbell's choice of Charest's campaign manager,Jodi White, as her Chief of Staff. But supporters of Charest and Campbell still vied for positions, especially in Quebec, which meant that Tory's freedom to choose people as he saw fit was constrained.

Campbell and her advisors were confronted with the question of whether the negative inheritance from Mulroney could be attenuated. Would it be possible to distance the new leader from the previous government, of which she had been one of its most visible members, so that a new electoral coalition could be formed? The post-war electoral record suggested that the prospects were daunting. Over 12 elections since 1953, no party had won three successive majority governments. And, although the party's standing in the polls had improved over the weeks since Mulroney's retirement announcement, there was still antipathy toward the Conservatives. Campbell's inclination was to stay in Ottawa over the summer and master the reins of government. But such passivity was not seen as being sufficiently dramatic to embody the spirit of "doing politics differently." The strategy adopted, primarily on the advice of Tory and Gregg, was to present the new prime minister as a person who was very different from her predecessor, both in personality and policy direction. Tory believed that the new leader and the new government had to establish markers that would sharply differentiate the new government from its predecessor. The emphasis was to be on hope and the future, with the new leader talking about jobs and economic development, the quality of life that Canadians enjoyed through their social programs, and the necessity of deficit reduction. The personality element of the strategy called for Campbell to meet people in a series of "soft" settings over the summer months. The second element was for Campbell to give a number of speeches in which new policy initiatives would be announced.

The personality element worked well. As Campbell went around the country attending Canada Day events, rodeos, ploughing matches, and barbecues, polls indicated that Canadians were increasingly interested in the new prime minister. Her accessibility and joie de vivre gave her an unusual political persona that seemed attractive to Canadians tired of, and disillusioned with, politicians. The policy element worked less well. By the end of August, Campbell had made only six policy speeches rather than the eight to 10 that had been deemed desirable. And the speeches, while generally well-received, reflected two constraints that were dominating discussions in the Political Operations committee which met four or five times between the swearing in of the new ministry and the dropping of the writ. This committee included senior cabinet ministers (Perrin Beatty, Bernard Valcourt, Doug Lewis, Lowell Murray, Charlie Mayer, Jim Edwards, Pierre Blais, Tom Siddon, and Gilles Loiselle) and a number of Campbell's closest advisors. Some were unhappy because dramatically new policy directions would imply criticism of the Mulroney government.Some, fearing a run on the Canadian dollar, cautioned against any suggestion of changes in fiscal and monetary policies. The committee never coalesced and focused its approach because many of its members were unaccustomed to being at the centre of the system and were concerned with their own election problems. Nor did the Prime Minister's Office require ministers to develop policy ideas that could form the basis of an election platform. So the party took the cautious route: "Doing politics differently" became "Staying the course."

Another constraint emanated from Quebec where the Bloc Québécois was threatening to erode a significant component of the electoral coalition that had produced the Conservative majorities in 1984 and 1988. Both ministers and political advisors were concerned that new policies could invite the Bloc to criticize "oppressive federalism" and build support for sovereignty association. Education exemplified the problem. Campbell,in Kitchener, Ontario, in August, spoke about initiatives such as distributing used government computers to school boards, and changing the Canada Student Loans Program. What she did not talk about were such things as national voluntary testing, the development of national standards, and working with the provinces to make it easier for students to move from jurisdiction to jurisdiction. Each of these had been ideas put on the policy table by both the Mulroney government and Campbell's policy advisors, but the decision was made not to talk about them, primarily because of the fear of how such nationally oriented initiatives would be interpreted in Quebec. A similar restraint was evident in Campbell's speech on social policy given in Quebec in late August.

Overall, however, by the end of August the strategy had worked reasonably well. The party was the beneficiary of a post-convention boost and seemed to have considerably strengthened its competitiveness. For example, the proportion of voters willing to consider voting Conservative had moved into the 70s from the low 50s. The party's surveys found a broadening of the political marketplace, indicating that Canadians were much more likely to say that Campbell would make a better prime minister than Jean Chrétien. Gallup in mid-August reported that Campbell's approval-disapproval ratio was greater than 2:1 while Chrétien's was 1:1.[7] And, on the party vote question, the Tories were within hailing distance of the Liberals, the Reform party's vote was moving in a narrow range, and the Bloc Québécois seemed to have plateaued. Only on policy issues had there been less improvement. On most issues, the Liberals were ahead of the Tories as the party best able to handle matters, except for those pertaining to economic management, a traditional area of Conservative strength. On attitudinal dimensions, such as "empathy" and "caring," traditional areas of Conservative weakness, the party was faring much better than it ordinarily did.

The decision was made to focus the campaign on the personality and attributes of Campbell. Speeches, announcements, questions and answers were to reflect the theme of hope built on expanding the economy and developing long-term jobs, maintaining social policies that defined what most Canadians perceived to be central to the quality of life, and reducing the deficit. At the last campaign college, held in late August, newly nominated candidates were informed that they should identify themselves as part of the Campbell team rather than as the Progressive Conservative candidate. Since the campaign was to emphasize that new times required a new approach, candidates were to avoid references to the previous government and stress that they were new to federal politics, that there was a new leader who had put into effect a number of changes that Canadians were seeking, and that they represented a new approach, real change, and a "different way of doing politics." Candidates whose ridings participated in the party's extensive riding research program were told that their literature and advertisements should be built on close identification with Campbell. The stress was to be on the "Campbell government" rather than the "Progressive Conservative government." The local candidate and Campbell should be described as the combination that best responded to Canadians' desire for change, because over half of voters thought that the Campbell government was "on the right track." Candidates were to talk about the fact that Campbell had downsized the Cabinet from 35 to 24, reduced the number of government departments from 32 to 23 and re-organized them in new thematic areas. She had cut ministerial budgets and committed herself to parliamentary reform in areas such as more free votes in the House of Commons, the opening up of the budget process, the reform of MPs' pensions and perks, and the reduction of the role of patronage in government appointments. However, it would be wrong to infer that party strategists approached the election as if it were a beauty contest: Tory and Gregg advised the cabinet in June and September that the leader and the party had to articulate her specific understanding of what was required in the areas of economic growth, quality of life, and deficit reduction. On the other hand, it was clear that the primary focus of the campaign was to be on the new leader, and not on the previous government's record, or on detailed (and presumably expensive) new policies.

While many Canadians were intrigued by Campbell's personality, their identification of her as an agent of real change was not strongly established. As Table 1 indicates, only about 10 percent of respondents in the party's polls in selected constituencies perceived Campbell as representing "real change," and the largest fraction did not see her as an agent of change at all. These findings suggested caution on the change issue, particularly because public opinion had been sounded when the other parties and leaders had not been in the forefront of media attention. Nor could there be certainty about the strength of the apparent interest in the new leader. Voters had not been required to compare leaders and parties carefully while they were in intense competition with each other.

Table 1
Perceptions of Campbell as Representing Change

Great Change	10%
Some Change	30%
No Change	40%
Don't Know	20%

Source: Generalized distribution of perceptions of Campbell and change in party's pre-election constituency polling studies.

When the writ was dropped the PC vote was at about 32 percent compared to the Liberals' 36 percent. But the capacity of the party to engage the Liberals effectively was limited by its organizational weaknesses. Given that the campaign's focus was on the leader, it was ironic, to say the least, that no leader-oriented literature was available until near the end of September, when camera-ready pamphlet designs were distributed for adaptation by local campaigns. Candidates at the first all-candidates meetings had to rely on brochures aimed at military and youth voters. Candidates seeking detailed policy materials had little with which to work, so they developed their literature and advertisements independently of the national campaign. When "Kim" paraphernalia finally arrived in the constituencies by the end of September, the possibility of "Campbellmania" had long disappeared.[8] The advice from Tory and Gregg that the campaign should be built on Campbell as representing the best choice for Canadians because of the party's commitment to jobs and economic expansion, maintaining the quality-of-life social programs, and deficit reduction was not followed with specific policy statements. While Campbell opened the campaign by mentioning these themes, her responses in unstructured situations, such as when questioned by the media, were less focused on "hope" and more on such esoteric concepts as economic restructuring and the urgency of deficit reduction. It is noteworthy that even in the training sessions for candidates in August debt reduction was given greater emphasis than the other two themes. But the problem with the stress on the deficit – and the particularly the commitment to eliminate it in five years – was that the party's record on the issue was, at best, suspect. While it was true that the deficit had declined as a proportion of Gross National Product from 8.7 percent in 1984-85 to 5.2 percent in 1992-93, there had been an enormous increase in the accumulated national debt, and there was no reason to believe that the 1993 figures would show improvement. The obvious difficulty was the party's credibility: "Given what you say you will do to eliminate the deficit in five years, why haven't you already done these things?" The hope was that the Liberals' low credibility on the deficit, combined with fears that Reform's plan to eliminate the deficit in three years would radically cut into social programs, would mean that voters might still be attracted to the middle road offered by the Conservatives.

THE CAMPAIGN

The campaign can be broken down into four stages, reflecting both major events and shifts in patterns of voter support found in the party's national polling and in selected constituencies.[9]

Stage One: the first 10 days, from September 9 until the weekend of September 18 and 19. The party's voting strength was more or less stable at 32 percent. This suggested a minority Liberal government, although the number of seats available to the Tories was problematic given that its vote was distributed evenly across the country. Campbell's first forays were marked by media probing about unemployment and economic growth, and were not overwhelmingly successful. Media interest was so intense that she had to address the specific issue of jobs in a speech in Brockville just two days after the campaign's kickoff.

Stage Two: from the last part of September until the debates on the first weekend of October. The Liberals had surprised Conservative organizers by releasing early in the campaign their platform in the form of the visible and photogenic Red Book, *Creating Opportunity*. The Conservatives, expecting that their opponents would follow the traditional mode of releasing components of their platform over the course of the election, had nothing with which to respond. One reason for not having a national brochure had been that it would necessarily refer to the Mulroney government's record and force Campbell to debate policies that the Tories thought desirable but unpalatable. Another reason was that it was surmised that Canadians were tired of politicians promising spending programs. In this instance "doing politics differently" meant not having a long catalogue of expensive promises. Instead, the leader would talk about the campaign's three themes, not in the traditional speech format, but in informal question-and-answer sessions, with Campbell sitting in the midst of the crowd, listening and taking notes. Forced to abandon these plans, the Tories hurriedly prepared their version of a national campaign book, which appeared near the end of September, with the title of "A Taxpayer's Agenda."

This stage of the campaign was marked also by controversy about Campbell's comments on September 23 on social policy. Responding to questions arising from media reports that government departments were preparing background papers on ways to restructure social policy, Campbell said that "an election is no time to talk about social policy."[10] This comment was a surprise to her advisors; their advice had been to make the point that bureaucrats are constantly writing reports that are not necessarily adopted as government policy, and no social policy decisions had been made by cabinet. Her explanation two days later of what she had meant to say did not stop the deepening of the decline in the party's support. A drop in popularity had been presaged by declines in the proportion of respondents giving the party high marks for "honesty," "specificity," and "talking about issues," and by the end of September, the party stood at 23 percent. The perception of unpreparedness evident in the first stage of the campaign was reinforced by Campbell herself, who in interviews with the media, most notably *The Globe and Mail*, did not seem to comprehend the documents she was using to make her case, especially in the area of deficit reduction.[11]

Stage Three: from the debates of October 3 and 4 to October 14. This part of the campaign began with the two debates. Gregg and Tory advised Campbell that the drop in the party's strength necessitated a much clearer articulation and definition of the three themes of jobs and economic development, quality of life, and deficit reduction, but her speeches lacked the specificity of the Liberal Red Book. Tory organizers pinned much of their hopes on the debates, expecting that Campbell would outshine Chrétien, especially in the English-language debate. But, in addition to the lack of specific policies, there was another flaw. Party organizers wanted Campbell to participate in a number of practice debates with stand-ins for the other party leaders. Not only would she be acclimatized to the debate format, but negative and distracting mannerisms and speech habits would be corrected. Campbell refused, preferring to sit with others around a table responding to questions.[12] This failure to prepare fully proved fatal. Chrétien was calm, direct, and focused, whereas Campbell, embroiled in arguments, appeared otherwise: her finger-pointing and raised voice detracted from the image of competence and newness that she and the party wanted to convey. In the end, the party's organizers decided, perhaps optimistically, that the debates had been a draw, reinforcing perceptions and commitments. But what the Tories had needed was a big boost, not a flatline.

Stage Four: from October 14 until voting day. In the days following the debates, party polling showed the Tory vote oscillating within a narrow range, with a slight incline upwards. By the Thanksgiving weekend the party felt its constituency tracking was indicating a vote of about 27 percent. But the fundamental weakness in the structure of the vote had now become painfully evident. While the party was comfortably in second place overall, it had no regional base which would produce a healthy number of seats. The PCs were a national party in a political system that seemed to have few national elements and many strong regional interests and orientations. Indeed, the party's precarious position was compounded by the fact that it was fighting a national campaign with different opponents from region to region. In Atlantic Canada the only significant opponents were the surging Liberals. In Quebec, the battle was joined between Tories and the Bloc in French-speaking constituencies, while the Liberals were dominant in English-speaking ridings. In Ontario, the party had to confront mainly Liberals, but in certain parts Reform was cutting into traditional bases of Conservative support. In the western provinces, the battle was more complex, with Liberals strong in Manitoba and Saskatchewan,

New Democrats strong in Saskatchewan, and Reform especially strong in Alberta and British Columbia. Within each of the provinces, regional variations in party competitiveness made it difficult to present consistent messages. In Alberta, for example, at the beginning of the campaign, party organizers perceived that southern rural ridings pitted Tories against Reform; in Calgary, the Liberals, Tories, and Reform fought for dominance; in northern Alberta it was a battle of Liberals versus Tories; and in Edmonton the Conservatives had to deal first with Liberals and then Reform. As the party of government and with the self-image of being a national party, the PCs found it difficult to mount a national campaign when two of its former bases of support had been fragmented by the emergence of two very different parties – Reform in the West and the Bloc Québécois in Quebec – which could reflect regional orientations and interests without worrying about the effect in another region. The collapse of the NDP meant that the Liberals, fearing no widespread challenge from the Left, could stress economic development rather than redistributive issues which would have given the Tories a clear target.

The party's best estimate now was that it could win between 20 and 40 seats. Even British Columbia, Campbell's home province, looked increasingly hostile, and decisions had to be made in the attempt to restore the party to competitiveness and deny the Liberals a majority government.[13] First, the Liberals would be the target, because Reform and Bloc voters tended to be more committed than were Liberal voters. Indeed, there were in the Liberal camp a significant fraction of voters, 10 to 12 percent, who had serious reservations about Chrétien. This group became the object of Conservative advertising. The party had started to run two negative advertisements on October 6. One was directed toward soft Liberals concerned about the efficacy of the Liberal job creation program and showed a worker shovelling coins into a ditch. A second targeted potential Reform voters by suggesting that only a magician could effect its proposed budgetary reductions without dismembering social programs. These advertisements had prompted what party organizers thought were the normal number of adverse reactions, but they had been at best only minimally effective in moving voters. New advertisements starting on October 14 centred on Chrétien's face. Party organizers claimed that the pictures used came from a photographer assigned to take two rolls of film at a campaign event the previous week in Toronto.[14] The combination of glaring red background, focus on Chrétien's facial features, and very negative voice-over text resulted in an outpouring of protests. Candidates, incumbents (including cabinet ministers), and newcomers, party workers and voters protested vehemently. From across the party there were calls for the withdrawal of the advertisements, with some candidates even threatening to disavow the party and its campaign. Party organizers frantically debated the question of what to do until Campbell, who had not seen the advertisements before they were run, decided, after much heated discussion with Tory and Gregg, that they would be withdrawn.[15] The cancellation of the advertisements left unanswered the question of their effectiveness, though the party's polling had shown an upswing on the nights of October 14 and 15, suggesting that perhaps soft Liberals were being affected.

The party's only hope of denying the Liberals a majority government was to unsettle voters who were uncomfortable with Chrétien. The Conservatives believed that they had turned their fortunes around in 1988 with their "attack" advertisements on John Turner, in which he was portrayed in an unflattering, even goofy, pose. The new advertisements were tested in focus groups, where no unusual negative reactions were expressed, and Liberal supporters with reservations about Chrétien's competence to be prime minister moved into the "undecided" category – precisely the effect that was desired. But such an approach toward Chrétien was risky since it could be perceived as unfair. Whatever one thought of Chrétien, one could not but admire his record of public service in national politics, despite his facial disability and his unilingualism when he arrived in Ottawa in 1963.[16] Three factors were not considered or adequately anticipated when the decision was made to run the advertisements. First, candidates and campaign managers had only slight indications of what was in the new advertisements, and in many instances they had to answer calls from angry voters without having seen the advertisements or knowing much about them.[17] Second, the Liberals, especially Chrétien, took advantage of responding to the advertisements. The Tories were scuppered when Chrétien appeared on television the next morning talking about how the advertisements attacked his appearance. His statement that "God gave me a physical defect and I've accepted that since I was a kid" immediately defined the advertisements as an attack on physically disabled Canadians. Third, the advertisements were hard to reconcile with the premise of the party's campaign that Campbell represented "a different way of doing politics." If anything, the advertisements had the effect of reminding voters of negative qualities of the previous Tory government.

The second devastating event of that weekend involved controversy in Quebec arising from remarks Campbell made to the media in which she implied criticism of Mulroney, Charest, and other Quebec cabinet members. The response of Quebec Tories was quick, angry, and pointed, and resulted in scrambling efforts to control the damage. But the damage had been done. The party's support dropped rapidly from the high 20s in the middle part of October to 17 percent by October 21. In the last week of the campaign, Tory candidates were quoted as saying that things had fallen apart, and that the party was doing badly. The media were full of stories about how well the Liberals were doing, that the Bloc was far ahead in Quebec, and that Reform's support was rising. Voters, especially in Ontario, who might have considered voting for the

PCs were cross-pressured, as it became apparent that the Tories were headed toward a debacle. They were tempted either to vote Liberal to elect a majority government able to handle the Bloc, or to vote Reform because, suddenly and unexpectedly, it was replacing the Conservatives as the party best able to defeat the Liberals. And so, on election night the party confronted the fact that it had won barely 16 percent of the vote and just two seats, Charest's constituency of Sherbrooke, and the New Brunswick riding of Saint John, won by a new Tory candidate, the city's long-serving mayor, Elsie Wayne.

CONCLUSION

In February the party's national election budget had been set at $23.5 million with a deficit of $5.5 million. In July it was pared down to $21.5 million, and the deficit to $3.5 million. By October the budget was at $18 million, and the overall deficit was between $7.5 and $8 million because contributions had dropped in tandem with the party's standing in the polls. Given that the party's 295 constituency organizations spent at least $12 million on their local campaigns, over $30 million was spent by the PCs in the 1993 election. The large debt and doubts about its ability to raise money forced the laying off of a large number of party workers. Many constituency organizations found themselves in debt because their candidates had not passed the 15 percent threshold necessary for federal subsidies of campaign expenses.[18] On December 13, six months to the day after she had won the party's leadership, Campbell, facing internal pressure from the party, resigned, and was replaced on an interim basis by Charest.

The easiest explanation is that Canadian voters simply wanted to turf the Conservatives out of office. Despite the best efforts of Tory strategists, memories of Mulroney reverberated in the minds of many voters, and after a couple of weeks of the campaign the PC vote was more or less at the levels that it had been prior to Mulroney's retirement announcement. From this perspective, the positive response to Campbell in July and August can be seen as a summer flirtation that cooled with the onset of autumn. Some Tory strategists, however, blamed the media for the party's disastrous showing. Their account is that Campbell was subject to much more searching discussion and criticism than the other party leaders, especially Chrétien. Campbell's utterances were misinterpreted by media trying to compensate for their soft coverage of her summer activities. One example was that the media's coverage of Campbell's response to a question about unemployment – at her press conference after the election was called – focused on her projections about unemployment at the turn of the century when her actual words combined unemployment and the deficit. The party's explanation is that Campbell was thinking as much about the latter as the former. Her comments about discussion of social policies during an election was similarly seen as being distorted by the media. But the real problem was that the Conservatives allowed, for whatever reason, Campbell's comments to take on a life of their own instead of making sure that her propensity for off-the-cuff remarks did not give her opponents material.[19]

Given the strong positive evaluation of Campbell and the relatively poor evaluation of Chrétien at the beginning of the campaign, the Conservatives were competitive. But, within a short period, Campbell and the party were, in the words of Dalton Camp, "all hat, no cattle." The leader, although dressed in fine attire, had neither the organizational preparedness nor clear and defensible policies to sustain the image so carefully nurtured. When times became difficult, she did not have the track record or personal constituency – as a new prime minister and a relatively new national politician – to sustain her.[20] In fact, once the campaign was underway, Campbell quickly created the impression of uncertainty, indecisiveness, and weakness while her main opponent was successfully portraying himself in the opposite terms. The lack of preparedness that marked the debates and press interviews were hallmarks of a campaign that produced nothing but bad news which became worse. As one senior party organizer put it: "It is absolutely amazing that over two million Canadians resisted the very strong reasons not to vote for us."

NOTES

[1] A number of media post-mortems analyzed the party's election campaign. Notable examples appeared in the *Ottawa Citizen* (Oct.30,1993), *The Globe and Mail* (Oct.27 and Dec.17, 1993), Global Television (Jan.16, 1994), and *Saturday Night* (Feb, 1994). Early in the campaign press commentaries contained references to problems confronting the Tory campaign. By the third week in September, even commentators such as Dalton Camp, whose close ties to the party extended to his son who was Kim Campbell's campaign manager in Vancouver Centre, were criticizing the party's campaign. *The Globe and Mail* in its lead editorial on Sept.25 said the Conservatives were "running the most incompetent campaign in modern political history."

[2] The Reform Party elected its first MP in a by-election in the Alberta constituency of Beaver River shortly after the 1988 election as a result of the death of the riding's newly-elected MP. After the failure of the Meech Lake Accord in 1990, Lucien Bouchard, a former cabinet minister in Mulroney's government, left the Tory caucus to form the Bloc Québécois. By the time of the election, as the result of by-election victories and defections from both the Liberals and Conservatives, the Bloc had 8 MPs.

[3] David Stewart and Ken Carty argue that the conventional wisdom that choosing a new leader has positive effects is wrong. See David K. Stewart and R. K. Carty, "Does Changing the Party Leader Provide an Electoral Boost? A Study of the Canadian Provincial Parties: 1960-1992,' *Canadian Journal of Political Science* XXVI: 2 (June 1993), 313-30.

[4] Campbell, in the course of acknowledging the decision of the convention, said: "And if I might be permitted a special word to my friend and colleague, Jean Charest. Jean, you are one hell of a tortoise."

[5] This failure to prepare for the post-convention period is not unique. In the 1976 Conservative leadership convention, the organizers on the Joe Clark campaign had given no thought about what would be required in the event of an admittedly-unexpected victory. Indeed, so many organizers had airline reservations to keep after Clark's victory that only a skeleton group was available to handle the organization of Clark's time and activities.

[6] Thorsell's article, published on October 27, entitled "How Mulroney's strategy failed," argued that the former Prime Minister had a seven-point plan in place that was intended to give the new leader the basis for victory in the next election. No person interviewed for this essay thought that such a "carefully honed strategy" existed.

[7] Gallup Canada, Inc, August 16, 1993. Gallup in its report of August 5, 1993 showed that Campbell was far ahead of Chrétien on the question about which leader would make the best Prime Minister to represent Canada internationally and was slightly ahead in terms of resolving problems between Quebec and the rest of Canada.

[8] Nationally-produced posters had a close-up photograph of Kim Campbell and the slogan "It's Time". In the subsequent weeks of the campaign there was no iteration of what was meant by this slogan.

[9] Decima's polling throughout the campaign entailed two alternating activities. The first, running over ten days, was in selected constituencies across the country. The second occurred in the next four days when a national sampling was taken.

[10] Some Tory workers tried to blame the press for exaggerating Campbell's comments and not testing Jean Chrétien in the same way that they thought Campbell was. In this instance, Campbell made more or less the same point in a number of different ways, which had the effect of reinforcing the media's interest in the issue. See, the *Globe and Mail*, September 24, 1993.

[11] *The Toronto Globe and Mail*, September 28, 1993. Peter Newman in an interview carried by Global Television on January 16, 1994, referred to briefing papers not read over the weekend prior to the release the party's social policy and deficit reduction programme.

[12] Campbell during the PC leadership campaign, after one negative instance that lasted less than half an hour, refused to participate any more in mock debates in preparation for policy forums. On one occasion, she was unprepared for the forum's physical setting as she did not take advantage of the opportunity to have a preview of the hall and stage structure.

[13] A tabloid, entitled "A Warning to all Taxpayers", was distributed to constituency campaigns in English-speaking Canada over the weekend of October 10 and 11. It was prepared in an attempt to define a middle position between the Liberals and Reform by suggesting that the Liberals were "soft" on the deficit and would increase taxes and Reform would eviscerate essential programmes by its "hard" position on the deficit. The PCs portrayed themselves as prepared to eliminate the deficit in five years without increasing or imposing new taxes.

[14] Kenneth Whyte in an excellent discussion of the Tory advertising campaign makes the point that two advertisements had a Quebec flag in the background; see Kenneth Whyte, "The face that sank a thousand Tories", Saturday Night, February, 1994.

[15] The plan was to run the "attack" ads for only a few days, when they would be replaced by a number of positively-oriented messages. The decision to withdraw the advertisements was made late on Friday afternoon, a time when tracking departments for the networks would be shutting down for the weekend. The timing of the cancellation ordinarily would have meant that the ads would run until the following Monday, which in fact was the original plan. However, as luck would have it, the new advertisements were already at the television networks so it was possible to replace the discredited ones with the positive messages.

[16] The advertisements were defended by John Tory in a number of media interviews on the grounds that they represented fair comment. The voice-over text, however, contained personal references, such as "Is this a Prime Minister?" and a comment about Chrétien perhaps being a source of international embarrassment, that for many were unacceptable.

[17] The party's "PC Express", an internal daily communique, referred to the new advertisements appearing on television the night of October 14 but gave no idea about how they were structured, their purpose, and no advice about how to reply to inquiries about them.

[18] According to preliminary results produced by the Chief Electoral Officer of Canada (November 10, 1993), 147 PC candidates got less than 15 percent of the vote.

[19] Political losers often quickly blame the media for their misfortune. It is worth noting that the Fraser Institute's analysis of the 1993 election concluded that Chrétien's Liberals were treated better by the national media than were Campbell's Conservatives; furthermore, Jean Chrétien and Kim Campbell were judged by different criteria. Data came from samples of CBC and CTV news stories and news programmes from September 8 to October 24, 1993. See, *On Balance*, 6(9) (Vancouver: The Fraser Institute).

[20] In addition, the shortness of the period between the convention and the election meant that Campbell and her senior organizers did not develop the empathetic relationship that Brian Mulroney had with his senior political advisors in 1984 and 1988. This was most evident in the worsening relationship over the course of the campaign between the national campaign committee and the people travelling with Campbell on her bus. The latter group comprised almost exclusively Campbell supporters while the former was perceived as being less obviously so. Every person interviewed for this essay reported that he or she had never seen such tense political relationships. Allan Gregg, for his part, was put into an unusual, perhaps untenable, context because he served as the campaign's pollster and the campaign's chief strategist. The normal practice was to have a sharp distinction between the two roles. See Ross Howard, "The Man Who Fell to Earth," *The Globe and Mail*, December 17.

CHAPTER 3

YESTERDAY'S MAN AND HIS BLUE GRITS: BACKWARD INTO THE FUTURE

STEPHEN CLARKSON

While Jean Chrétien had been first in the hearts of Liberal delegates at the 1984 convention which chose John Turner as leader, he was far from being the sentimental favourite on June 23, 1990 when he finally achieved his ambition.[1] He may have had a superior organization and sounder finances, but other contenders had stolen the limelight. Sheila Copps, the brilliant daughter of a former mayor of Hamilton, had wowed Quebec with her bilingual support for the constitutional recognition of Quebec's distinctiveness. Paul Martin, son of the Mackenzie-King era social reform minister from Windsor, was the preferred choice of the business communities of Montreal and Toronto, thanks to his mentor, Paul Desmarais of Power Corporation, and to his successful record as CEO of Canada Steamship Lines. Where Copps and Martin had proven articulate rivals, one slightly to the Left, the other slightly to the Right of the ample Liberal middle, Chrétien appeared to have lost his grip, unable to express any values. Like Turner before him, he had managed, while working in the private sector as leader-in-waiting, to lose his appeal with business, English Canada, and, worst of all, his own province.

The gold he finally grasped after almost 30 years of dogged service in the Liberal party turned to dross. Without a seat in the House of Commons for six months, he seemed to be in shock and to have lost his fabled common touch. His handlers gave him long speeches to read from a prompter, suppressing the spontaneity and folksy humour that had been his endearing hallmark once upon a time. Unable to communicate his own ideas or those of others, refusing to take English lessons to improve his delivery, he appeared completely incapable of offering a Liberal alternative to what the party considered to be Brian Mulroney's implacably neo-conservative agenda – devastating the industrial sector via the Canada-United States Free Trade Agreement (FTA), shifting the tax burden from corporations to individuals via the goods and services tax (GST), dismantling the institutions of the federal state and curtailing its social services. With their leader appearing so weak, Copps and Martin kept their organizations at the ready should a Chrétien collapse or a caucus coup precipitate another leadership campaign. Personal tensions between Copps and Martin, Chrétien and Copps, Martin and Chrétien kept the rivals' supporters within the party continually at odds. Although the 1988 election had more than doubled the size of the Liberal caucus – from 40 to 83 – morale among the MPs was low.

It was far from obvious, even to the most committed Grit, that the party was positioned to win the next federal election. Out of power for almost six years, it had developed a losing-party syndrome,[2] a set of self-perpetuating characteristics that had caused it to lose the last two elections: weak leadership, debilitating factionalism, policy confusion, and organizational disarray. Quebec, which had been a Liberal bastion for 90 years, had become its wasteland. By the spring of 1990, during the final stages of federal-provincial negotiations over the Meech Lake Accord, Chrétien was undecided for two weeks about whether to endorse the concept of a distinct society for Quebec, and this seriously undermined his credibility in his home province. Fear of alienating Pierre Trudeau, who was jealously guarding his absolutist a-province-is-a-province-is-a-province position, stopped him giving rein to his instinct to support a deal that might lay Quebec's discontents to rest. The francophone news media let no one forget that on the day that Chrétien was elected leader and that the Accord failed, Chrétien had hugged Clyde Wells, the Newfoundland premier who had been the its nemesis. This self-inflicted damage was serious. Two members of parliament, Jean Lapierre and Gilles Rocheleau, quit the party on the spot branding Chrétien a traitor to Quebec. The once popular "little guy from Shawinigan" had become anathema among his own people, francophone Quebeckers shunning his outstretched hand in airport cafeterias and accosting him with insults and anger in the street.

Chrétien's trauma as an outcast in his own society was partly linked to his party's ideological confusions. How to square Trudeau's hard line on the constitution with Quebec's demands for greater powers was far from being Chrétien's only policy dilemma. The question of free trade had left the party deeply divided, since John Turner had fought the 1988 election on the promise to tear up the FTA even though many in his party were in favour of endorsing continental economic integration. Equally difficult was bridging the gap between the party's business Liberals, whose top priority was reducing the federal deficit, and its welfare Liberals who wanted to maintain universal social-welfare programs, whatever their budgetary cost. On breaking issues such as the Gulf War, Chrétien reversed positions often enough to become a national joke.

Chrétien brought his own people into the Leader of the Opposition's Office (LOO) – notably his personal adviser of long standing, Eddie Goldenberg – but his new broom did not sweep clean Turner's old disorder. The LOO remained in an organizational uproar. The extra-parliamentary wing, which had not been revitalized by Turner, was not reanimated by his successor. The party's debt of several million dollars remained on the books because business was so in thrall to the Mulroney government's American-style conservatism that the Liberals' entrepreneurial friends had not been able to raise the kind of corporate cash needed to return the party to solvency. The vicious circle created by these mutually aggravating factors was perpetuated by a press gallery for whom Chrétien had become "almost a non-person, written off by many and ignored by the rest."[3] It was not only passionate Quebec nationalists who had bolted the party in disgust. Two respected policy activists – the lobbyist Rick Anderson and the political scientist Blair Williams – also quit, in their case to join Preston Manning's Reform party. With such substantial figures abandoning ship, the wreck seemed imminent.

The Pre-Campaign: Subverting the Syndrome

Two and a half years later, by January 1993, Chrétien was still not taken seriously, but his party was nevertheless poised to win office. Not only had Mulroney made himself and his government irremediably unpopular; Chrétien had made significant progress in turning each of his liabilities into assets. He recruited his old friend Jean Pelletier, the former mayor of Quebec City, to take charge of the LOO. At the same time two other Liberals were brought in to bolster Chrétien's image and policy. Peter Donolo, a bright and energetic young Liberal, was put in charge of communications, and Chaviva Hosek, a former president of the National Action Committee on the Status of Women, former professor of English, and former Ontario Minister of Housing was taken on to direct the party's policy research. A professional management team was hired to bring the party's debt under control and reassure its creditors. Old loyalists such as John Rae, executive vice-president of Desmarais's Power Corporation, remained in the background, ready to manage the leader's campaign. Young loyalists such as Dominic LeBlanc, son of the regional minister for New Brunswick in the Trudeau cabinet, remained active, and senior caucus members André Ouellet and Senator Joyce Fairbairn were named co-chairs of the planning committee for the next election.

With order re-established in the parliamentary party, Chrétien quietly courted the business community with the short-term goal of raising cash and the long-term goal of gaining its confidence. Corporate contributions increased 12 percent in 1992 to $8 million, while donations to the Conservatives fell slightly.[4] Business, like other potential supporters, wanted to know where the Liberals stood on the major issues. To provide an answer, Chrétien put Hosek in charge of a process to redefine the party's ideology, instructing her to start with a thinkers' conference on the model of the famous Kingston meeting of 200 leading intellectuals in 1960 with which his mentor, Mitchell Sharp, had helped Lester Pearson's Liberals work their way back to power.[5] Held in Aylmer, Quebec in November 1991, the weekend seminar was designed to provide intellectual grist for the party's policy. The roster of speakers was ideologically balanced, from the cautious on the Right who emphasized the country's economic straits, to the activist Left calling for a reaffirmation of the welfare state and its cultural institutions. The overall message lay somewhere to the Left of centre as defined by Lester Thurow of MIT: government had to be active in the new age of tougher global competition. But the media spin put on the conference by Chrétien was a clear message that the Liberal party had put its welfare-statism and nationalism behind it: "At this conference, we have learned that the old concepts of Right and Left do not apply to the world of today and tomorrow. ... Protectionism is not Right-wing or Left-wing. It is simply passé."[6] The Chrétien party was not going to resist globalization but embrace it, and such Left-leaning nationalists as Lloyd Axworthy would have to concur.[7]

Whereas the party leadership was signalling to business that the high-spending days of the Trudeau era were over, delegates who came to debate policy at the party's biennial convention in April 1992 seemed to be cut from the same Left-Liberal cloth as their predecessors. Apart from a few off-the-wall resolutions (oxygen was to be recognized as an exportable resource of countries with tropical rain forests), the consensus on social policy questions was decidedly Left-Liberal. On constitutional reform it reflected Copps's and Martin's neo-federalist views with a nine-point position that accepted the recognition of Quebec's distinct-society status.[8] With Martin, Hosek toured the country twice, consulting Liberal activists on the proposed campaign policy.[9] By July, a binder of two dozen papers, reflecting key ideas from the Aylmer meeting, the convention, the caucus's own policy committees and the extra-parliamentary activists had been readied to introduce the candidates to the Liberal positions.

Attracting good candidates was a critical problem for Chrétien. The recruitment process within the Liberal party had come under intense pressure, particularly in metropolitan areas where ethnic groups had learned how to capture riding nominations by mobilizing thousands of supporters. The bitterness of the fights and damaging allegations made by the losers had jeopardized the party's capacity to assemble a credible roster of candidates. The ethnic activist who could deliver a nomination did not generally provide the high-profile material Chrétien needed for his cabinet, yet prospective candidates who might have made good ministers were repelled by the prospect of waging nomination campaigns that could cost well over $50,000, require many months of slogging, and still offer little assurance of success. In contrast to Turner's passivity in the face of this dilemma, Chrétien acted. The 1992 convention amended the party's constitution to give the national campaign committee (appointed by the leader) carte blanche to "adopt and publish rules regarding the procedures to be followed in the nominations of candidates."[10] Using – some felt abusing - this authority, Chrétien's provincial campaign chairs exercised draconian control over the nomination process, sometimes recommending that the leader impose a candidate over the heads of the constituency's rank and file. At the cost of considerable unhappiness on the part of aspirants who were shouldered aside, Chrétien's people helped position prominent citizens in winnable ridings across the country. Six women were appointed as candidates, along with stars such as Arthur Eggleton, former mayor of Toronto, Douglas Peters, vice-president of the Toronto-Dominion Bank, Ann McLellan, former dean of the University of Alberta law school, Robert Blair, president of Nova Corporation, Marcel Massé, former senior federal civil servant, and Michel Dupuy, a former ambassador. Once the press gallery had duly rapped Chrétien on the knuckles for his anti-democratic propensities, it went on to take note of the Liberal team's high quality and to take the party's chances more seriously.[11]

Opinion polls, which consistently showed the Progressive Conservatives at historic lows and their leader even more unpopular, were a tonic for Liberal solidarity. Dissension among the MPs declined. In contrast to Turner, Chrétien had proven a healer in caucus, more ready to listen to his colleagues, better able to sustain their morale and to delegate responsibility. Copps and Martin sublimated their ambitions, partly because they had been co-opted by the leader – Copps was made deputy leader, and Martin co-chair of the platform committee – and partly because self-interest dictated that they present a united front to elect the party, and for them to have a crack at the leadership next time round. Chrétien made André Ouellet, a former Turner supporter, his key constitutional spokesman, representing the federal Liberals on the Bourassa government's important Bélanger-Campeau committee and the Mulroney government's Beaudoin-Dobbie committee. However, Quebec remained hostile territory. With no social base left to the party – business, the trade unions, and new social movements found their allegiances elsewhere – it was extremely difficult for Ouellet to obtain quality candidates. Bourassa maintained close ties to the Mulroney regime, and the media continued to treat Chrétien as a pariah.

Beyond Quebec, Chrétien's major liability in early 1993 was his low credibility as leader. He had turned inward, stricken by a health crisis (requiring a difficult lung operation) and a family disaster (his adopted aboriginal son was found guilty of sexual assault after a painfully long trial). But as the months passed his confidence gradually rose. With Margaret Thatcher ousted and George Bush on the run, neo-conservatism was demonstrably in decline. Chrétien withdrew as much as he could from the public eye so that the Tories would have no target to attack while they self-destructed. When Mulroney failed to get the Charlottetown Accord accepted in the Quebec and Canadian referendums in October 1992 it looked as though victory was assured for the Liberals with their 28 point lead in the polls. But within weeks, all the Liberals' best-laid plans seemed to have come to naught. Mulroney announced his resignation, and the Conservatives rallied round a dazzling political newcomer who was not just a feisty intellectual from the West but a forty-something woman of the Clinton generation able to champion the Mulroney policies while distinguishing herself from the Mulroney persona. When Kim Campbell launched her summer prime ministership by courting photo opportunities at PC barbecues from coast to coast and eclipsing the Liberals in the media, Chrétien kept his nerve, waiting for the honeymoon to end and the campaign to begin. He would then have a chance to challenge the Conservatives on a level electoral playing field. Showing a new resolution, he rallied his caucus by chiding its "nervous Nellies" and set off to try out his campaign technique in BC where the local media operated independently of the national news services.

Even at Campbell's moment of triumph in June 1993, when she became leader and prime minister, the Conservative party stood at only 21 percent in the polls compared to the Liberals' 43 percent. The disapproval rating for the GST remained almost 80 percent, opposition to free trade over 50 percent, dissatisfaction with the federal government at 75 percent, consumer confidence low and feelings about the economy bad.[12] Canadians hated the PCs and liked the Liberal party but they loved Campbell and had more negative than positive feelings about Chrétien. The Liberal leader's challenge was to change public rejection of the Conservative record into support for himself, the least popular of the party leaders.

GAFFES, GOOFS, AND GODSENDS: THE BATTLE OF THE NEWS CLIPS

The shape of the election campaign was visible from the first day, September 8, when Campbell, in indicating that employment rates were unlikely to improve before "the turn of the century,"[13] offered Chrétien a foil for his main message: "For us, the priority is to create jobs in 1993, right now, and we'll start in November."[14] The pattern had been set: Campbell would make a gaffe she would be forced to correct, thereby giving Chrétien the chance to make an immediate, often humorous reply that would transmit his message of hope.

The Liberal game plan for the news media was modeled on the Democrats' recent presidential campaign, in which Republican communications were monitored, enabling Governor Clinton to respond nearly instantaneously to statements by President Bush. A high-tech Liberal "war room" of half a dozen, led by Warren Kinsella, monitored the Tory campaign.[15] At 5 pm on September 23, to take one example, the Kinsella team alerted Donolo that Campbell had said "You can't have a debate on such a key issue as the modernization of social programs in 47 days."[16] He faxed the wire story to the Liberals' press room in Vancouver so that the reporters covering Chrétien there could attend an impromptu news conference at which Chrétien, in time for the evening news, responded: "In my judgment it is almost contemptuous. It's not [showing] a great respect for the electorate."[17] When the Conservatives unveiled their first commercial slogan, "It's time," Chrétien appeared on TV news the same night crowing: "It's a fantastic slogan. Yes, it's time for a change. It's time to get the truth. It's time to throw them out." In the face of this derision, the commentator reported, "The Conservatives may find it's time to change their slogan."[18]

Chrétien enhanced the impact of his campaign by making fun of the Conservatives without attacking them in the aggressively partisan style with which, according to the party's pollster, the Canadian public had become increasingly disenchanted. Rather than denouncing Conservative policies, Chrétien would hold up an empty blue binder in a mocking gesture that suggested to his audience the Conservative campaign had no substance. When Campbell tried to escape Mulroney's shadow, he feigned sympathy: "Poor Brian. Just think how disappointed he must be that the woman he took in ... and made her prime minister won't even mention his name. What ingratitude! But don't worry, Brian, I won't let people forget you."[19] Attacking the Conservative decision to buy helicopters for sophisticated anti-submarine warfare, he wondered if they were designed "to protect us against North Koreans coming up the St. Lawrence."[20]

Marketing Integrity: The Strategy of the Plan

When Chrétien said "It will be like the good old days. Canadians will be working again,"[21] some commentators felt he had made a major mistake, calling attention to his weakness – his unflattering label as "yesterday's man." But his appeal to nostalgia at a time of economic distress and political anomie was deliberate. The old days had been better days for most Canadians. For those who could remember them, the 1960s and 1970s had been decades of relatively secure employment and relatively low interest rates. Unveiling a political manifesto on Day 8 of the campaign was old-fashioned, equally deliberate, and risky. When the Liberals attempted this with Turner in 1988 the strategem proved disastrous. But Chrétien's advisers knew from Insight Canada's polling and focus group analysis that the public was deeply sceptical of all politicians, their self-serving motives, and their unkept promises. Remembering the fiasco of Turner's inadequately prepared positions, they had instructed Hosek to turn her 1992 policy material into a coherent campaign platform with each promise carefully costed. The 1993 document, *Creating Opportunity: The Liberal Plan for Canada*, was more than just a detailed presentation of the party position. It was a brilliant prop. For a leader who was short on intellectual agility but long on political experience, the document signalled – as Chrétien repeated ad nauseam in TV interviews and on the hustings – that he was the man with a plan. He told voters they could accost him at any time after the election and ask which of the promises he had kept. The document had been professionally edited with the kind of graphics and summaries more typical of a government report than a partisan campaign document, and the media were briefed at a closed session on the day the document was released so that reporters could appreciate the high quality of the research and budgeting. Once the figures and the logic had proved to be solid, the implicit messages of what quickly came to be known as the Red Book were that the Liberals were competent and the party was accountable.

Beyond its symbolic value, the platform positioned the Liberal party flexibly on a middle ground which appeared responsible in relation to the deficit problem while still appealing to its Left-Liberal constituency. On the hard, macro-economic issues the document took the position developed by Douglas Peters while still chief economist at the Toronto-Dominion Bank: the deficit could not be solved by reducing inflation to zero as the Conservatives and the Bank of Canada's governor had insisted, but was related to four other factors, economic growth, employment, interest rates, and the debt, which had to be handled together as a complex whole. As Martin expressed it to a seminar of CBC reporters on September 18, the twin spectres of the national debt and high unemployment could not be traded off one against the other. The root cause of both was the same: the economy had fallen behind.[22] On the CBC's Prime Time Town Hall debate on September 20, he asserted that unemployment and the deficit were caused by economic decline and insisted, "Economic growth is not a matter for market forces alone." If the private sector was to be the motor of the economy, government had to play a positive role by reducing the cost of capital through lowering interest rates and inflation. Taxes were not to be used to fight the deficit because companies could not pay more. Monetary policy should not be used to prop up the dollar or to achieve a zero inflation which really meant an actual deflation of the economy. The role of a Liberal government would be to help change the culture of the private sector, pushing it toward innovation by linking business to university researchers.

Creating Opportunity had two policy ranges to propose. In the short term, funds for housing rehabilitation and a $6 billion infrastructure program, to be launched in co-operation with the provinces and municipalities, would provide immediate economic stimulus and raise consumer and business confidence. In the longer term, the deficit would be reduced by requiring that new projects cost less than programs that had been cut. The cost of the infrastructure program, for instance, would be lower than the Conservatives' helicopter program which would be cancelled. Rejigging the unfair and overly complex GST, enhancing education and job training, introducing a youth service and an apprenticeship program, providing capital for small and medium enterprise where levels of Canadian ownership were high and female participation significant, diffusing innovation through a technology network, and converting military industries to peaceful purposes covered the main issues of economic policy. Chrétien's personal stamp on the economic platform was its overall prudence: the deficit would be reduced over three years to 3 percent of GNP.

On the softer, social-policy issues, the Red Book emphasized the decidedly Liberal values of human dignity, justice, fairness, and opportunity. On the environment, industry was to be greened with rules to address ozone depletion, parks were to be expanded, and the Law of the Sea implemented. When it came to social programs, the platform spoke of a "society of reciprocal obligations in which each of us is responsible for the well-being of the other."[23] Equality of social conditions was the objective. Health care was to remain universal, portable, comprehensive, publicly funded, and publicly administered. Pre-natal nutrition programs for expectant mothers living in poverty (an idea taken from Michael Wilson's prosperity action plan) addressed both the needs of children and the need to save future medical costs.[24] The public was to be made safe from crime through gun control, amendment of the Young Offenders Act and, above all, allieviating poverty, which had been increased by the PCs' cuts in social programs and was the basic cause of crime. Immigration was a dynamic force to be fostered with careful refugee programs. Aboriginals were to get "head start" programs and support in achieving self-government. National identity had to be nourished with support for the CBC and cultural development policies.[25] Political institutions would be reformed, starting with parliament, and lobbying would be brought under public control. Finally, a Liberal foreign policy would emphasize peace keeping, the United Nations, independence, and an arm's-length relationship with the US. These policies could as easily have been expressed in the 1960s and 1970s by the Pearson/Trudeau party in its more generous moments. Chrétien's stamp of businesslike caution could be seen on the social-policy side with its caveat that the day-care plank was conditional on the economy achieving real growth of 3 percent. His political shrewdness was evident in the omission of the Liberals' constitutional reform proposals. Chrétien believed—and his polling indicated—that the public was sick of constitutionalism. Government was central to the Liberal vision, but it would have to live within its means as it had in the good old King/St. Laurent days of the 1950s.

On Day 19 of the campaign, September 26, a major survey by CBC's Sunday Report showed the Liberals at 36 percent, compared to the Conservatives' 31 percent. The Liberals had achieved the magic quality of "momentum."[26] Equally important, the Liberals appeared to be winning control of the agenda. The survey reported a "massive" shift on what the public considered to be the major issue for the election. Now 36 percent believed it to be not the deficit but unemployment, and the Liberals were thought best able to deal with the problem by 32 percent, compared to 17 percent crediting the Conservatives. Two obstacles remained on the Liberals' path. They were in third place in Quebec at 24 percent, compared to 45 percent for the Bloc Québécois and 27 percent for the Conservatives. And 40 percent approved Campbell's leadership compared to 28 percent favouring Chrétien's. Coping with the leadership question would be the task of the campaign's next phase.

Making the Man Prime Ministerial

On Sunday, October 3, viewers of the French-language debate saw a Chrétien who had given up brawling. Where Campbell was aggressive, Chrétien tried to stay above the fray. He turned aside Lucien Bouchard's attacks on his constitutional position by insisting that the public wanted its politicians to create jobs. Chrétien was trying to play the statesman, a man with dignity enough to pass as prime ministerial. The next night on English-language television Chrétien turned in another adequate performance. Although he did not win the debates by being the most articulate, he conveyed his positions with enough coherence to reassure voters – who had long since indicated they wanted to vote Liberal – that he was sound enough to cope with the top job.[27] By this time the Liberals' advertising group, Red Leaf Communications, was airing its commercials. Consisting of political neophytes working out of the Liberal agency, Vickers & Benson, the creative team decided to reverse the original, poll-driven strategy of emphasizing the party and hiding Chrétien. Defying the notion that people vote for parties rather than leaders, Red Leaf decided to focus its small budget on commercials that featured Chrétien talking quietly about his policies and reflecting on his campaign: "I have the plan. We will make a difference."[28]

Although the Liberals were out-spent three to one by the Conservatives, Insight Canada's tracking indicated that their ads bested their rivals' by a factor of two. Viewers sampled rated Liberal ads better than Conservative ads on several scales: "most interesting," 30 percent to 15 percent; "most believable," 28 percent to 14 percent; "most informative," 28 percent to 16 percent; "make most sense," 32 percent to 17 percent; "deal with issues important to you," 33 percent to 15 percent.[29] But if Chrétien's image problem had been largely rectified by the end of the fourth week that was as much due to chance as to the cunning media campaign and Campbell's pratfalls. In large part Chrétien's luck lay in his timing. He had been dismissed for so long by the national media ("Chrétien mangles his syntax in both official languages while his words echo the concepts and values of the seventies"[30]) that reporters found themselves compensating for their past sins.[31] Outstanding facilities provided by the Liberals in their campaign bus helped create a positive mood in the press entourage. Chrétien, whom veteran journalists remembered as affable, communicative, informal, and helpful a decade earlier, turned out to be more accessible than Prime Minister Campbell and more capable, humorous, and likeable as a politician than younger reporters had expected. In contrast to the many scandals they had revealed about the Mulroney regime, they could find no skeleton in Chrétien's closet. They knew that when he had moved into Stornoway, the home of the Leader of the Opposition, and found the kitchen cupboards to be bare, he had bought china with his own money. Of all the stories written about the Conservatives during the campaign in *La Presse, The Globe and Mail* and the *Toronto Star,* 42 percent were negative, compared with 32 percent for the NDP, and only 26 percent for the Liberals.[32]

After Audrey McLaughlin declared the Liberals would get a majority, further boosting the Grits' momentum,[33] Chrétien seemed to live a charmed life. Conservative commercials that played on his facial deformity produced an immediate outcry. In the 1988 election that kind of negative advertising would scarcely have raised an eyebrow, but after four more years of politics characterized by overt government manipulation, and after two weeks of Liberal commercials that had been boosting Chrétien's prime ministerial qualties, the media were ready to play up the public's outrage. Although the Liberals had themselves pointed out his facial distortion in their own commercials in Quebec ("Drôle de tete. D'accord. Mais quelle vision!")[34] Chrétien's wounded plea about the Conservative ads – "They try to make fun of the way I look. God gave me a physical defect and I've accepted that since I was a kid" – was given generous treatment in the news.[35]

In a time of cynicism, this populist from rural Quebec turned out to have experience and savvy. He was not too aggressive, compared to Campbell whose style was belligerently partisan, not too scary, compared to Manning's fierce commitment to a zero deficit, and not too charismatic, compared to Bouchard's unabashed determination to lead francophones to his promised land. Chrétien was a team player, appearing at rallies with his candidates from the region, not as a superior like Campbell, but as a leader in touch with his associates. When he made mistakes (attending a $1000-per-person event which promised special access for donors to Chrétien, who had just given a speech promising to restore integrity to government) he addressed the problem directly by answering reporters' questions, then joking that the only person with preferential access was his wife, Aline.

Having successfully navigated the debates and beaten off the Conservatives' final attack, the last phase of Chrétien's campaign shifted to the regions where he was weakest. In British Columbia and Alberta, where Reform was surging, he urged voters not to waste their votes in protest but to elect Liberals so that the West would be represented in the cabinet. "I want Western Canada to be on the inside."[36] In Quebec he insisted that le vrai pouvoir—the Bloquiste slogan

— meant having the province's representatives in the government rather than in the opposition, a not-too-subtle reference to the power of government to dispense patronage and public works. As the Quebec press published polls indicating Chrétien might lose in his own riding, he returned to Shawinigan to remind his electors that he was their favoured son and would bring the benefits of the prime minister's good offices to them if elected.

THE MEANING OF VICTORY

Chrétien's success was historic. In the Atlantic provinces, where the Liberals already controlled every provincial legislature, the party carried every seat but one. It was an indication of the extent to which the Conservatives had alienated the Maritimes, dependent as they are on federal funding to maintain the quality of social services and even the capacity of the private sector to provide jobs. In Ontario, the Liberals also managed to win all but one seat. Free trade, the GST, and a Bank of Canada-induced recession had devastated the manufacturing economy, notwithstanding the panacea the Conservatives and the economics profession had promised. Comparatively speaking, the Liberals' breakthrough in the West was just as spectacular: 45 percent of the vote and 12 seats in Manitoba; 32 percent of the vote and five seats in Saskatchewan; 28 percent of the vote and two seats in the Territories; 25 percent of the vote and four seats in Alberta, the first time that the Liberals had carried a constituency in that province since 1968.

It had taken till the end of the campaign for Chrétien to overcome his personal deficit. It will take still longer for him to deal with his Quebec problem, although he has made considerable progress. Liberal support had risen from 23 percent in the first week of the campaign to 33 percent at the end when his party won 19 seats. Outside the anglophone area of West Montreal, the Liberals had done better than most expected, coming second in 44 ridings and re-establishing themselves as a substantial force. Being endorsed by two senior members of Robert Bourassa's government (Health Minister Marc-Yvan Côté and Security Minister Claude Ryan),[37] having his infrastructure program applauded by the mayors of Montreal and Quebec, turning in a decent performance in the debates, and getting his own message across through the party's commercials had led to a steady rise in his popularity throughout the campaign. He had not been able to counter the nationalist protest in the wake of the 1992 referendum on the Charlottetown Accord, but he did so well on election day that Quebeckers started to revalue the man they had come to despise.

The importance of the election lay mainly in the questions it raised about the future of the country. Did the devastation of two national parties – the PCs and the NDP – by the Bloc Québécois and the Reform party herald the beginning of the end for Canada? Or did the fact that the other national party, the

Liberals, won a clear majority with representatives elected from each province indicate that Canadian federalism had been given a reprieve from sea to sea? If neo-conservatism had really been rejected, had it been replaced by the humanistic welfare liberalism of the Pearson/Trudeau years, by a leaner, meaner neo-liberalism adapted to tough economic times, or by some tough-love blend of the two ideological variants? In the longer run, the nature of Chrétien's liberalism will depend on two factors largely beyond his control. The willingness of the Quebec public to remain within the Canadian state will be decided in the province, not in Ottawa. And the capacity of the private sector to produce enough jobs and tax revenue to sustain an advanced social structure will depend on North American free trade delivering prosperity not just to the United States but to the territory to the north. Only time will tell whether blue Grits is the appropriate diet for managing the continuing crisis in the Canadian political economy.

NOTES

[1] I am grateful to Jeffrey Johnstone for assistance in researching this chapter.

[2] George Perlin, *The Tory Syndrome: Leadership Politics in the Progressive Conservative Party* (Montreal: McGill-Queen's University Press, 1980), ch. 10.

[3] John Fraser, "Jean Chrétien: The Sequel," *Saturday Night* (February 1994), p. 12.

[4] Geoffrey York, "Liberal coffers grow as business smell a winner," *The Globe and Mail* (July 20, 1993), A3.

[5] Mitchell Sharp, *Which Reminds Me ... A Memoir* (Toronto: University of Toronto Press, 1994), pp. 88-93.

[6] Right of centre: Peter Nicholson, "Globalization: The Economic Impact," pp. 24-37; left activist: Mary Eberts, "Politics and the Community in an Information Age," pp. 209-13; active government: Lester Thurow, "The Need for Strategic Approaches," pp. 72-83; social programs: Ken Battle, "The Economy, Social Policy and the Environment," pp. 145-68; cultural institutions: Rosemary Kaptana, "Developing Institutions for the 21st Century," pp. 221-27 in Jean Chrétien, ed., *Finding Common Ground* (Hull: Voyageur Publishing, 1992); "passé", Chrétien, *ibid*, p. 245, and Hugh Winsor, "Liberal conference tests icy economic waters," *The Globe and Mail*, (November 26, 1991), p. A1, A8.

[7] Rosemary Speirs, "Where is Chrétien taking the Liberals?" *Toronto Star* (February 16, 1992), B1, B5.

[8] Adopted Resolutions, Biennial Convention, The Liberal Party of Canada, 1992. Martin's views: Carol Goar, "Martin sets Chrétien agenda," *Toronto Star* (February 25, 1992), A21.

[9] Interview with Chaviva Hosek, February 7, 1994.

[10] Section 14 (6) Liberal Party of Canada Contribution. Amended at the 1992 Biennial Convention, Hull, Quebec.

[11] Carol Goar, "Liberal candidates give substance to leader's bravado," *Toronto Star*, May 13, 1993, A23.

[12] Opinion data courtesy Environics Ltd.

[13] Jeff Sallot, "Jobless rate won't drop soon, Campbell warns," *The Globe and Mail* (September 9, 1993), A6.

[14] Susan Delacourt, "Election crossfire begins quickly," *The Globe and Mail* (September 9, 1993), A6.

[15] William Walker, "Hidden high-tech `toys' help big parties battle for voters," *Toronto Star* (September 21, 1993), A11.

[16] Rosemary Speirs, "Election not time to debate cuts: PM," *Toronto Star* (September 24, 1993), A1.

[17] CBC Prime Time News, September 23, 1993.

[18] CBC Prime Time News, September 26, 1993.

[19] Hugh Winsor, "The two faces of Jean Chrétien," *The Globe and Mail*, (September 20, 1993), A4.

[20] Richard Gwyn, "Momentum shifting to Chrétien as tired PM falters," *Toronto Star* (September 26, 1993), B3.

[21] Edison Stewart, "Jobs: Battle lines drawn," *Toronto Star* (September 9, 1993) p. 26.

[22] Author's notes.

[23] *Creating Opportunity*, p. 11.

[24] *Creating Opportunity*, p. 82.

[25] *Creating Opportunity*, p. 88.

[26] Richard Gwyn, "Momentum shifting to Chrétien as tired PM falters," *Toronto Star* (September 26, 1993), B3.

[27] Rosemary Speirs, "Chrétien gained most in debates, pundits say," *Toronto Star* (October 6, 1993), A14.

[28] Interview with Marlene Hore, January 31, 1994.

[29] Interview with Marlene Hore, January 31, 1994.

[30] Hugh Winsor, "The two faces of Jean Chrétien," *The Globe and Mail* (September 20, 1993), A1, 4.

[31] Interview with Robert Sheppard, November 1, 1993.

[32] Jim Bridges, "Media and the 1993 Canadian Federal Election," unpublished paper, p. 8.

[33] CBC Prime Time News, interview with Peter Mansbridge, October 13, 1993.

[34] CBC Prime Time News, October 11, 1993.

[35] CBC Prime Time News, October 15. The over reaction is analyzed by Kenneth Whyte, "The face that sank a thousand Tories," *Saturday Night*, February 1994, pp. 14-18, 58-60.

[36] CBC Prime Time News, October 19, 1993.

[37] In offering his support for Pierre Trudeau's constitutional hatchet man, Ryan was magnanimous: "You cannot live perpetually with bad memories." Susan Delacourt, "Liberal campaign gets a huge shot in the arm," *The Globe and Mail* (October 16, 1993), A7.

CHAPTER 4

The NDP's Quest For Survival

Alan Whitehorn

Echoing Charles Dickens, the New Democratic Party's newspaper in British Columbia, *The Democrat,* in Autumn, 1993, referred to the past two federal elections as the best of times, the worst of times. The 1988 election produced the best electoral results for the party – 20.4 percent of the vote and 43 seats – and the 1993 campaign the worst.[1] But because expectations were high in 1988, with many New Democrats hoping finally to overtake the Liberals, it did not then look like the best of times, and there was disappointment despite the strong showing. Optimism revived in the following year when the party elected Audrey McLaughlin as its new federal leader, the first woman to lead a national party in Canada. This was followed by increased in support in the polls both for the party and the new leader.[2] One reason was the electrifying NDP victory in Ontario, in September 1990. This breakthrough in the industrial heartland was followed in 1991 by expected but nevertheless important provincial victories in British Columbia and Saskatchewan. Half the country's population was now guided by provincial social democratic governments. In addition, the Liberals, the NDP's main electoral rival, seemingly had made a mistake in opting for an aging leader, Jean Chrétien, at its federal convention in June 1990. Preliminary public opinion polls showed Liberal party support dropping from 50 percent that month to 31 percent by January 1991.[3] All in all, things looked solid for the NDP. It seemed again the best of times, but difficulties were developing.

The disappearance of Social Credit from the House of Commons in the 1980s had left the Western protest vote to the NDP by default. However, with the growth in the 1990s of the Right-wing populist Reform party in the West, the NDP – like its predecessor the CCF – was once more challenged by another populist party.[4] Also, the fracturing of Conservative leader Brian Mulroney's electoral alliance of Western neo-conservatives and Quebec nationalists had important and long term negative implications for the NDP. As dissatisfaction with Mulroney's Conservative party grew, citizens in the West seemed increasingly to transfer their allegiance to the Reform party, not the NDP.[5] The failure of the Meech Lake constitutional accord encouraged nationalism in Quebec and gave rise to the separatist Bloc Québécois (BQ). The BQ swiftly and decisively undercut the NDP's fragile support in Quebec.[6] While that province rarely provided the NDP with a parliamentary seat, it had a quarter of the population and decline in Quebec support for the party sent national polling numbers tumbling. This contributed significantly to the marginalization of the NDP and its leader. Part of the image-making of the Reform party and the BQ was to contrast themselves with the three older parties. In so doing, both had the potential to undermine the NDP as a vehicle for protest voters, whether they were alienated Westerners or discontented Quebec nationalists. Given that the bulk of NDP incumbent seats were in the West,[7] the Reform party proved to be the more serious challenge.

PARTY AND CAMPAIGN ORGANIZATION

The decision-making structure in the 1988 campaign left many in the party frustrated.[8] This was a factor in the resignation of the leader, Ed Broadbent, along with several of his key staff. Formal post-election reviews, both by the party and its labour allies, produced a number of recommendations on how to run the next campaign.[9] Among the more important were: (1) the campaign decision-making should be more inclusive;(2) the campaign needed to be more flexible when issues and polls warranted; and (3) the campaign should be one in which social democrats could take philosophical pride. The 1993 campaign tested those recommendations.

Normally, between NDP conventions, the federal executive and federal council are the party's principal decision-making bodies. Immediately prior to an election campaign, however, the Strategy and Election Planning Committee (SEPC) becomes the pre-eminent organ of the party although technically it is a committee of the federal executive. Working closely with its steering, working group and platform committees, the SEPC designs the strategic election plan.[10] Day-to-day administration and execution of the plan are left to the federal secretary, operating as the campaign co-chair, and his staff. As a result of a post-1988 recommendation, the SEPC was expanded to more than 50 members: the chair, the party leader, two associate chairs, all members of the federal executive including the federal treasurer and the federal secretary, MPs who were regional caucus chairs, the principal secretary to the leader, the House leader, the political action director of the Canadian Labour Congress (CLC), chairs of the multiculturalism and aboriginal committees, and several others. The SEPC started preparing for the campaign several years before the election was called and usually met at least twice a year. However, given the size and diverse membership of the full SEPC, it is not surprising that there were also smaller bodies. The steering committee was composed of about 25 people, almost all members of the SEPC. A still smaller body was the working group of just over 10 people, with federal staff assigned to assist. Most of the initial members were based in Ottawa and this group met more frequently (monthly in 1991) than either the full or steering SEPC.

The 14-person election platform committee, a sub-committee of the SEPC, culled the hundreds of resolutions passed at previous party conventions, and strove to draft a coherent policy platform to maximize electoral appeal. Its centrepiece publication was the Jobs Plan, a document distributed in a long, short and executive summary form to several hundred thousand people. The title of the document conveyed one of the main campaign messages.

In the year or so prior to the 1993 campaign, there was a continuing exodus of senior party personnel. Among the key staff changes were the party's federal secretary, the caucus research director, the federal fund raiser, the leader's principal secretary, the party's media co-ordinator, the director of organization, and the leader's communication co-ordinator. Even the leader offered to resign in the summer of 1993, just weeks before the campaign began; needless to say, this was not accepted. The reasons for the staff departures were varied, but resignations accelerated with the decline in the party's poll standings and increased friction between the leader and some of her staff on the one hand, and between senior party officials and caucus members on the other. During the actual campaign, a series of groups supervised and, where necessary, modified the election strategy. At the pinnacle of the hierarchy was the inner core of strategists: the two campaign co-chairs, Julie Davis (the SEPC chair) and Fraser Green (the federal secretary), Dave Gotthilf (party pollster) and Tessa Hebb (director of caucus research and travelling with the party leader). A slightly larger working group met daily in Ottawa for about an hour. Each Saturday afternoon, the SEPC steering committee composed of about 15-20 people discussed the past week's events and endeavoured to anticipate and plan the next. Among the participants were the two federal campaign co-directors (the SEPC chair and federal secretary), the party president, the tour director, the pollster and one of his colleagues, the director of organization, the director of communication, the leader's principal secretary, the party's treasurer, the assistant federal secretary, the media monitor, several labour representatives from the CLC and occasionally the director of research (normally on the plane). The committee discussed modifications to the leader's tour, daily tracking of polling results, focus group findings, ongoing testing of campaign slogans and phrasing, the final changes of the ads and when and how to replace the first round of ads with subsequent ones. The meetings usually lasted four to six hours.

ELECTION FINANCES AND INCOME

On the eve of the campaign, the proposed budget was $8.4 million – higher than in 1988. The media budget for 1993 was set at $3.28 million, mostly allocated to television advertising. This followed a trend: the percentage of the advertising budget that went to television had increased from 58 percent in 1979 to 80 percent in 1988.[11] The leader's tour, the second largest portion of the campaign budget, was projected to cost $1.493 million. The remainder of the campaign expenditures were primarily for public opinion research ($525,000), the new, computer-based predictive dialing campaign, described below($489,000), organization ($391,000), direct mail and fund raising ($269,000), riding support materials ($180,000), administration ($205,000), candidate support ($195,000), and riding support ($180,000).[12] However, as the NDP slid in the opinion polls, the actual campaign expenditures were cut. Funds for the campaign were to be raised as follows: riding rebate ($2.5 million),[13] central rebate ($1.7 million), labour ($1.4 million), direct mail ($800,000), goods and services ($650,000), and the income from the leader's tour ($400,000).

POLLING

Following the 1988 campaign there was criticism of Vic Fingerhut, the party's American-based pollster, who in the eyes of many activists had underestimated the importance of Canadian nationalism and its relationship to the issue of US-Canada free trade. One of those critics was Dave Gotthilf, the Winnipeg-based co-founder and driving force of Viewpoints Research. He was instrumental in the historic and unexpected electoral victory of the NDP in Ontario in 1990, and was the pollster for the BC NDP in its 1991 victory. He now became the architect of federal polling strategy for 1993.

NDP polling from 1988 to 1993 fell into two categories. Prior to the campaign, baseline surveys tended to be more in depth and designed to build a national data-base from which comparisons could later be made. During the campaign, shorter surveys daily posed about two dozen questions to samples of several hundred people which were then combined into a weekly rolling sample, large enough for regional breakdowns. They explored voting intentions, party identification, perceptions of the parties and party leaders on a range of issues, the most salient/effective messages and phrasing, and the viability of party commercials and literature. There were to be six waves of polling which began on September 12, but the polling was modified and cut short near the end of the campaign to save money as the party's popularity continued to slide and the campaign became increasingly regionalized and concentrated in fewer and fewer competitive ridings in the West.

During the campaign a parallel set of surveys was conducted in ridings already held by the NDP and other ridings thought to be competitive. As the campaign progressed, the number of ridings considered competitive declined, while the importance of this narrower band of polling increased as party strategists gave greater attention to trying to save the party from electoral annihilation. The NDP also made use of small focus groups in selected cities, such as Toronto, Montreal, Winnipeg, Regina and Vancouver, in which people were drawn into discussions about party ads and arguments pro and con voting NDP were tested. It was in the groups that the controversial first round of ads – the so-called angry streeters – took shape.

While not officially part of the formal polling,and sponsored by the labour movement, one new feature of the campaign was computer-based predictive dialing, an enhanced technique for telephone canvassing and fund raising by means of computerized telephone lists, automated dialing, and electronic data entry of the responses. It was also able to provide detailed voting information from the targeted ridings, and as the party's campaign increasingly focused on a few winnable seats, the utility of predictive dialing grew correspondingly.

CAMPAIGN STRATEGY

The original campaign strategy, inspired by a new leader and high standing in the polls in late 1990, assumed continued growth in votes and seats. But difficulties appeared and those planning the campaign were confronted with several image problems. The first was that sustained polling revealed too few people identifying themselves as NDPers. Even in targeted and incumbent ridings, identification with the NDP often ranked second or even third. In contrast to 1988 when pollster Fingerhut had encouraged the party to focus on the Conservatives as the main target, in 1993 the focus was on the Liberals. Pollster Gotthilf believed that the greatest potential expansion of NDP support could be found amongst soft-Liberal voters, and past polling evidence supported the belief that there could be an important overlap of reform liberals and social democrats in the "NDP universe."[14] Certainly Chrétien's age and record suggested to some that the Liberals might be vulnerable. On the other hand, there was the danger of strategic voting. In 1988 the anti-free trade forces had divided their votes between the NDP and the Liberals, with the result that the Conservatives were re-elected. Many of those on the centre-left were determined that such a situation would not happen again. They were resolved to get rid of a unpopular Conservative government. Accordingly, many social democrats considered voting Liberal.

National politics in the year prior to the election were dominated by constitutional issues and the referendum on the Charlottetown Accord. The federal NDP leadership, particularly the parliamentary caucus, and the NDP provincial governments, supported the accord. However, there was increasing evidence of rank and file opposition. Even more controversial to many NDP members was the leadership's decision to join as an official member of the YES committee, which was dominated by the party's opponents, the Liberal and Conservative parties. The NDP became locked into the government's constitutional advertising strategy, which many social democrats disliked, instead of running its own free-time referendum ads. Increasingly, the NDP was perceived as part of the political establishment. For a Left-populist party, this was perhaps a fatal transformation in image. When the referendum results were summed, Canada had voted No. In the NDP's Western heartland, voters in every province said No. In British Columbia, where the largest number of NDP seats (19) were held, a resounding 68.3 percent voted No, the highest percentage in the country. It was an important, but largely ignored, warning sign of the growing gulf between the party elite and its rank and file membership, particularly in the West. It seemed yet another example of the potential tension within a social democratic party between more affluent professionals and intellectuals, and the working class.

It has long been noted that the public viewed the NDP as weak on economic issues.[15] Ontario's mushrooming debt and unemployment under Bob Rae's NDP government did nothing to alter the image of social democrats as poor economic managers. Not surprisingly, the federal NDP was not perceived as credible on the twin issues of the government deficit and public debt. Given the continuing recession, the economy was bound to be the dominant focus, but for the NDP, job creation was a more important and better economic issue than the debt.However, without sufficient economic credibility, the NDP was vulnerable even on the issue of job creation.

After being criticized for paying insufficient attention to the issue of free trade in 1988, the party approached the topic of NAFTA with determination. There was a widespread desire to deal in a more forthright manner with the issue of free trade. It became perhaps a preoccupation and the NDP may have been one election too late. Even nationalist allies such as the Council of Canadians seemed less able to arouse the public on the issue in 1993.

In the 1988 federal campaign, the NDP had made extensive use of the one major political asset it possessed – the popularity of its veteran leader, Ed Broadbent. Now the party had a new female leader who was not very well known. In an effort to overcome this, McLaughlin was encouraged to write an autobiography/policy book which was released during the fall of 1992. However, the question lingered of whether a female leader was an advantage or a handicap. Some felt that with the electorate increasingly cynical about the old male-dominated style of politics, a female leader with a new and less confrontational style might be an advantage, if the message could be conveyed. The question then became, whether the mostly male national media would listen as well to a female leader. The strategy was based on the assumption that the appeal of the new leader could be kept fresh until the election campaign. In fact, McLaughlin's popularity plummeted. In Oct. 1990, she was rated first among party leaders,[16] aided by the fact that Mulroney was still leader of the Conservatives, while the Liberals had just elected a former Trudeau cabinet minister, Chrétien, as their leader. By January 1993 she had slipped to an overall negative rating – 41 percent negative vs. 38 percent positive. Many of the previous undecideds had gone over to a negative evaluation. Just prior to and during the election campaign, she slipped further. For example, on the question of who would make the best prime minister, McLaughlin was 8 percent and in third place in June, but 4 percent and fifth in the Gallup Poll on October 21, barely ahead of National party leader Mel Hurtig.

On the eve of the campaign, NDP strategists were encouraged to read Kevin Phillips's book, *Boiling Point,*[17] in which he developed the theme of the financial erosion of the middle class under the neo-conservative policies of favouring the rich and powerful. However,a populist campaign never fully took hold, although the closing weeks of the campaign did see greater use of the issues of medicare and fairer taxation. For the NDP, it was too little and too late.

In an effort to catapult the party back into higher poll ratings and appear competitive, the NDP opted for tougher and more negative ads, although personal attacks on the other leaders were ruled out. Angry ordinary voters were filmed in stark black and white newsreel style complaining about politicians in Ottawa. These ads were in dramatic contrast to the soft message and autumnal colour of the so called "On Golden Pond" ad used in 1988. But as there was no talk of a breakthrough in Quebec in 1993, the campaign was more modest and there were only slight regional differences in the editing of the ads. Later separate ads were prepared for the West, such as, BC's two anti-Reform ads. There were saturation TV buys in the West and moderate buys in Northern Ontario, but no national radio ads were produced.

In candidate selection, the federal NDP reiterated its policy of supporting affirmative action for women and visible minorities. Led by a feminist,[18] the federal party put considerable energy into achieving gender parity in candidates and, in addition to soft Liberal voters, targeted women, labour, youth and members of multicultural communities. The NDP nominated far more women (113) than any other party, but unfortunately, only one, the leader, was successful.

In 1991, with high expectations, about 140 ridings were targeted, 62 in the West where the party had always been strong, 52 in Ontario where the affiliated trade union movement was strongest and where after the 1990 Ontario provincial victory gains were expected, about 15 in Quebec, and 11 in Atlantic Canada. By the outset of the campaign, the number of targeted ridings was down to about 75, and by the end of the first week of October only about 23 seats were targeted even though the party had 43 incumbent seats. By the last days of the campaign, the NDP was fighting for its very survival as a party in parliament, and the campaign became even more defensive than it had been in 1984. The goal became simply to protect as much as possible the crumbling electoral base. Party strategists increasingly recognized the danger of squandering funds and experienced personnel in ridings where there was little hope of success. Accordingly, even in the last few weeks of the campaign, tough decisions were made about where to use additional funds, staff, and advertising and where to cut. The threat of a debt crisis for the party reinforced the urgency of these decisions. A key question posed by some was whether the shift to the West came soon enough. The fact that Ontario, with its NDP government, was base for most of the affiliated unions and both campaign co-chairs perhaps contributed to the Ontario focus remaining longer than it should have in the pre-election period.

THE CAMPAIGN AND THE LEADER'S TOUR

Because support had been slipping for more than a year, the pre-campaign was thought to be even more important than usual. The highlight was to be a one-hour television town hall special on August 11 in Ontario, where it was hoped to make gains. The television special was planned as an opportunity for the public get to know the new NDP leader, and included a five minute video and a toll-free telephone number to call for information. However, within a day of the broadcast there were negative comments suggesting the video had been made in the United States. In fact, only the final edit had been done there, but for a nationalist party the damage had been done. To stop the spread of negative publicity, Michael Balagus, the communications director, resigned. This episode gave the party the wrong momentum going into the campaign.

The leader's tour was intended to be the main vehicle to communicate the party's message during the campaign, but was less ambitious and more regionally based than in 1988. During the 47 days McLaughlin visited all major regions, but spent most time in the West – 22 days, or 28 if the Yukon is included – where the party had been most successful in past elections. She spent 17 1/2 days in Ontario, partly because the leaders' debates were held in Ottawa, where the campaign steering group also met, and national media interviews were often done in Toronto. A mere one day was spent in Quebec, and Atlantic Canada received one and a half days with some provinces not visited at all. The schedule reflected the fact that the NDP was in a survival mode and focused its efforts on regions in which victories seemed possible.

Week One of the actual campaign saw the party at a disappointing 10 percent, and in fifth place, in an Environics poll. Even more damaging was the fact that the party was often not even mentioned in newscasts. And when it was mentioned it was often as one of the "traditional parties" – a damaging, even fatal blow to a Left-populist party. McLaughlin addressed the problem of the unpopularity of the Ontario NDP government by meeting Premier Rae, talking about job losses threatened by NAFTA, and describing the party's Jobs Plan to create employment on public works.

In Week Two the party was still in single digits in the polls. McLaughlin continued to meet with NDP premiers, attacked excessive corporate profits on prescription drugs, and spoke of the need to defend social programs. Grim poll results continued in Week Three: CTV reported that the NDP was at an abysmal 6 percent and might win only five seats. Despite winning three provincial by-elections in Manitoba, the strategists were worrying privately. They hoped that things would improve with the start of the hard-hitting advertising campaign in which angry Canadians complained about military helicopters, the Senate, the GST, tax loopholes for the rich, free trade and unemployment, and finished with the line, "Ottawa hasn't got the message. Send it," with the image of a ballot showing a vote for the NDP. However, there were worries that because the NDP was being perceived as one of the traditional parties in Ottawa, the ads might actually send support to the Reform party.

Poll results were largely unchanged in Week Four, but regional breakdowns showed the NDP running fourth in British Columbia, Saskatchewan, and Manitoba where most of its MPs had their seats. Leading up to the TV debates, McLaughlin urged the election of New Democrats to preserve Canadian medicare against the threat of a US-style health care system.

In Week Five came the leaders' debates. In the 1980s equal television status with the Liberals and Conservatives had been a factor in the growth of NDP support, but now there were two new players to share the spotlight. Although neither Reform nor the BQ had official party status in the Commons their leaders gained access to the debates and they became major beneficiaries. The dynamics of the five-leader debates lessened the likelihood that the NDP leader would be able to get the struggling party back into the fight by scoring a knock-out blow.

Not fluently bilingual, McLaughlin was at a disadvantage in the French debate on October 3, and he was not helped by being placed on the far side of the stage. Her comments stressed a Left-populist theme of preserving public medical care and introducing a fairer tax system, and criticized Lucien Bouchard's Tory past and the Liberal party's abandonment of the free trade fight. She performed modestly well but was seen to be a distant finisher. The English-language debate the next day was extremely important for the NDP, and strategists hoped that Campbell would be handicapped by having a government record to defend, while Chrétien would be vulnerable as "yesterday's man." Unfortunately, the luck of the draw again placed McLaughlin at the far end of the studio. This visual image of being off to the side, with the low poll numbers, contributed to the marginalization of the leader and her party. McLaughlin did score points on the issues of medicare, fairer taxes, and the Liberal's abdication of the struggle to stop NAFTA. However, McLaughlin was not part of the most dramatic moment, the riveting exchange between Campbell and Bouchard over the size of the deficit, and in the five-person debate there were no dramatic NDP gains. The hope that the party would move up in the polls after the debates was not fulfilled, and post-debate polling showed that NDP remained low at 8 percent and in fifth place.

Accordingly, Week Six saw a risky shift in strategy. The decision was made that McLaughlin would boldly announce that as the Liberals had sufficient support to form a majority government, wavering social democratic voters, who had wanted to drive a stake into the Tory heart, could now safely "come home" and vote NDP.[19] Tying into her message were new ads which reminded voters of the need for New Democrats to protect medicare and keep the Liberals honest. But in the last week of the campaign polls placed the NDP between 6 and 7 percent, still stuck in fifth place. McLaughlin, stoically completing the last act of the NDP script, continued to warn of the dangers to medicare.

ELECTION RESULTS

From its best ever showing in votes and seats in 1988, the NDP fell to its worst ever percent vote (6.9 percent) and number of seats (9). It went from the best of times to the worst, without enough seats to be recognized as an official party in parliament. Only the free fall of the Conservative party cushioned the NDP loss and distracted political commentators and social democratic activists. In terms of votes it was in fifth place among the parties, with 939,575,[20] the lowest since 1958 in the CCF era.Most ridings gave the NDP less than 15 percent of the vote, the crucial level required to receive financial reimbursement. However, the regional bias and quirks in the electoral system helped the NDP to lose fewer seats than the Conservatives, and thus to place fourth in number of MPs in parliament. It was a moral victory of sorts, but with a hollow ring. Instead of the giant leap forward that had been hoped in the heady days of 1990 and 1991 when three NDP provincial governments had been elected, the federal NDP took a major step backwards towards oblivion.

In terms of regional distribution, the largest number of NDP votes came from Ontario (291,658), British Columbia (252,257), and Saskatchewan (129,649). Each of the other provinces provided less than a hundred thousand. Every single province saw a decline in the party's vote. In terms of percentages of the vote, Saskatchewan led the way with 26.6 percent, followed by Manitoba with 16.7 percent, and British Columbia with 15.5 percent.[21] In all the other provinces, including Ontario, home of an NDP provincial government, the party won less than 10 percent. Again every province saw a decline, and Quebec hit rock bottom at 1.5 percent, a level not seen for four decades. In terms of seats in the Commons, there were 9 winning NDP candidates. Saskatchewan led with five out of a possible 14 seats. All nine seats were won with significantly less than 50 percent of the vote. The range was from 43.3 percent in McLaughlin's Yukon riding to 31.1 percent for Vic Althouse in Saskatchewan, and the average was 35.1 percent. In other words, the NDP victories were based on only about one-third of the votes cast. Ridings in which the party placed second offer a realistic chance of winning next time, and there were only 22 of these for the NDP – despite the fact that the party went into the election with 43 incumbent seats. The plight of the federal NDP in Quebec is indicated by the fact that none of its candidates, in 75 ridings, placed first, second, or even third.

Both Left and Right variants of populism have had long and important traditions in Canada. Often the two streams have been in competition: Social Credit vs. CCF, and, more recently, Reform vs. the NDP. In this election the Reform party had a higher vote than the NDP in 173 ridings in the nine provinces in which it campaigned, and this of course translated into far more seats. The NDP was ahead of the Reform party in only 46 ridings. There was a regional pattern to the losses. In the West, the NDP lost 17 seats to the Reform party and six to the Liberals. In Ontario all 10 NDP seats were lost to the Liberals. In Quebec, the solitary NDP seat won in a by-election fell to the Bloc Québécois.

As was the case for the CCF in the difficult era of the 1950s, the West – Saskatchewan in particular – largely saved the federal party from oblivion.[22] The NDP elected no members east of Manitoba, which had never before occurred in its history, and, in terms of social democracy, it had not happened since 1945 in the CCF era. Thus the central industrial heartland of Ontario and Quebec has no federal NDP representation, nor does economically impoverished Atlantic Canada. These results seem to belie socialist doctrine,[23] and as the NDP was created precisely to overcome the limited appeal and skewed regional profile of the CCF, there seems little progress in 1993. One obvious consequence of the regionalized pattern of support is that the NDP, like its predecessor the CCF, continues to be seen by many as a Western-based party. A leader from the Yukon in the distant Northwest accentuates that image.

The consequences of the most dramatic realignment of the party system in Canada's history are serious and potentially enduring. Accordingly, many, both within and outside the party, have begun to reconsider the future prospects of the NDP.

POST-ELECTION REACTION

The original campaign planning team had been led by two brothers-in-law, Les Campbell and Michael Campbell-Balagus – part of the so-called Manitoba boys. Both were bright and articulate, but also young and relatively inexperienced as top party strategists. They were replaced before the campaign actually commenced, but their optimistic scenarios based on a new style of politics probably should have been countered earlier by more realism, scepticism, and caution by party veterans, on the SEPC or elsewhere.

In years leading up to the campaign, the party was pre-occupied with fighting the free-trade issue and was relatively slow to adjust when the leader and the party fell in the polls. This indicates that there was a lack of flexibility in the long-range strategic plan, although that had been one of the key recommendations following 1988. However, during the actual campaign, the party did make dramatic shifts in organizational focus. The increasing concentration in the end on only two dozen ridings in the West was probably the reason the NDP did better in winning seats than the Conservatives. The question posed by some was, "Could it have been done sooner?"

Advertising was the NDP's largest expenditure in both the 1988 and 1993 elections. Yet both ad campaigns became the target of significant criticism. In 1988 the ads were seen as too soft and not sufficiently addressed to the dominant issue of free trade. In 1993, the ads were perceived by many as too negative. The "angry outsider" tone was seen to have benefitted the Reform party, not the NDP, particularly in the West.

Despite more sophisticated use of polling, the party did not fare as well as expected, and after two consecutive NDP campaigns that seemed flat, questions about polling have arisen. Party veterans ask, whether more scope should be given to old-fashioned political speech writers and less to modern-day pollsters.[24]

Several difficult post-election meetings were held concerning the party's financial status. The loss of official party status in parliament decimated the party's income. The central office had counted on a considerable number of rebates from ridings in which the party had expected to receive at least 15 percent of the vote, but this was the case in only about 50 ridings, a sharp decline from 1988. As a result of the shortfall in income, staff cuts at the party's national headquarters were more drastic than usual. Even the recently purchased federal headquarters was not immune.

As in 1988, labour, one of the partners in the creation of the NDP, began a post-mortem and explored the relationship between the party and the labour movement, commencing with a November meeting of the National Political Action Committee.[25] An obvious question is the extent of the gulf between the labour movement and the NDP, particularly in Ontario where most labour affiliations to the party have occurred. Significantly, only 52 of the 295 NDP candidates were from the labour section of the party. This was fewer than the number of women who ran for the NDP, and it may be appropriate to ask, whether there should be an affirmative action program for labour and working-class candidates in a social democratic party.

The election posed major problems for the NDP. First was the question of leadership: ultimately, a leader who guides a party to such a devastating loss must accept considerable responsibility. McLaughlin picked the staff who planned the campaign in the early stages, she accepted the strategy, and she delivered the message. No one bore more responsibility, but perhaps no one worked harder, a fact which the press belatedly recognized. At a specially-converred federal executive meeting in April, 1994, McLaughlin announced her intention to step down as leader. The method by which her replacement will be chosen is as yet inclear.[26] Another key question is whether the NDP will be able to rebuild itself organizationally in central Canada. Most urgent is the party's status in Ontario where the Rae government, with its controversial social contract legislation, has alienated the Ontario Federation of Labour, one of the party's most important allies. The Rae government has also seemingly disoriented a great multitude of NDP activists. Declining party income and drops in affiliated and individual memberships are serious and growing problems. Quebec, always difficult terrain, seems a wasteland for the NDP in the foreseeable future.

Ultimately, the experience of the federal party and that of the NDP provincial governments brings into focus another and more crucial issue. Like so many social democratic parties, the NDP must consider what policy direction to take in the 1990s and the new century.[27] The period of 1990-1991 seemed to many Canadian social democrats to be the best of times. Several years later, it seems more like the worst of times. The 1993 federal election produced the most dramatic realignment of the party system in Canadian history. The NDP, as it currently exists, may no longer be the best vehicle for Canadian social democracy. Like its predecessors, the Progressives and the CCF, the NDP may be coming to the end of its role, and it may be necessary to pass the torch to another and more vibrant standard bearer.

NOTES

1 I wish to thank the members of the NDP Strategy and Election Planning Committee (SEPC) and the Saturday election steering group for allowing me to observe their meetings. Many staffers in the federal office provided assistance, but I particularly wish to express my thanks to Fraser Green, Brian McKee, and Carmel Belanger. I also wish to acknowledge the many individuals who consented to interviews, particularly after a difficult campaign. Chris Page of Queen's University also provided able research assistance. Lastly, special mention and gratitude is expressed to Dave Gotthilf of Viewpoints Research. Amid an impossibly hectic schedule, he always took the time to discuss his company's polling data with grace and dignity. His death at the age of 35 was a loss of one of Canada's most promising pollsters.

2 From August 1990 to January 1991, there was a dramatic rise from 22 percent to 41 percent in federal NDP support (Gallup Reports). The primary causes seemed tied more to the federal Liberals' selection of Jean Chrétien as their leader and the consequences of a provincial election in Ontario than the earlier selection by the NDP of a new federal leader.

3 Gallup Reports, Novovember 22, 1990 and June 20, 1991.

4 David Laycock, *Populism and Democratic Thought in the Canadian Prairies, 1910 to 1945* (Toronto, University of Toronto, 1990).

5 This tendency was accentuated by the federal NDP's strategy of trying to woo soft Liberals, not disgruntled Tories, and by the belief that Ontario with its 99 seats was to be the major battle ground on which the NDP could win electoral gains.

6 For example, in January 1991 federal NDP support in Quebec was at 23 percent but by December was a mere 8 percent. In mirror-image fashion the BQ in the same period shot up from 26 percent to 41 percent, while Liberal and Conservative support remained stable (Gallup Report, February 18, 1993.)

7 See A. Whitehorn "The CCF-NDP and the End of the Broadbent Era" in H. Thorburn, ed., *Party Politics in Canada* (Toronto: Prentice-Hall, 1991); A. Whitehorn, *Canadian Socialism: Essays on the CCF-NDP* (Toronto, Oxford, 1992) #1.

8 See A. Whitehorn, "The New Democrats: Dashed Hopes" in A. Frizzell, et al., *The Canadian General Election of 1988* (Ottawa, Carleton University Press, 1989); *Canadian Socialism* #8.

9 NDP, "Report of the Election Review Committee," September 9, 1989.

10 SEPC, Steering Committee Minutes, March 7, 1991.

11 Whitehorn, *Canadian Socialism*, op. cit., p. 216; see also "Dashed Hopes."

12 At the time of the writing, accounting was not complete. Thus the numbers represent only preliminary estimates.

13 These figures proved to be excessively optimistic in view of the failure in many ridings to meet the 15 percent vote criterion.

[14] See for example K. Archer and A. Whitehorn, "Opinion Structure Among New Democratic Party Activists: A Comparison with Liberals and Conservatives." *Canadian Journal of Political Science*, March 1990; K. Archer and A. Whitehorn, "Opinion Structure of New Democrat, Liberal and Conservative Activists." In H. Thorburn, ed., *Party Politics in Canada* (Scarborough, Prentice-Hall, 1991).

[15] G. Caplan et al., *Election: The Issues, The Strategies, The Aftermath* (Scarborough, Prentice-Hall, 1989).

[16] McLaughlin was rated positively by 43 percent as NDP leader vs. a 25 percent equivalent rating for Chrétien as Opposition leader and 16 percent for Mulroney as Prime Minister (Gallup, January 28, 1993).

[17] *Boiling Point: Republicans, Democrats and the Decline of the Middle Class Prosperity* (N.Y., Random House, 1993). See also Kevin Phillips, *The Politics of Rich and Poor* (N.Y., Random House, 1990). In an ironic twist, for the second consecutive Canadian election the NDP had gained inspiration from a prominent American.

[18] Audrey McLaughlin, *A Woman's Place: My Life and Politics* (Toronto, Macfarlane, Walter and Ross, 1992).

[19] It appears that the message worked most effectively in Saskatchewan, a province with the longest and strongest social democratic heritage.

[20] At the time of writing, only unofficial returns were available from Elections Canada.

[21] The Yukon with one seat saw NDP leader Audrey McLaughlin receive 43.2% of the vote. It was the highest vote for any NDP MP. Since it represents only one riding, however, it is not listed in the regional averages.

[22] A whopping 89% of CCF federal seats came from the West (*Canadian Socialism* pp. 4-5); see also A. Whitehorn, "The CCF-NDP and the End of the Broadbent Era" in H. Thorburn, ed., *Party Politics in Canada*, (Prentice-Hall, Scarborough, 1991). Perhaps, a measure of the degree of popularity or unpopularity of the three NDP provincial governments is the number of seats the federal NDP won: 5 from Saskatchewan, 2 from British Columbia and zero from Ontario.

[23] See also L. Erickson, "CCF-NDP Popularity and the Economy", *Canadian Journal of Political Science*, 1988, March.

[24] Even the late Grace MacInnis made her concerns known about what she felt was excessive reliance on polling (see S.P. Lewis, *Grace: The Life of Grace MacInnis* (Harbour, Madeira Park, 1993). p. 9

[25] See Alan Whitehorn, "Some Preliminary Reflections On the Labour Movement and the New Democratic Party," paper presented to the Canadian Labour Congress, Ottawa, 1993; see also Keith Archer and Alan Whitehorn, *Canadian Trade Unions and the New Democratic Party* (Queen's University Industrial Relations Centre, Kingston, 1993) and Keith Archer *Political Choice and Electoral Consequences: A Study of Organized Labour and the New Democratic Party* (McGill-Queen's, Montreal, 1990).

[26] S. Hayward and A. Whitehorn, "Leadership Selection: Which Method?" paper presented to the Douglas Caldwell Foundation, Ottawa, April, 1991.

[27] See Whitehorn, *Canadian Socialism*, #9. See also John Richards & Don Kerr, eds., *Canada, What's Left: A New Social Contract: Pro and Con* (Edmonton, NeWest, 1986); Donna Wilson, ed., *Democratic Socialism: The Challenge of the Eighties and Beyond* (Vancouver, New Star, 1985); Simon Rosenblum & Peter Findlay, eds., *Debating Canada's Future: Views From the Left* (Toronto, Lorimer, 1991); John Richards, Robert Cairns & Larry Pratt, eds., *Social Democracy Without Illusions: Renewal of the Canadian Left* (Toronto, Mclelland and Stewart, 1991); Daniel Drache, ed., *Getting on Track: Social Democratic Strategies for Ontario* (Montreal, McGill-Queen's, 1992).

CHAPTER 5

REFORM: ELECTORAL BREAKTHROUGH

FARON ELLIS AND KEITH ARCHER

The Reform party's prospects heading into the election campaign were highly uncertain. Reform leader Preston Manning had been campaigning tirelessly since the party's formation in 1987. But by the late summer of 1993, Manning's efforts and those of the party had yielded mixed results. The party had won no seats in the 1988 federal election, but it did manage a by-election victory the following year. In addition, although its membership ranks, income, and standing in national polls all swelled in the early 1990s, by the eve of the election its growth had halted and in some areas the party was in decline. By election night, those setbacks were a distant memory, as Manning led his party to 52 seats in the Commons, just shy of official opposition status.[1]

The party's success, while owing a considerable amount to the collapse of the Conservatives, was also a product of organizational work between elections and an effective campaign strategy. The organizational efforts developed a campaign infrastructure, as well as providing an opportunity to test-market party platforms. The campaign strategy combined an extraordinary focus on the party leader with an army of volunteers at the local level canvassing door-to-door and dropping campaign literature, on a shoe-string budget.

BUILDING A NEW PARTY

Following the 1988 election, the ongoing politics of constitutional renewal provided Reform with a foothold in the political arena. The party's 1989 convention in Edmonton was an opportunity to clarify its position on the constitutional question, and to illustrate its distinctiveness from the other parties.[2] In his keynote address, Manning outlined what would become the party's constitutional stand for the next three years. He argued that Canada currently existed as a "house divided" that could only be reunited through sweeping institutional and economic reform. In responding to the "leadership crisis" in the country, Manning argued that Western Canada must insist on equal status in confederation: "Our goal of one united Canada is achievable. But if these principles of confederation are rejected by Quebec, if the house cannot be united on such a basis, then Quebec and the rest of Canada should openly examine the feasibility of establishing a better but more separate relationship between them, on equitable and mutually acceptable terms."[3] Delegates later adopted Manning's proposals in what became known as the Quebec Resolution. Throughout the Meech Lake debate, Reform membership continued to grow. In occupying the anti-Meech issue space, the party capitalized on the representational vacuum that existed as a result of the all-party support for the accord in parliament. By mid-1990 the party boasted over 40,000 members. The failure of the Meech Lake Accord, the nine- month delay by Prime Minister Mulroney in appointing Stan Waters to the Senate,[4] and the continuing GST controversy gave the party ample opportunity to promote its platform of institutional reform. In September the party announced that membership had topped the 50,000 mark and was growing at a rate of 3,000 members per month. The party began to register in national public opinion polls capturing 8 percent of the national vote by late 1990,with 24 percent support on the prairies and 20 percent in BC.[5] Further, the party organized its first interim constituency associations in Ontario in preparation for the assembly in Saskatoon in 1991.[6]

At the assembly, delegates addressed over 70 policy resolutions. They upheld the party's opposition to comprehensive bilingualism. They reaffirmed the policy opposing government financial support for multiculturalism. They accepted a resolution sponsored by Manning endorsing unconditional federal funding to permit the provinces to decide how best to operate their health care systems. Delegates supported resolutions basing immigration on Canada's economic needs without regard to race, creed or national origin. But undoubtedly the most important decisions were those not to contest provincial seats, and (by a 94 percent vote) to hold a binding vote of the membership on the proposal to expand the party east of Manitoba.[7] In his keynote address, Manning outlined his vision of what he called the "New Canada."[8] He explained,"New Canada should be a balanced, democratic federation of provinces, distinguished by the conservation of its magnificent environment, the viability of its economy, the acceptance of its social responsibilities, and recognition of the equality and uniqueness of all its provinces and citizens."[9] With its policies and principles now more fully articulated to appeal to a more "national" constituency, the party embarked on its expansion.

CANDIDATE RECRUITMENT

While the party organized in Ontario and the Atlantic provinces it also expanded and reorganized its national office in Calgary and began recruiting and nominating candidates in the West. At the Saskatoon Assembly the party had developed a code of conduct for Reform MPs and a set of guidelines and procedures for candidate recruitment. Included was a two-part Candidate Information Sheet designed to "enable the potential candidate, and his or her spouse, to assess whether he or she should seek a Reform party nomination," and "to enable Reform Party Constituency Nominating Committees to assess the qualifications of each candidate and to conduct necessary background checks."[10] The first part was a personal resumé, while the second contained a comprehensive list of questions a candidate could expect to be asked. These questions included items about the candidate's "Values and Motivation," "Electability and Acceptability to Constituents," familiarity with and commitment to the party platform, "Knowledge and Experience","Skill Requirements," "Political Vulnerability,"and commitment to the party's Code of Conduct. Candidates were requested to inform the nominating committee of any potential conflicts of interest. Constituency nominating committees were to interview each potential candidate. They could advise that the candidate not seek a Reform nomination, gain further experience before seeking a nomination, or seek nomination. But no bona fide member of the party was barred from contesting a Reform nomination.[11] By the spring of 1992 membership had grown to over 100,000. Many of the new members were a result of Manning's Ontario tour and of the competitive constituency nominations in Alberta and BC. By way of example, in the southern Alberta riding of Lethbridge membership expanded from 1,500 to over 5,500 before the cut-off period (30 days prior to the nomination meeting). Almost 3,200 members cast ballots at a meeting attended by over 4,000 people. Other Alberta meetings regularly drew over 1,000 voting members:1,300 in Medicine Hat, 1,000 in St. Albert, 1,400 in Ponoka, 1,500 in Red Deer.[12]

Reform's continued momentum affected the Tories. After test-marketing a negative advertising campaign in two Ontario ridings, the Alberta Tories implemented a similar campaign in Calgary, aiming to discredit Reform in its most supportive province. A series of billboard advertisements, radio ads, and over 300,000 flyers were designed to "give Calgarians 'second and third thoughts' about Reform policies."[13] The campaign foreshadowed the Tory strategy in the general election campaign.

TESTING THE ORGANIZATION

The referendum on the Charlottetown Accord allowed Reform to test its organization and electoral readiness. Each of the members, now more than 130,000, was mailed a questionnaire, and a "constitutional hotline" to the National Office enabled members and the general public to express views. While an Angus Reid-Southam News survey was showing 61 percent of English Canadians and 49 percent of Quebeckers initially backing the accord, the hotline recorded overwhelming opposition.[14] With the membership demonstrating similar contempt for the accord, Manning announced the Reform party's intention of campaigning for the NO side. A six-point plan included registering a Reform Party Referendum Committee on the NO side, development of the

KNOW MORE campaign theme with a "principled, knowledge-based communications effort," and a challenge to the YES side to public debates. Reform also sought to establish, through its hotline and 1-900 number, that a NO vote was a vote by a "proud citizen of Canada which includes Quebec."[15] Understanding that the NO forces could not match the YES forces dollar-for-dollar any more than Reform would be able to match the three traditional parties in a federal election, the party also tested its grassroots campaign organization. By promoting a word-of-mouth NO campaign as opposed to a high-profile media campaign, the party tested the ability of its members, volunteers, and constituency organizations to win public support and financial contributions. The effort centred on a widely distributed household flyer that attempted to capitalize on the public desire to resolve the constitutional issue. Calling the accord "no final constitutional agreement at all," Reform argued that a resounding NO vote would demonstrate to the political and special-interest elites that Canadians would no longer tolerate constitutional debates dominating the public agenda at the expense of economic and fiscal matters.

Reform's position as the only national party to have campaigned on the winning NO side affirmed for many the wisdom of the party's populist approach. However, this success did not translate into more generalized support. For over a year public opinion polls had been measuring a steady decline in Reform support. Environics had measured 19 percent support for Reform nationally as early as March of 1991.[16] By December of 1991 it had slipped to 12 percent and by October of 1992, despite the referendum campaign, it had dropped to 9 percent nationally, and to 34 percent in Alberta.[17] To rebuild support,the party reverted to its economic agenda.

PREPARING FOR THE ELECTION: THE CAMPAIGN THEME

Reform delegates met in their final assembly before the election in the week prior to the referendum. While most of the informal proceedings centred on the coming constitutional vote, delegates debated 19 planks for their election platform and 10 amendments to the party's constitution. An indication of electoral strategy came in the fact that 10 of the 19 planks dealt with economic and fiscal priorities, while only three dealt with the national constitutional debate.[18] The assembly produced the details of three planks: economic reform through deficit reduction, law and order, and non-constitutional parliamentary reform. In three major speeches in this pre-election period, Manning unveiled the party's "Zero in Three" strategy to eliminate the federal deficit within three years by spending reductions and economic growth, and without tax increases. Phase I, released in a March address in Toronto, established the party's position that "it is the mounting deficit and debt, and the interest payments thereon, that constitute the greatest threat to Canada's social services safety nets, including medicare."[19] Based on the finance minister's December 1992 projections of a $34.6 billion deficit and a predicted growth rate of 3.5 percent a year over the three year period, Reform calculated that balancing the budget would require a total of $19 billion in spending cuts. The bulk of the cuts would come in the form of reductions in transfers to provinces and individuals. Federal funding would remain at current levels in areas deemed to be of the highest priority to Canadians -healthcare, education, child benefits, guaranteed income supplements, and veterans' pensions. Contributory programs like the Canada Pension Plan and Unemployment Insurance would be put on a self-sustaining basis. Finally, non-contributory programs like Old Age Security would be focused on families with below average incomes. Savings in these areas would total $9 billion. Phase II, released in Vancouver in early April, concentrated on job creation and the reform of federal subsidies to business and special interests. Spending cuts proposed in Phase II included the elimination of some regional development programs, reduction in grants to defence contractors, elimination of financial support for the Hibernia off-shore oil project, elimination of business tax concessions, business grants and loans, and elimination of funding for special-interest groups. Total savings in Phase II would amount to $5 billion. Phase III was announced in Ottawa in late April and dealt primarily with reductions in expenditures on parliament and other federal institutions. Total savings from cuts in the budgets of the Prime Minister's Office, Commons, Senate, and Governor General's office, redirection of foreign aid, and elimination of funding for multicultural and bilingual programs among others were projected to save $5 billion, bringing total cuts to the required $19 billion.

Rounding out the platform were Reform's policies on criminal justice, including the Young Offenders Act, and parliamentary reform which included a Triple-E Senate, popular ratification of all constitutional changes, better constituency representation by MPs, and support for popular participation by way of referendums, initiatives, and recall of MPs.

The Campaign Organization

Like most aspects of the Reform party, the structure of the campaign organization was unique. It consisted of two tiers, the national campaign team and the candidates' campaigns at the constituency level.[20] After meeting with the leader in Ottawa in late June, candidates were regularly updated on National Office activities by fax and, once the campaign began, daily by way of the national headquarter's newsletter, *The National Informer* and supplementary documentation on the leader's tour, press releases and strategies reacting to developments. The national team consisted of the six-member Campaign Management Committee (CMC), the Campaign Committee made up of National Office managers, and campaign advisors including a candidate liaison network called

Figure 1
Reform Campaign Organization

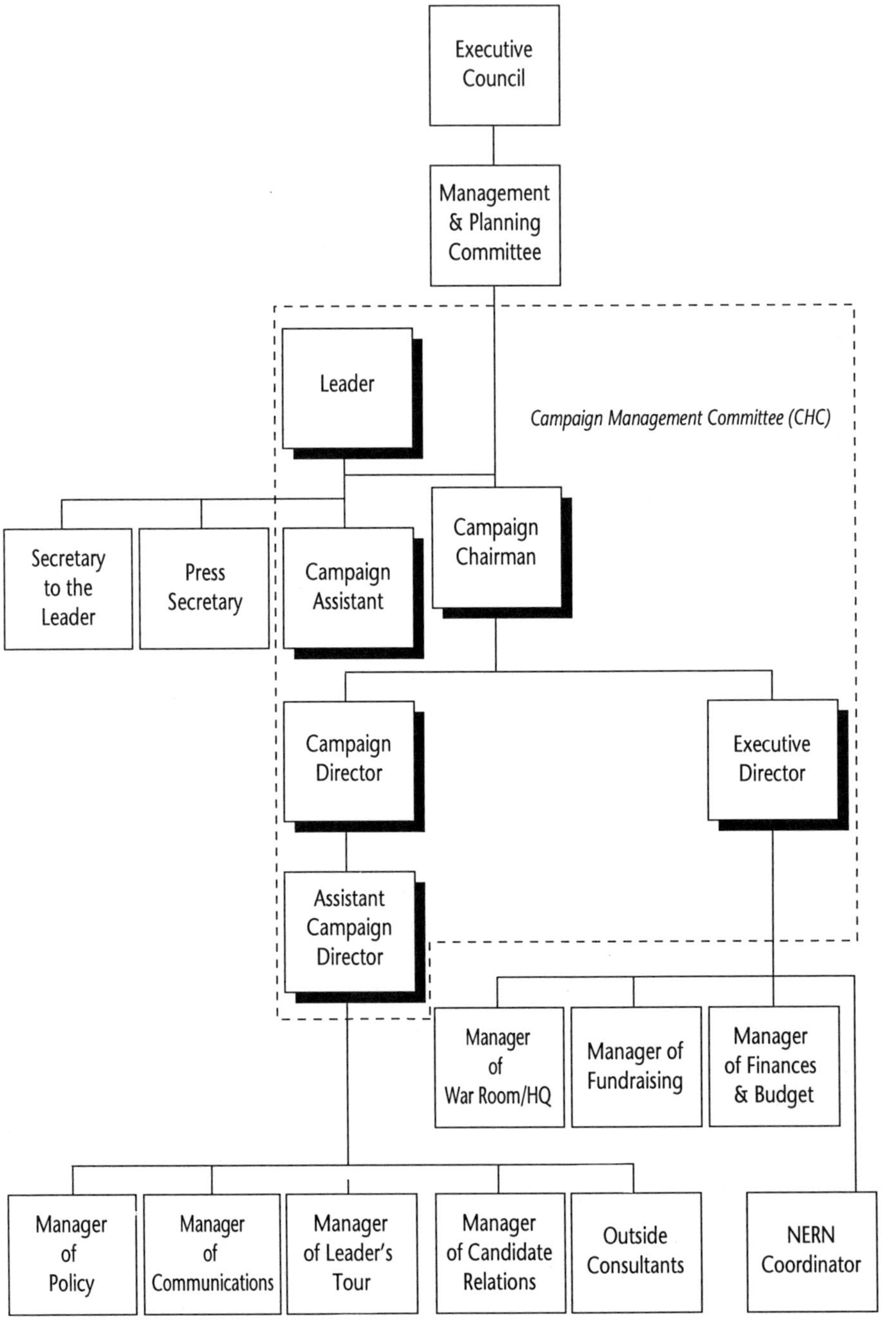

Note: Revised September 3, 1993

NERN, and consultants. CMC members included the leader, campaign chairman Cliff Fryers, campaign director (with special responsibilities for the leader's tour) Rick Anderson, assistant campaign director (with special responsibilities for support of constituency campaigns) Virgil Anderson, the executive director, National Office, Gordon Shaw and liaison to the leader's office Ian Todd. All members of the CMC had been long-time Reform organizers, with the exception of Rick Anderson whose appointment as campaign director was an initial source of controversy amongst some policy advisors and members.[21] Noticeably absent from the team were two long-time strategists, Stephen Harper and Tom Flanagan. Harper had been the party's chief policy advisor since its founding but declined to sign on with the national campaign, preferring instead to concentrate on his own candidacy in Calgary West, where he faced his former boss and Tory Whip Jim Hawkes. Flanagan had left his position as research director in January 1993 following disagreements over the referendum campaign. He stayed on in an informal advisory capacity until the summer when further disagreements became public and the party formally severed the association.[22]

The campaign committee worked out of the National Office in Calgary and consisted of seven members supported by National Office staff and ad hoc policy advisors and co-ordinators. Key members included Manager of Policy, Dimitri Pantazopoulos, Manager of Communications, Allan McGirr, Manager of the Leader's Tour, Ellen Todd, Manager of Candidate Relations, Ken Suitor, Manager of the "War Room" at Campaign Headquarters, Fraser Smith, Manager of Fund Raising, Don Leier, and Manager of Finances and Budget, Glenn McMurray.[23] Other key personnel included Mitch Grey who acted as a policy assistant and a spokesperson, Neil Weir who managed constituency development and election readiness, Jennifer Grover in communications and media strategies, and Harry Robinson who, with the assistance of Sandra Manning, ran the leader's campaign, with Faron Ellis providing polling and consulting for the leader's local campaign. Ron Wood acted as press secretary in charge of the leader's tour, media logistics, and Bob van Wegon co-ordinated youth projects and served in several capacities on the leader's tour.

Financing The Campaign

Reform party financing is a two-tiered operation. National Office maintains a national membership list and communicates directly to every member a half dozen or more times a year through sustainer letters, issues statements, Reformer newsletters, and opinion surveys. Members are automatically members of both their constituency association and the federal party between which the $10 fee is split. In 1991 the party collected over $6 million. Of that, 16 percent came from the sale of memberships ($990,000), while members and other individuals donated over $5 million, up from $2.5 million in 1990. The party continued to collect funds in these proportions through 1992, most of which were used to build up constituency war chests, fund the leader's activities and those of the national office, and to communicate with the membership. By the summer of 1993 many constituency associations in Alberta and BC had, or were close to having, enough money to exceed their campaign limits – on average, $41,000 each in campaign funds.[24] But many of the recently organized constituencies, particularly in Ontario and Atlantic Canada, were still far below their campaign limits.

The initial campaign budget was established in the pre-election summer meetings of the Campaign Management Committee, when the party had less than $500,000 to spend on the national campaign. It was in the process of raising advertising funds through its co-operative program with key, well-funded constituency associations. However, if the party was to keep its pledge of running a debt-free campaign, the national campaign would have to be financed through individual donations by members and supporters attending tour events. The National Office sent out two fundraising letters and conducted a phoneathon during the campaign, and the leader's tour events often charged an admission fee, usually in the $10 area. At all events, cash donations were solicited. The candidates raised funds through membership sales, local sustainer letter campaigns, and at local campaign events.

During the first three weeks of the campaign the party and its candidates raised more than $3 million, including more than $2 million by the candidates. The national letter campaign had raised $560,000 while another $500,000 had been raised through memberships, donations to the national campaign, the leader's tour, and business donations.[25] By mid-campaign the national letter/phone campaign surpassed $600,000 while candidates had raised an average of $11,500.[26] With two weeks remaining the party had raised a total of $5.1 million, with the two sustainer letters collecting $890,000, the national campaign another $800,000, and candidates $3.5 million.[27] By campaign's end the party and its candidates had collected over $6 million and it ended with a surplus.[28]

POLLING

The party leadership had always been suspicious of politicians and parties guided in their policy decision by the latest opinion poll. Reformers tended to seek out public opinion by way of open-ended question-and-answer sessions at public forums. However, party officials realized that, despite budgetary considerations, they needed polling data to gauge voter response to their campaign. They also had requests from constituency organizations and candidates to set up local polling organizations. As with the campaign organization, polling operations were divided into two tiers. The national party purchased from

Environics Research Group Limited of Toronto its standard package of national, regional, and provincial breakdowns of voter support, demographic breakdowns, and daily tracking polls.[29] The constituency polling operation was initiated by the National Office, and Gorgias Research Consultants of Calgary developed an inexpensive standardized polling package that could be implemented at the local level, using campaign volunteers. In the end, few constituency associations opted for the package.

Leader's Tour

Manning's personal importance in the success of the party and the campaign cannot be overstated. His tour was designed to serve several key functions. It would promote the party by way of media coverage – uniquely important for Reform because it could not afford a national advertising campaign. With few high-profile candidates and none with Manning's national stature, the tour would also serve as the sole vehicle for announcing new positions on issues and strategic reactions to campaign dynamics. Third, it would solicit money to finance the campaign. In planning the tour it was recognized that as the leader of a populist party dedicated to constituency representation, Manning would have to spend more time than other party leaders in his own riding. He spent at least parts of 21 days in Alberta, on 15 of which he appeared in Calgary.[30] Twelve days were spent in Ontario, including three in Ottawa for the debates; approximately nine days in BC; and four days in Saskatchewan and Manitoba combined. There were two trips to the Maritimes. Partly as a result of budgetary consideration and partly because it reflected Manning's personal style, the tour began as a modest affair. All personnel including the leader, and the accompanying media, flew economy class, travelled in the same tour buses, stayed at the same hotels and often ate the same volunteer-packed lunches. One observer commented that "all in all, Manning is leaving himself open to closer scrutiny than any other leader. So far, he is handling it well."[31] The smooth functioning of the early tour was achieved in large part by the membership and constituency organizations. Local volunteers often managed to gather large crowds with just a few days notice. For example, early in the campaign a decision was made to stage the first big Alberta rally in Red Deer, rather than a larger centre. Despite being a high-risk and audacious decision according to some organizers, with less than three days' notice the central Alberta constituency campaign volunteers managed to turn an expected crowd of 1,500 into over 3,000.[32] Similar organizational efforts were achieved in every province. Less than two weeks into the campaign so many constituency associations were demanding a tour stop that the party had to send a memo outlining the focus and objectives of the tour and Manning's commitments in the Calgary campaign.[33]

As momentum grew, so too did the crowds and financial contributions. Toward the end of the campaign the party chartered a plane and the tour took on a more traditional look. Finances had improved to such an extent that the party could afford a 12-stop, cross-country push, a task that would have been both physically and logistically impossible without a charter plane. The final week of the tour saw some of the largest rallies of the campaign. Initial estimates were for over 45,000 to attend the 12 scheduled events, with over 6,000 gathering for the final event in Calgary.[34]

ADVERTISING

Reform's advertising strategy was dictated by two factors: the amount of air time the party would be legally allowed to buy and the amount it could afford to buy. The original formula under the federal Elections Act based on party performance in the previous election gave Reform only 11 minutes. Calgary North Reform candidate Diane Ablonczy challenged that allocation, and in December, 1992, the Alberta Court of Queen's Bench agreed with her arguments that the formula was discriminatory and unconstitutional. The court gave parliament six months to devise a more appropriate formula,[35] and the independent broadcasting arbitrator, Peter Grant, allocated Reform 23 minutes (later reduced to 17).[36] In view of its court victory, it is ironic that the party could afford to purchase no national advertising during the campaign. Instead, certain regional markets in the Western provinces were targeted by the national office in conjunction with local candidates' associations, and this advertising was purchased on a cost-shared basis.[37] Further advertising was the responsibility of the local candidates and their campaigns. To assist them, media packages including television, radio, and newspaper ads were produced in the second and third weeks of the campaign and sold for $500. The party also made used of its free-time allocations (9 minutes on CTV, CBC English and French radio and TV). However, the party's major advertising effort was literature drops. Over 19 million pieces of Reform literature were delivered by local volunteers. National office produced and printed these brochures and initially sold but then gave them to the local campaigns.[38]

THE CAMPAIGN

Reform began the campaign in fourth place in the national opinion polls. After an initial boost in the polls generated by media attention surrounding the "zero in three" deficit reduction promotion, the party settled back to 7 percent. Party strategists were privately conceding that no seat, including the leader's, was guaranteed. Nevertheless, the party continued to work for the electoral breakthrough that many believed was possible. The campaign was divided into three stages. Reform defined its agenda by opening the campaign with its "Let the people speak" message, introducing voters to Reform's democratic populism.[39] During the second stage it promoted its economic strategy. The third stage would include an emotional plea urging the electorate to vote on the basis of personal conviction of the right thing to do at the present time rather than from fear or tradition. The dynamics of the campaign allowed the party to stick to its general agenda while modifying and adjusting it in response to attacks by the other parties as well as responding to the agenda set early by the Liberals. The leader's tour was used to promote Reform's national platform, tailored to regional subtleties across the country.

Manning kicked off the campaign at a Calgary news conference by declaring,"This election is not just about what the politicians have to say to the people. This election must be about what the people want to say to the politicians."[40] During the first week he attempted to establish a link between the very future of democracy in Canada and Reform's electoral prospects: "For six years, over 100,000 Canadians have been building a constructive alternative to the old political parties – a political movement based on democratic principles...If Reformers are beaten down by special interests or whichever old-line party has the most money, then it won't be just Reform that fails the test, it will be democracy itself that fails."[41] Populism was used extensively to sell the Reform message in Alberta and BC. In Ontario Manning urged voters to "break with tradition" because "if Canadians vote the way they always have, they'll get what they've got. If they want something better, then they should look at Reform."[42] Arguing that the NDP no longer represented working Canadians and union members, Manning articulated his belief that Reform's brand of populism could involve a much broader coalition than simply the disaffected of the Right. In the Maritimes he urged a break with tradition by arguing that Maritimers ought to "vote for their children rather than for their grandfathers."

With the Liberals successfully establishing their agenda on employment as the early campaign theme, Manning began to adjust his deficit-reduction message by attempting to convince voters of the connection between debt and jobs. He attacked Liberals and Tories without yet spelling out Reform's plans, other than to state that the party would not be advocating government intervention in the economy to manufacture jobs. On the heels of Campbell's reported comments that the employment situation would not improve until the next century, he urged voters to "ask hard questions about the connection between debt and jobs,"[43] criticizing the Tories' record on deficit control and declaring that Campbell's team had no new plan. He attacked the Liberal economic plan for ignoring the connection between high levels of government spending, high taxes, and jobs. As the Tory fortunes sank, Manning moved to establish Reform as the only legitimate party for the Right. The Prime Minister's remark that she could not release details of her own deficit-cutting plan presented Manning with an opportunity to go on the offensive with details of Reform's "zero in three" plan: "If a party such as ours, with relatively little staff and resources, can provide details of our approach to deficit elimination, surely Ms. Campbell's government with its thousands of accountants and officials, can manage to do the same before this election is over."[44] Campaigning in Manitoba later that week Manning attempted to move from the negative, program cuts and deficit reduction, to the positive, what he called the "light at the end of the tunnel." Canadians could look forward to the "benefits that will flow if Canada gets its spending under control, gets its agricultural house in order, and gets more accountable politicians... We should start to see disposable incomes rise as consumer confidence rises, and we see the truth of the proposition that a dollar left in the pockets of a lender, investor, taxpayer, or consumer is more productive than in the hand of bureaucrat, politician, or lobbyist."[45] Returning to Calgary later that week, Manning added tax reform and relief to his list of rewards for voters willing to suffer $19 billion in cuts to reduce the deficit: "If the country commits to a genuine deficit elimination program, and stops adding to the size of the national debt, we envision a National Tax Reform Initiative to run concurrently with the implementation of 'zero in three,' and the changes agreed to during the course of the initiative would be implemented as soon as the budget is balanced."[46]

Reform received its strongest editorial support to date during this phase of the campaign. *The Globe and Mail* editorial on September 23 commended Manning and Reform for having "the only deficit plan we've seen."[47] This was representative in two important ways of the positive media coverage the party had begun to receive. First, Reform had established itself as the party with a detailed plan on deficit reduction, and second, with the Tory campaign becoming increasingly disorganized, Reform increasingly came to be seen as the only alternative for voters chiefly concerned with government financing. The favourable editorial also signalled the beginning of the increased media attention – often far less favourable – that would be paid to the party during the remainder of the campaign. Up to this point both the Tories and the Liberals had been content to ignore Reform, or to dismiss it as a fringe player. As the party picked up momentum, all three major parties would begin counterattacks focused on social policies such as health care, education, and welfare reform.

Campaigning in southern Alberta in the third week of the campaign, Manning introduced the theme of trust as he unveiled the parliamentary reform plank of the party's platform:

> Elections are battles for the trust and confidence of voters, and the old-line parties have lost that trust... The way for politicians to earn public trust and confidence is to let the people speak first, learn how to tell painful truths in a way that wins respect, and provide substantive alternatives on issues of

> concern to voters... If you want to get trust you have to earn it. Politicians have to demonstrate that they are prepared to trust the people by putting tools into the hands of the people that will give them some real control over the political process and politicians.48

Later that week, at a rally in Red Deer attended by over 3,000 supporters, Manning delivered a speech tailored specifically to Alberta voters and reminiscent of the early, pre-expansion days. "The rhetoric, Mr. Manning's fiercest yet, appeared to shift the tone of the Reform campaign," wrote one reporter. "Unlike his recent speeches in Ontario and other parts of the country, his address purposely hit the hot buttons for the Reform party's core membership and for last night's home-town crowd: regional alienation, spendthrift Liberals and Tories and the emergence of a separatist movement in Quebec."[49] The address indicated the party's strategy in that, despite attempts at gaining support in other regions, its electoral prospects hinged on success in the West and in Alberta and BC in particular.

THE DEBATES

The debates offered an interesting set of organizational and strategic choices. The broadcasters and the three traditional parties were forced to address the question of what role the leaders of the new parties would play and how much the traditional debate format would be changed to accommodate them. As Manning was unable to speak French one possibility was that he would be excluded from the French-language debate while the "regional" party leader, Lucien Bouchard, could participate in both. Initially, the three traditional parties attempted to exclude both leaders from full participation in both debates. But when it became evident that Bouchard would have to be allowed to participate fully in the French debate, it also became impossible to exclude Manning from full participation in the English debate. However, the problem of the French debate remained. With none of the traditional parties willing to risk handing Manning a quintessential Reform issue – a unilingual Canadian being given "second class status" – it was eventually decided that Manning would be allowed an opening and closing statement, in English, in the French-language debate, with limited participation in the question-and-answer session. Both "regional" leaders participated fully in the English-language debate. The format of this debate proved beneficial to Reform and its leader in that it "levelled" the playing field. As one observer commented, "The format treated all leaders equally, and thus it was easy to forget that Campbell leads a national majority government while Manning's party has only a single MP."[50]

Manning used his brief time in the French debate to explain to Quebeckers his vision of the "New Federalism" and to invite Quebec federalists to join in building it. He warned that there was no market for sovereignty association outside Quebec. His real test came a day later in the English-language debate. The strategy was to have him appear statesmanlike by not entering into personal attacks on the other leaders while, at the same time, urging voters to base their judgments of the leaders not on personality or debate performance but on how they addressed the issues. The strategy worked well for the first half of the debate with Manning, at times, acting as moderator between two other excited combatants. However, as the debate progressed, Manning often used his scarce time to ask questions of the other leaders rather than enunciating party policies. Post-debate polls indicated no leader had emerged a clear winner but Manning had at least held his own, and with three weeks remaining had solidified his standing as a national presence and Reform as a distinctive political alternative for voters outside Quebec.

POST-DEBATE MANOEUVRES

The three-week period following the debates saw Reform emphasize two main themes. With the Tory vote continuing to collapse and Reform fortunes rising, especially in Alberta and BC,[51] the party attacked the Liberal economic plan and the rise of the Bloc in Quebec.[52] In both instances it argued that a large bloc of Reform MPs would keep the Liberals fiscally responsible, and prevent the Bloc and the Liberals from negotiating any new constitutional initiatives or developing unacceptable programs designed to appease Quebec. Reform continued to be on the defensive in explaining its social policy and health care proposals, and in dealing with charges of racism.[53] The charges emerged in a highly controversial context with less than two weeks remaining in the campaign. On October 13, Manning was in Toronto discussing the party's approach to the criminal justice system in a speech at Osgoode Hall Law School.[54] Toronto area Reform candidate John Beck was accused of making racist comments while promoting his views about Canada's immigration policies and its effects on employment. After he reiterated his views to a local television reporter investigating the allegations, the party's Campaign Management Committee demanded and received his resignation. Manning's response to the incident was that the national office had placed a great deal of pressure on new constituency associations in Ontario and the Maritimes to get candidates nominated and that a few undesirable candidates may have gotten through the screening process. Beck had completed the candidate nomination questionnaire but did not reveal anything that would have suggested he harboured racist opinions. The party's quick action on this potentially explosive issue helped to minimize the damage. More importantly, the issue was moved off the front pages by the publicity surrounding the Tory "Chrétien ads."

Manning spent the final week of the campaign on his cross-country tour campaigning on the themes of trust, accountability and institutional reform while urging voters not to give the Liberals a blank cheque majority government. With Reform leading the Tories in the polls, party insiders were becoming increasingly confident that Reform would sweep BC and Alberta to win a majority of seats in the West, pick up as many as a dozen seats in Ontario, and possibly three in the Maritimes to form the official opposition. Although it did not do quite that well, Reform placed second in popular vote with almost 19 percent nationally despite the fact that it did not contest seats in Quebec. In capturing 52 seats (and running second in 79 ridings) the party took its place in parliament with the third largest caucus. Reform winners defeated incumbent MPs in 35 ridings (19 Tories, 15 NDP, and one independent).

The results mean that Reform is now operating in a changed environment. No longer given the luxury of political outsider status, its challenge is to pursue its agenda within parliament, far removed from its supporters in the cities and towns of the Canadian West. History has shown that few parties have been able successfully to bridge that distance. Reform's continued success will be measured by its ability to do so.

NOTES

1 This research was supported by the University of Calgary Research Grants Committee and by the Social Sciences and Humanities Research Council grant 410-93-0400. Generous assistance was provided by the Reform party of Canada national office. Helpful comments were provided by Tom Flanagan, Glen McMurray, Virgil Anderson, and Jennifer Grover.

2 The Reform party held its founding convention in 1987, under the slogan "The West Wants In!" at which time E. Preston Manning, son of former Alberta Social Credit Premier Ernest Manning, was chosen leader. The party ran 72 candidates in the four Western provinces in the 1988 election, but failed to elect a single MP.

3 "Leadership for Changing Times," an address to the October 27-29 Assembly of the Reform Party of Canada by E. Preston Manning, leader.

4 Reform candidate Stan Waters won the Alberta Senate selection election in October 1989, but was not appointed to the Senate until June of 1990, on the eve of the ratification deadline for the Meech Lake Accord.

5 CBC News/*Globe and Mail* survey as reported by Kenneth Whyte, "Filling a vacuum: The RPC is short of organizational expertise," in Terry O'Neill, ed., *Act of Faith*, (Vancouver: B.C. Report Magazine Ltd., 1991) p. 117. Originally published in *Alberta Report*, November 12, 1990.

6 By the time Assembly 91 took place, the party had organized 50 interim constituency associations in Ontario and was preparing to organize in the Atlantic provinces.

7 The party membership later overwhelmingly (92 percent) endorsed the expansion proposal.

8 "The Road to New Canada," an address to the 1991 Assembly of the Reform Party of Canada by E. Preston Manning, leader, Saskatoon, April 6, 1991; see also Preston Manning, *The New Canada* (Toronto: Macmillan Canada, 1992).

9 Ibid., p. 10.

10 "Candidate Recruitment and Selection Manual," Reform Party of Canada, August, 1991.

11 Ibid., and Preston Manning's letter of intention and information sheet to Calgary Southwest Constituency Association, March 18, 1991.

12 Lorne Gunter, "Experience wins by a hair: Speaker's self-effacing speech gained him his nomination, but only just," *Alberta Report*, April 6, 1992, p. 10 and Jim Johnston, "New Party, old tricks: Overspending charges follow a Reform nomination meeting," *Alberta Report*, April 27, 1992, p. 14.

13 Calgary Centre MP Harvie Andre as quoted by Jim Johnston, "The Tories swing left to hit Reform: Money pours into billboards, radio ads and flyers to halt the RPC's march," *Alberta Report*, June 8, 1992, p. 10 and Jim Johnston "Protesting too much: The Tory anti-Reform ad campaign is imported from Ontario," *Alberta Report*, April 20, 1992, p. 12.

[14] Of the 500 calls that came in during the first 36 hours, even before the party publicized the hotline, 61 percent were from members, of whom 93 percent rejected the package while 83 percent of non-members opposed it. Lorne Gunter, "A moderate 'No' Campaign," *Alberta Report*, September 14, 1992, p. 7.

[15] "Statement by Preston Manning for the Official Launch of the Reform Party of Canada's Referendum Campaign," Reform Party of Canada, September 18, 1992.

[16] Kenneth Whyte, "Ontario by Storm," *Alberta Report*, June 24, 1991, p. 15.

[17] George Koch, "Frustration on the first plateau: As its enemies grow increasingly vigilant, the Reform party adjusts to the big leagues," *Alberta Report*, December 16, 1991, p. 8 and Lorne Gunter, "Canada after the uprising: The rejection of the accord and its elite backers augers well for the RPC," *Alberta Report*, November 9, 1992, p. 10.

[18] For an indication of the attitudes and opinions of delegates attending the 1992 Assembly see Keith Archer and Faron Ellis "Opinion Structure of Reform Party Activists," *Canadian Journal of Political Science* (forthcoming) 1994.

[19] "Stop Digging! A plan to Reduce the Federal Deficit to Zero in Three Years (Phase I)" an address to a joint luncheon of the Canadian Club and the Prospectors and Developers' Association, Toronto, by E. Preston Manning, March 29, 1993.

[20] An adjunct advisory group called NERN (National Election Advisory Network) existed at the fringes of the campaign and consisted of approximately 50 regional advisors across the country.

[21] Anderson had served as an unofficial advisor to Manning for approximately two years prior to being appointed campaign director. An Ottawa "insider," Anderson had worked for the lobbying firm of Hill and Knowlton for the past 13 years, managing its Ottawa office for the last four. A former Liberal, Anderson worked for Paul Martin Jr. in his bid for the Liberal leadership. He also publicly backed the Yes side in the Charlottetown referendum campaign. Despite being considered too moderate and centrist by some members of the party, Anderson's appointment proved a benefit to the party as it ran an extremely effective and well organized leader's tour due, at least in part, to his "insider" experience and expertise.

[22] Harper won his seat for Reform in Calgary West. Flanagan returned full-time to his professorial position at the University of Calgary. Parenthetically, Flanagan was not Manning's only contact in the Political Science Department at the University of Calgary. As early as 1990, Manning organized monthly informal discussion sessions at the university during which he exchanged views with interested department members.

[23] Reform Party of Canada Memoranda, September 7 and 8, 1993.

[24] Lorne Gunter, "Steal from Reform, win re-election: Campbell copies the RPC's plans for cabinet reform, and snatches Manning's popularity," *Alberta Report*, July 12, 1993, p. 6.

[25] Reform Party Memorandum, September 26 and 27, 1993.

[26] Reform Party Memorandum, October 3, 1993.

[27] Reform Party Memorandum, October 9 and 14, 1993.

[28] Tom Flanagan, "Corporate and Union Political Donations Are Unwise and Should Be Illegal," *Alberta Report*, December 13, 1993, p. 9.

[29] The association between Reform and Environics dates back to 1991. The party first flirted with establishing an in-house polling operation to gather both public opinion data and an accurate demographic profile and political history of the party membership. The party commissioned U.S. consultant Frank Luntz to conduct a base-line study of electoral support with Environics providing data collection and compilation support. The membership study was conducted by Gorgias Research Consultants of Calgary, run by Faron Ellis. For a demographic profile of the Reform party see Tom Flanagan and Faron Ellis, "A Demographic Profile of the Reform Party of Canada," paper presented to the Annual Meeting of the Canadian Political Science Association at Charlottetown, P.E.I., June, 1992.

[30] The Calgary South West constituency was not a sure seat for Manning. Running against newly appointed Energy Minister Bobbie Sparrow who won her seat in 1988 with over 65 percent of the vote. Early polling showed Manning in the lead and Reform support solid but by no means overwhelming. As late as the first week in October, a Gorgias poll showed that while Manning had a substantial lead (31.9 percent versus 13.9 percent for Sparrow) 43.6 percent of Calgary South West voters remained undecided.

[31] Sean Durkan, "Travels with Preston plainly interesting," *Calgary Sun*, September 19, 1993, p. C4.

[32] Reform Party Memorandum September 26, 1993.

[33] Reform Party Memorandum, September 17, 1993. The four-point tour objectives were outlined and explained under the headings 1) logistics: size of tour and problems with no charter aircraft; 2) strategy, get the biggest bang for the buck so go to major media centres; 3) national campaign commitments, debates and high profile nationally scheduled media events; 4) constituency activities of leader in Calgary South West.

[34] Mark Miller and Sean Durkan, "Reform hopes to detour Grits," *Calgary Sun*, October 25, 1993, p. 18.

[35] Jim Johnston, "The right to buy airtime: A court ruling favours Reform against the old-line parties," *Alberta Report*, December 21, 1992, p. 11, reporting on the decision of Court of Queen's Bench of Alberta Justice Virgil Moshansky in Ablonczy vs. the Attorney General of Canada.

[36] Lorne Gunter, "New heights in federal paranoia: A second gag law would further curb non-party election ads," *Alberta Report*, May 31, 1993, p. 13.

[37] Reform Party Memorandum, September 7, 1993.

[38] Reform Party Memorandum, September 9 and 25, 1993.

[39] For a discussion of "issue priming," see Richard Johnston, Andre Blais, Henry Brady and Jean Crete, *Letting the People Decide* (Montreal and Kingston: McGill-Queen's University Press, 1992).

[40] "Let the People Speak" remarks by Preston Manning, Leader Reform Party of Canada to Reform Meetings/News Conferences, opening week of 1993 federal election campaign, Draft 7, September 8, 1993 – Calgary.

[41] Reform Party News Release, "Let The People Speak: This election is a Test of Democracy Itself," September 9, 1993 – Edmonton.

[42] Reform Party News Release, "Let The People Speak: Manning Encourages Voters to Break with Tradition," September 10, 1993 – Oshawa/Toronto.

[43] Reform Party New Release, "Let the People Speak: Manning Urges Canadians to Ask Hard Questions about the Connection between Debt and Jobs," September 13, 1993 – Vancouver.

[44] Reform Party News Release, "Manning Challenges Other Parties to Release Detail on Deficit Control," September 20, 1993 – Peterborough. "Stop Digging: A Presentation of the Reform Party's Plan to Reduce the Federal Deficit to Zero in Three Years," by Preston Manning, Peterborough, Ontario, September 20, 1993.

[45] Reform Party News Release, "Manning Points to Light at the End of the Economic Tunnel," September 23, 1993 – Carman, Manitoba.

[46] Reform Party News Release, "Manning Pledges Tax Reform and Tax Relief When Deficit Eliminated," September 27, 1993 – Calgary.

[47] "The only deficit plan we've seen," *Globe and Mail*, editorial, Thursday, September 23, 1993.

[48] Reform Party News Release, "Manning Says Election is a Battle For Trust," September 25, 1993 – Medicine Hat, Alberta.

[49] Miro Cernetig, "Old-line parties betray Alberta, Manning says: Make Ottawa change its ways, leader exhorts Reformers," *Globe and Mail*, September 27, 1993.

[50] Roger Gibbins, "Debate Taught Few Lessons," *Calgary Sun*, October 8, 1993.

[51] Jim Cunningham, "Poll says Reform ready to conquer Alberta," *Calgary Herald*, October 8, 1993, A1.

[52] Reform Party News Release, "Manning Says Liberal Economic Program Dangerous," October 7, 1993 – Prince George, BC.

[53] Martin Mittelstaedt and Susan Delacourt, "Attacks on Reform Intensify: Survey indicates party has seized second place," *Globe and Mail*, Friday, October 8, 1993, p. 1. Sean Durkan and Bill Kaufmann, "Heat's on Reform: PM and Chrétien attack Manning," *Calgary Sun*, October 19, 1993, p. 24. Preston Manning, "Personal Message to Canadians from Preston Manning," open letter, October 10, 1993. Diane Francis, "Right-wingers must vote Reform if PCs keep sliding," *The Financial Post*, October 7, 1993. Reform Party Press Release, "Manning Says Liberals Don't Deserve a Majority Government; Minority Parliament is best for Canada," October 12, 1993 – Cambridge/Sarnia.

[54] Reform Party News Release, "Manning Sets Out Proposals to Restore Faith in the Criminal Justice System," October 13, 1993 – Toronto.

CHAPTER 6

The Bloc Québécois

André Bernard

Although the Bloc Québécois (BQ) was a new party in the 1993 election, its success is explained by the fact that it was simply the long-overdue expression in federal politics of the sovereigntist movement that had developed in Quebec over the past 25 years. The phrase "Bloc Québécois" had been in use long before the party took form. It was a reference to the Bloc Populaire, formed after the conscription crisis of 1942, which ran in the provincial election of 1944 and the federal election in 1945, and also to the dream of placing a group of sovereigntists in the House of Commons. The emergence of a "Bloc Québécois" was advocated by Gilles Grégoire after his resignation from the Social Credit caucus in the Commons in 1966 to sit as the first "indépendantiste" MP. He did not succeed in forming a bloc but he did influence the choice of a name by the provincial coalition united by Réné Lévesque in 1968 – the Parti Québécois (PQ).

The BQ Forerunners

After the birth of the PQ several sovereigntists tried to develop a BQ to run in the next federal election, but the PQ leaders discouraged them because, in their view, the electorate was not yet ready for such a venture. But in 1979, in view of the growing popularity of their "constitutional option" and despite the objections raised by the PQ hierarchy, several sovereigntists created a new party, christened the Union Populaire, to compete in the federal election on May 22. The PQ leaders objected to the Union Populaire mainly because Liberal incumbents were benefiting from the popularity of Pierre Elliott Trudeau among French-speaking Quebeckers and, according to several of its advisers, the PQ was likely to lose more than it would gain by supporting the new party because it would give the Liberals an argument in the rest of Canada. Outside Quebec, however, the Ottawa Liberals were facing an uphill battle and the PQ leaders hoped for a victory of the Conservative party led by Joe Clark. They reasoned that if the PCs won solely outside Quebec, and if the Social Credit improved its position in Quebec, it would be a boost for the sovereigntist movement, enhancing its chances in the Quebec sovereignty referendum planned for 1980. Accordingly, the PQ leaders gave some unofficial support to the Social Credit party led by Fabien Roy, a former member of the Quebec National Assembly, who opposed the constitutional stand of the Ottawa Liberals. The PQ strategy was not a success. The Social Credit party got only 16 percent of the votes in Quebec, and the Union Populaire, which had persisted despite the PQ boycott, attracted less than 1 percent. When a new election was called for February 18, 1980, the PQ followed the same strategy, and this time the results were disastrous from a sovereigntist viewpoint. The Social Credit vote fell from 512,995 in 1979 to 174,583. The PC party in Quebec went down from 432,199 votes to 373,317. Together, the 54 candidates of the Union Populaire gathered less than 15,000 votes. The total of valid votes fell and with an addition of less than 43,000 votes, the Liberals were able to claim 74 of the 75 Quebec seats.

The defeat of the PQ government's proposal in the sovereignty referendum of May 1980, followed by the constitutional amendment of 1982, forced a reconsideration of the PQ strategy. A member of the government, Marcel Léger, got permission to form a new front, the Parti Nationaliste, uniting most of those who had worked for the Union Populaire in 1979 and 1980, and many others. Unfortunately for Léger, Premier Lévesque became convinced that it was foolish to try and develop the new party with Brian Mulroney heading the PC party. A native Quebecker who spoke perfect French with the proper accent, Mulroney could easily reach the level of popularity that had served Trudeau so well. Lévesque believed Mulroney's promise of special status for Quebec, which could be seen as a step toward the long-term objective of sovereignty. In the 1984 election the PQ sided unofficially with Mulroney's PCs, and let the Parti Nationaliste run a lonely and discouraging campaign: only four of its candidates were able to reap more than 5 percent of the votes in their ridings. But the PQ felt it had won when the PCs, led by Mulroney whose personality and message had gained great popularity in French-speaking Quebec, won 58 of the 75 Quebec seats in the Commons. The PQ organization had been successful, and, above all, the Liberals had been condemned: after the 1980 referendum, the sovereigntists could not forget and did not want to forgive what the Liberals had done. As Lévesque said, the PQ strategy of supporting the PCs had been "le beau risque," and Lévesque now wanted a satisfactory deal from Mulroney's government.

A deal was made in 1987, but it was by a Liberal, Premier Robert Bourassa, who had beaten th PQ in the 1985 election, and it was not the deal for which the PQ had hoped. Nevertheless, sovereigntists thought the Meech Lake Accord a step in the right direction. To maintain Mulroney in power, the PQ again supported him and his party in 1988. So when, in 1990, the PC government began to retreat from its commitments, the reaction in the ranks of the PQ was almost emotional. At the grass roots the support for Quebec sovereignty soared to 60 percent, and to 70 percent among French-speaking Quebeckers.[1]

THE BQ: BORN IN THE ASHES OF THE MEECH LAKE ACCORD

The name Bloc Québécois was available and sounded familiar when the idea of forming a group of sovereigntist Members of Parliament became newsworthy, in the spring of 1990. It was used by several commentators when François Gérin resigned from the PC caucus on May 18 because, he said, he could not accept the decision of the government to revise the Meech Lake Accord in an effort to convince the premiers of New Brunswick, Manitoba, and Newfoundland to ask for its formal ratification. Going further, a second dissenter, Lucien Bouchard, stated his reasons in a long letter addressed to Prime Minister Mulroney. He explained that he had joined the PC party because he was willing to support the efforts of his friend, Mulroney, who had pledged to amend the Canadian Constitution to make it acceptable to a majority in Quebec. The Meech Lake Accord was the minimum acceptable, and since the Accord was to be modified in a way that was not satisfactory, from the viewpoint of a majority in Quebec, he had decided to resign from both the government and the caucus.[2] The same day, May 22, a third member of the PC party, Gilbert Chartrand, left the caucus also to protest the "betrayal." He could not endorse what was known as the Charest Report, the PC proposal meant to placate the premiers of New Brunswick, Manitoba, and Newfoundland.

The initial members of the BQ were given plenty of encouragement. Having been prominent as a federal minister from 1988 to 1990, Bouchard was the best-known member of the group and able to attract media attention to explain his resignation. Various organizations invited him to be a guest speaker, and friends in the PQ and in the Quebec trade union movement gave him a central place in several meetings. Premier Robert Bourassa, on July 3, appointed him to the Commission sur l'avenir du Québec which was chaired by Michel Bélanger and Jean Campeau and produced, in March 1991, a report concluding that sovereignty was feasible.

Many other Quebec members of the PC caucus were dissatisfied with the decision of their leaders concerning the Meech Lake Accord, but they decided to postpone resignation and await developments. Finally, only three other PC MPs resigned, to condemn the treatment given to the Accord. On June 26, three days after the deadline for ratifying the Accord had passed, Nic Leblanc, Louis Plamondon, and Benoît Tremblay joined the original three. In their view, the refusal to ratify the Accord, even after it had been diluted, showed it was impossible for Quebec to obtain even the smallest of concessions within the federal framework. They agreed with the belief held by Quebec sovereigntists that a sovereign Quebec, within a Canada-Quebec economic association, would satisfy both Canadians living outside Quebec and the "nation" formed by Quebeckers. In their view, under the arrangement proposed by sovereigntists, Canadians living outside Quebec would be able to pursue their own political objectives, without being forced to compromise with Quebeckers and, conversely, Quebeckers, would be able to suit themselves in areas they considered important. On July 25, the initial group was joined by Jean Lapierre, who had previously resigned from the Liberal caucus because he could not serve under Jean Chrétien, the new leader of the Liberal party. Lapierre had supported Paul Martin who, in his view, was more willing than Chrétien to accommodate Quebec. Because he hoped for a constitutional compromise favourable to Quebec, Lapierre could not rally to a leader who was opposed to any compromise.[3]

On July 25, the dissenters – now seven in number – made it known that they were uniting formally as a parliamentary group under the name suggested by their supporters, Bloc Québécois. The group pledged to promote the aims of the Quebec sovereigntists.[4] One of the reasons for hastening the formal creation of the parliamentary group was the need to endorse officially the BQ candidate in the by-election in Laurier-Sainte-Marie, in Montreal. Bouchard has written that Michel Lepage, the PQ's pollster, had found that a sovereigntist could get elected more easily if he had the "support of Lucien Bouchard." Reversing its previous strategy, the PQ gave full support to the BQ candidate, Gilles Duceppe, who won the by-election on August 13. With a member elected under its banner, the new BQ could now claim a legitimacy that many Canadians were not willing to recognize.[5] On September 19, the group admitted a ninth member, former Liberal Gilles Rocheleau, elected in the riding of Hull-Aylmer in 1988 with 49.8 percent of the votes. In a public statement, Rocheleau called himself a "convert."[6] In 1988, he had still been opposed to Quebec sovereignty but the rejection, by a majority of English-speaking Canadians, of the Meech Lake Accord had persuaded him to join the sovereigntists. According to some surveys, a substantial number of federal Liberals in Quebec followed the same line of reasoning,[7] and when the two former federal Liberal MPs, Lapierre and Rocheleau, maintained their membership in the Parti libéral du Québec, the BQ was able to present itself as a coalition open to sympathizers of any political party. Sovereigntists not only from the PQ and the Parti libéral du Québec joined the BQ but also from the three traditional parties in Canada, especially the New Democratic Party (NDP). On October 25, Bouchard announced the group's decision to form a full-fledged party, and to recruit candidates to run in all Quebec ridings in the next federal election. In November a fundraising campaign was launched with a one-million dollar objective.

Gilbert Chartrand rejoined the PC caucus in April 1991, in an effort to stop the splitting of the PC vote in Quebec which, at the time, seemed to make a victory possible for the Liberal party, the real enemy. But his action had no effect. Less than 11 months after their first formal meeting, the founding members of the BQ held a convention of delegates from the riding associations that had been formed. Some 900 people attended the convention, held in Tracy on June 15,

1991.[8] It adopted the "statutes" of the new party and confirmed Bouchard as leader. Two months later another MP, Pierrette Venne, resigned from the PC caucus and joined the BQ.[9] She also had been convinced to join the ranks of the sovereigntists by the rejection of the Meech Lake Accord by a majority of English-speaking Canadians. As a party, the BQ developed a grass-roots organization of its own and, one year later, was able to claim a membership of some 75,000 sympathizers.

THE REFERENDUM BATTLE

From September 1991 to the referendum of October 26, 1992, the BQ and the PQ worked together to defeat the Charlottetown agreement – the constitutional overhaul proposed by the federal government as a substitute for the defunct Meech Lake Accord. Their leaders condemned the various reports produced in Ottawa, and finally passed a death sentence on the agreement on August 28, killing it in Quebec. In the referendum, 1,709,075 Quebec voters said "Yes," but 2,236,114 (57 percent of the 3,945,189 valid votes) said "No." Riding by riding, the proportion of the "No" votes was closely related to the percentage of French-speaking voters. While around 90 percent of English-speaking voters sided with the government in support of the agreement, close to 70 percent of French-speaking voters sided against the government and the agreement. Bouchard took these results as corroboration of his view that further constitutional negotiation was futile. Once again Quebec had shown that it could not accept the compromises proposed by the political elite – compromises that appeared equally unacceptable to more than half of English-speaking Canadians living outside Quebec but for diametrically opposed reasons.

The BQ came out of the referendum campaign stronger than before. It had been ahead in the polls in the last months of 1990, and had kept its lead despite a substantial decline in public support for its long-term and primary objective, sovereignty association. After the referendum, it benefited from the support of disillusioned federalists, and its share of the vote reached a new high. From then on, the BQ remained the first choice of a solid plurality of voters. This stability encouraged Bouchard to say repeatedly that, come the election, the BQ would succeed in electing 40 or more of its candidates.

THE ELECTION

The BQ had several advantages over its opponents. It had the support of many of the activists on the Quebec political Left, notably many former members of the NDP, some of whom had even been delegates at the BQ founding convention. The support of the PQ organization was open and official. In addition, the Ottawa Liberals, led by Chrétien, were handicapped by the stigma of the 1982 constitutional amendment which had been adopted without the consent of the

Quebec Assembly, and by the memory of their opposition to the Meech Lake Accord. If it could avoid mistakes, the BQ could keep its edge over its opponents despite financial disadvantages. But unlike the Liberals and the PCs, it could not count on the indirect help of large Canadian corporations and pressure groups. Also, with only 75 candidates, the BQ was restricted in the scope of its publicity campaign.

Bouchard deserves much of the credit for the election of 54 BQ candidates. Already well-known as a member of the Mulroney government when he resigned, he had increased his popularity and become the first choice of voters who were not firmly opposed to Quebec sovereignty. During the election campaign, his performance in the media, notably in the two television debates,[10] undoubtedly contributed to the BQ's increased support. At the beginning of the campaign, the BQ was credited with 40 percent of the vote, but during the last week it consistently recorded 50 percent or better.[11] Its electoral success was also a reflection of its policy position. Its moderate posture did not frighten the voters who had taken the time to listen to its leaders. The platform included proposals quite similar to those of the larger parties. The BQ favoured substantial reductions in military expenditures, probably more so than the Liberal party. It wanted to see most tax shelters disappear, and in this seemed to agree with the NDP. It supported the free trade agreements, in tune with the PC party. Together with the Liberal party and the NDP, it advocated public investment to provide work and improve the competitiveness of the economy. The BQ welcomed the interest rate reduction proposed by the Liberal party, and applauded the pledge made by other party leaders to continue the universal social security and health care programs. Taken together, the BQ proposals fell closer to those of the NDP and the Liberal party than to those of the PCs. The few proposals that were really different concerned topics of special interest to Quebec. The BQ, for instance, would like to see the development of a speed-train link between Quebec and Montreal and between Montreal and Windsor, Ontario. It would like also to see the federal government getting out of programs that could be administered in Quebec by the Quebec government, in accordance with the 1867 constitution and its amendments. On the whole, the BQ looked like a catch-all party, leaning on the side of more government involvement in the economic and social development of the country, and determined to pursue the long-term objective of the sovereigntists in a peaceful, democratic, and orderly manner.

VICTORY

On election day, the BQ won 49.5 percent of the votes cast in Quebec, and 54 of the 75 Quebec seats in the House of Commons. It took every riding where French-speaking voters constituted more than 70 percent of the population, with four exceptions: Saint-Maurice (where the Liberal leader was elected); Sherbrooke (represented by Jean Charest, second to Kim Campbell in the PC leadership race in June, 1993); Beauce (retained by a former PC, Gilles Bernier); and Bonaventure-Iles-de-la-Madeleine (won by Liberal candidate Patrick Gagnon with 44 percent of the votes). The pattern of representation in Quebec was completely changed, in favour of the BQ and at the expense of the PC party, just as it had been changed in 1984 in favour of the PC party and at the expense, then, of the Liberal party. Winning 72 percent of the seats with 49 percent of the vote, the BQ was overrepresented in Quebec. But in Canada as a whole the Liberal party was similarly overrepresented, winning 60 percent of the seats with 41 percent of the vote. Bouchard said that the new House of Commons would better reflect the Quebec reality than before when almost none of its members were sovereigntists.[12]

ANALYSIS

By the end of 1990, although not yet a party, the BQ had won the support of 40 percent of Quebec voters, which proved to be its cruising speed. According to public opinion surveys, disillusion engendered by the failure of Prime Minister Mulroney's efforts to achieve a constitutional agreement was the driving force. Nevertheless, leaders of the other parties argued that the support gathered by the BQ was the expression of dissatisfaction with the economic recession. The Liberal leader, Chrétien, said that the BQ supporters were likely to become Liberals by the end of the election campaign. This viewpoint was endorsed by several commentators who described the BQ as a regionalist protest movement.[13]

However, according to public opinion surveys, the characteristics of BQ sympathizers were similar to those of PQ sympathizers. Younger people, the better educated, those who work in the public sector or in the co-operative segment of the private sector are overrepresented in both parties. Membership is primarily among French-speaking Quebeckers, but a number of English-speaking people are active in both parties, and surveys tend to show that approximately 10 percent of the English-speaking voters in Quebec have decided to side with the sovereigntists.[14] Two-thirds of the BQ sympathizers support the long-term objective of the sovereigntists. The remainder prefer a devolution of some federal powers to Quebec. These "federalists" side with the BQ because they cannot approve of the constitutional *status quo*. The survey conducted for the Canadian Broadcasting Corporation (Société Radio-Canada) in September 1993 found the same proportion of hard-line sovereigntists (15 and 14 percent respectively), in the BQ and PQ, the same proportion of supporters of sovereignty association (53 and 54 percent), and the same proportion of "devolutionists" (26 percent).[15] According to the CBC survey, of respondents planning to vote for the BQ who had a preference for a provincial party, 88 percent supported the PQ.[16] Approximately 10 percent of BQ voters intended to vote, provincially, for the Parti libéral du Québec.

Not all sovereigntists voted for BQ or PQ candidates. According to the CBC survey, among Liberal voters in federal and provincial elections between 10 and 15 percent (the actual figure of 12 percent in the survey was based on a small sample) would prefer a sovereign Quebec to any other constitutional option. Among Quebec voters who intended to vote PC, around 20 percent preferred sovereignty.

On the whole, the votes reaped by the BQ came from PQ sympathizers. The two parties have roughly the same electoral base. They also have the same long-term primary objective: to make Quebec a sovereign country, hopefully associated with the rest of what is now Canada. The BQ is meant to promote that objective in the House of Commons and in areas to which the PQ does not have access. The BQ is doomed to disappear if (or when) Quebec becomes a sovereign country.[17] As long as Quebec is not sovereign, the BQ, like the PQ, plans to foster friendship between the people of Quebec and those of the other provinces, while defending the interests of Quebec. Lucien Bouchard has stated repeatedly that his own views on the Quebec-Canada relationship and on the relations between language groups make for respect and mutual adjustment.

If their plans unfold as they wish, the sovereigntist leaders will form the government of Quebec this year after the provincial election, and in 1995 they will hold a referendum to legitimize a declaration of independence. In Ottawa, the BQ would play the go-between to ease the process of devolving federal powers to Quebec.[18]

Notes

[1] For an analysis of this phenomenon, see Edouard Cloutier, Jean H. Guay, and Daniel Latouche, *Le virage. L'évolution de l'opinion publique au Québec depuis 1960, ou comment le Québec est devenu souverainiste* (Montréal: Québec/Amérique, 1992).

[2] This long resignation letter is reproduced in Lucien Bouchard's biography, *A visage découvert* (Montréal: Boréal, 1992), pp. 319-25.

[3] "Le Bloc convertit le député de Shefford," *La Presse*, July 26, 1990, p. A1.

[4] This pledge (protocole) is reproduced in Lucien Bouchard's biography, *A visage découvert* (Montréal: Boréal, 1992), pp. 340-41.

[5] According to one public opinion survey: "Une légère majorité de Canadiens s'insurgent contre l'entrée des indépendantistes aux Communes," *La Presse*, September 13, 1990, p. B1. For other comments, see Lucien Bouchard, *A visage découvert* (Montréal: Boréal, 1992), pp. 342-44.

[6] Gilles Paquin, "Gilles Rocheleau travaillera à sortir le Québec du Canada," *La Presse*, September 20, 1990, p. B4.d

[7] Gilles Paquin, "Une poussée souverainiste inégalée: indépendance: 58 p. cent: souveraineté-association: 66 p. cent," *La Presse*, November 26, 1990, p. A1. See also Edouard Cloutier, Jean H. Guay, and Daniel Latouche, *Le virage. L'évolution de l'opinion publique au Québec depuis 1960, ou comment le Québec est devenu souverainiste* (Montréal: Québec/Amérique, 1992).

[8] Among these 900 people, 145 were volunteer members of the BQ, 587 were delegates of the riding associations who had disbursed $50 each, and 200 or so were observers with no right to vote. See Paul Roy, "Le Bloc québécois réussit un autre test. A peine né, ce parti 'pas comme les autres' parle déjà de disparaître," *La Presse*, June 16, 1991, p. A1.

[9] Josée Lapointe, "Pierrette Venne joint le Bloc québécois," *La Presse*, August 13, 1991, p. A1.

[10] Among the available survey results, three refer specifically to the debates (either one). See *Le Journal de Montréal*, October 5, 1993 (Léger et Léger), *La Presse*, October 6, 1993 (SOM), *The Gazette*, October 8, 1993 (Angus Reid).

[11] *La Presse* published a daily survey account of voters' intentions in Quebec during the last four weeks of the electoral campaign (these surveys were conducted by SOM, a Quebec polling firm).

[12] Quoted in Paul Cauchon, "Donner à Ottawa la température exacte du Québec," *Le Devoir*, October 23,1993 p. A6.

[13] Examples: Sarah Scott, "Bouchard grabbing Quebec's protest vote," *The Gazette*, September 23, 1993, p. A10; Editorials - "The danger in the margins. Protest movements attract loose cannons," *The Gazette*, October 23, 1993, p. B4; Peter Cook, "How to lose

a Canadian election," *The Globe and Mail*, October 15, 1993, p. B2; Philip Authier, "Bloc win won't help PQ: Bourassa," *The Gazette*, October 27, 1993, p. B1.

[14] *Journal de Montréal*, October 9, 1993, p. 11 (survey conducted by Léger et Léger); André Pratte, "Au *Bloc*, un profil de candidat qui se rapproche de la clientèle du PQ," *La Presse*, October 23, 1993, p. B5; Bloc québécois, *Caractéristiques des candidats* (1993).

[15] Direction de la recherche, Radio-Canada, *Résultats préliminaires*. Sondage SRC/CBC sur l'opinion des Canadiens pendant la campagne fédérale 1993, Montréal, September 24, 1993.

[16] The PC party does not have a provincial counterpart to run candidates in Quebec provincial elections: its main support necessarily comes from voters who side either with the PQ or with the Parti libéral du Québec. Among the respondents interviewed for Radio-Canada in September 1993, many were planning to vote both federally and provincially: those of them who sided with the PC party were divided into two main segments, one (30 percent) made up of PQ sympathizers, the other (58 percent) favouring the Parti libéral du Québec.

[17] Paul Roy, "Le Bloc québécois réussit un autre test. A peine né, ce parti 'pas comme les autres' parle déjà de disparaître," *La Presse*, June 16, 1991, p. A1.

[18] See Lucien Bouchard (sous la direction de), *Un nouveau parti pour l'étape décisive* (Montréal: Fidès, 1993), 122 pages.

CHAPTER 7

The Press and the Prime Minister

ALAN FRIZZELL AND ANTHONY WESTELL

Some scholars argue that the mass media directly affect the way in which people behave; for example, how an election is reported affects how people vote. Others believe the influence is indirect and occurs over the long term by forming attitudes. But whatever the theory, there are at least two groups of people, journalists and politicians, who are certain that the media have a great and immediate influence. A study of 126 journalists conducted jointly by the Carleton University School of Journalism and Communication and Anderson Strategic Research just prior to the 1993 election found that 81 percent thought the media would have a very significant effect on the outcome of the election. Convinced of their role and responsibility media organizations devoted considerable resources to election coverage. The day after the election, the *Citizen* in Ottawa, for example, produced a 14-page supplement giving the national and local results, with commentary and analysis – a costly exercise for any newspaper. Politicians are so convinced of the influence of media on voting behaviour that they devise media strategies intended to ensure that what they want reported is reported and, equally important, what they don't want reported, isn't. In the past, this meant arranging leaders' tours, providing briefing documents, and scheduling events and photo opportunities to coincide with deadlines, thereby giving the media little choice of what news to report that day.

But this time was different: as the *Citizen* put it in a front page headline on September 8, "Space Age Campaign Starts Today." Everyone expected that a new style of campaign would emerge, reported in a new way. Well aware that their standing in the community was low, politicians would use more technology and money to give at least the impression of a campaign directly in touch with the people. At the same time news organizations would change strategy. As Elly Alboim, former CBC-TV bureau chief in Ottawa and now a respected media consultant, has argued, in the wake of the Charlottetown referendum debacle, journalists were regarded as the handmaidens of the political elite, and new approaches were thought necessary to involve average Canadians in coverage of the election. This was most evident in television coverage, but newspapers also got into the act. For example, *The Globe and Mail* introduced a Vox

Populi space, and another innovation in the press was the Reality Check feature to evaluate politicians' claims and promises.

Murray Campbell, writing in *The Globe and Mail* on September 10, commented: "The prospect is that this campaign will – if the best intentions hold – move beyond the tyranny of the photo opportunity that has prevailed since whirlwind jet tours by party leaders were introduced a generation ago." Others were more sceptical. In a September 28 article in the *Globe,* Allan Levine quoted the paper's own Ottawa columnist, Giles Gherson, as writing, "...the media...will devote most of their substantial energies not to explaining the basic policy issues that move voters, but to charting the horse race – who's ahead and who's behind." Levine asserted that elections emphasize the weakness in current journalism, "The misinterpretations, the biased reporting, the quick judgments, the fascination with the trivial, the lack of historical perspective and the conflict with making news informative and making it entertaining."

The following content analysis suggests that in fact the broad pattern of coverage changed very little. Attempts to involve readers may indeed have guided journalists in editorial choices and made the news and commentary more accessible. On the other hand, far less attention was paid to polls which seek out the opinions of thousands of citizens on a variety of issues and choices. On balance ordinary Canadians may actually have had less input to the news than in past elections. As noted in chapter 1, some Conservatives complained that the news media were less than fair in reporting on Prime Minister Kim Campbell. This survey certainly shows that she was under attack more than her opponents and received more unfavourable coverage, but it cannot say whether she deserved it, whether the press was merely recording her failures. There have also been suggestions that Campbell and NDP leader Audrey McLaughlin were treated severely by the media because they were women, but there is no evidence of gender bias in the coverage.

The analysis covered seven newspapers, each a market leader in its region: *The Sun* in Vancouver; the *Free Press* in Winnipeg; the *Star* in Toronto; the *Gazette* and *La Presse* in Montreal; the *Chronicle-Herald* in Halifax; and the national edition of *The Globe and Mail* which is edited in Toronto but printed in centres across the country. These were the same newspapers analyzed in the election studies of 1984 and 1988, making comparisons possible. While the papers are not completely representative of the press in Canada, they are influential in their markets and provide a picture of news coverage from most of the regions of the country. Every journalistic item dealing with the election for every day of the campaign was analyzed and coded – 3,744 items, including news reports, analysis of the news, articles by columnists, editorials expressing the opinion of the paper, photographs, cartoons, even letters to the editor.

Our researchers read and classified each item in a number of ways. For example, they measured the length, recorded the type of journalism – news report, backgrounder, opinion, etc. – noted the principal person and topic identified in the item, and so on. Those are objective measures, but we also applied subjective tests in the sense that the researcher had to make judgments, assessing whether the average reader would obtain a neutral, favourable, or unfavourable impression of the person, party, or policy featured in the item. Most items are, of course, neutral, and even when they are judged to be favourable or unfavourable this is not a measure of bias: a report may be entirely fair and accurate yet still reflect favourably or unfavourably on the subject. But this measure does allow us to determine how coverage might have influenced the attitudes of reasonable readers. However, reading newspapers is only one way a person gathers information and forms an opinion or, more likely, modifies an opinion already held.

For the first time we have tried in this study to measure the extent of negative campaigning – that is, direct attacks on a politician or a policy or even, heaven forbid, on the media or the polls. When researchers found an item that contained an attack, they reported the target of the attack.

One interesting finding in the study is that the quantity of coverage is sharply down from previous elections.

Table 1
EXTENT OF COVERAGE *
(actual number of items)

	V.Sun	W.FP	T.Star	M.Gaz	M.LP	H.C-H	G&M
1984	739	768	1035	581	1043	631	812
1988	831	915	1378	897	1143	849	922
1993	524	435	822	571	680	230	484

* Where a series of short articles on a single topic were grouped together they were coded as one article.

Some of the difference is explained by the fact that the election campaign was shorter – 47 days as compared to 51 in 1988 and 57 in 1988. More of the difference is probably due to the recession reducing advertising revenues for papers, which has meant smaller editorial budgets and less news space. One might also argue that the campaign was less newsworthy because it lacked a dominating topic such as the Free Trade Agreement in 1988 or the surprising rise of the Tories in 1984. Another factor, as we shall see, is that the press was far less interested in poll results.

Between 1984 and 1988 there was a marked swing from news coverage to analysis, commentary, and opinion. If anything that trend has continued, but the overall pattern in 1993 seems to be similar to that in 1988.

Table 2
TYPE OF COVERAGE
(percentages)

News	60.1
Backgrounder	6.5
Editorial	6.6
Column	12.8
Letter	10.6
Cartoon	2.3
Photograph with Caption	1.1

This breakdown was common to most newspapers with the exception of *La Presse* where 23.4 percent of the coverage was in the form of columns, reflecting the personal style of journalism in Quebec.

About two-thirds of the items were under 500 words in length, and most coverage came from staff sources. CP/PC accounted for 14.9 percent of all election coverage, with other news services contributing a further 4.1 percent. As in previous years, the *Chronicle-Herald* carried most wire copy; 36.9 percent of its election coverage came from CP.

Table 3
ORIGIN OF STORY
(percentages)

	V.Sun	W.FP	T.Star	M.Gaz	M.LP	H.C-H	G&M
Ottawa	9.9	7.4	13.9	28.7	11.5	8.3	29.8
Home Province	61.3	59.1	40.3	30.5	52.6	46.1	32.2
Other/ Unclear	28.8	33.5	55.8	40.8	35.9	45.6	38.0

We have noted in past elections that BC and Quebec papers tend to pay more attention to the campaign in their own province than other papers, but this may be explained in part in this election by the fact that they were home base for party leaders: Kim Campbell from Vancouver, and Jean Chrétien and Lucien Bouchard from Quebec. It is not so obvious why in this election the *Winnipeg Free Press* stayed close to home, unless it was an economy measure. It is possible that the leading role of TV in covering the national campaign may encourage even major newspapers to concentrate on local or regional news.

Table 4
COVERAGE OF LEADERS
(percentage of all election items)

	V.Sun	W.FP	T.Star	M.Gaz	M.LP	H.C-H	G&M
Campbell	20.1	20.4	20.0	18.1	14.4	16.8	21.4
Chrétien	11.4	8.0	13.0	13.2	14.9	16.9	13.9
McLaughlin	6.7	6.9	8.2	6.3	5.0	4.9	5.1
Manning	10.9	9.7	10.6	8.0	6.2	7.0	13.9
Bouchard	4.2	3.5	4.2	17.8	17.6	2.8	7.8
Other Leader	3.1	2.8	2.4	2.9	2.1	4.9	2.0
Other Coverage	43.6	48.7	41.6	33.7	39.8	46.7	35.9

Campbell received substantially more coverage than Chrétien in the West and Ontario, and even in the English-language *Gazette* in Montreal. As might be expected, Bouchard was a major figure in Quebec, outstripping even Chrétien, but he was not of much interest elsewhere – despite which he became Leader of the Opposition. Coverage of the other emerging party leader, Preston Manning, was fairly consistent in Ontario and the West, but fell off in Quebec and the East in part no doubt because his Reform party was barely visible in those regions. Thus the attention to party leaders seems to reflect the regional nature of this national election.

Elections are supposed to be primarily about issues: after careful reflection, voters choose the party whose policies promise the best government for the country. In fact, research shows that a minority of voters base their choice on issues, and political experts consider campaign strategy more important to electoral success than detailed policy statements. This is reflected in media coverage. While the media argue that they concentrate on issues, analysis of coverage shows that they usually devote more space to such topics as campaign strategy, party organization, the individuals involved in running the campaigns, and candidate nominations. We group these items under the heading of "Process". We group under the "Other" heading non-issue coverage dealing with topics such as opinion polls, criticism of party leaders, debates about the quality of leadership, and interpretation of the TV debates. These three broad subject areas – "Policy", "Process" and "Other" – are necessarily grab-bags for hundreds of subjects. There are scores of different policies and a variety of items about party organization, tactics, the nomination of candidates, and so on. Caution is required when making comparisons among the three elections covered in this study since the contents of the grab-bags change from campaign to campaign. But there appeared to be more attention to policy in 1988 than in 1984 because the Free Trade Agreement dominated the political debate, and there was less emphasis on the political process. In this election the situation seems to have reverted to that of 1984: more attention to process and less to policy. While the budget deficit emerged as a major issue, all the parties said it had to be reduced, so the difference between them was not as sharp and exciting as was, for example, the clear difference of policy over free trade in 1988.

Table 5
TYPE OF ELECTION COVERAGE
(percentages)

	1984	1988	1993
Issues	26.0	36.8	31.0
Process	39.1	29.1	34.4
Other	34.9	34.1	34.6

The Globe and Mail was the paper most concerned with campaign strategy, and the two Western papers disproportionately covered candidate nominations. Though the percentages in the "Other" category are similar we must bear in mind that the total number of items – the extent of coverage – was sharply reduced. The reality, therefore, is that the press paid far less attention to polls in this campaign than in the past.

Table 6
ISSUES COVERED
(percentage of all items mentioning issues)

	1984	1988	1993
Economy/ unemployment	28	3	38
National unity	15	6	2
Peace/defence	11	4	4
Patronage	10	1	—
Women's rights	11	4	5
Tax reform	5	5	5
Energy	4	1	—
Social	4	6	22
Free trade	—	58	2
Immigration	—	—	4
Other	12	12	14

The Economy/Unemployment item includes such policy topics as inflation, interest rates, and the budget deficit, and the problem with making comparisons is that the weight of each topic changes from election to election. For example, unemployment was not a big issue in 1988 but accounted for about 9 percent of all items this time. Similarly, the budget deficit became a major issue accounting for over 7 percent of all items. In 1984 the issue of free trade was invisible; in 1988 it far outstripped all other policy issues; this time in the form of NAFTA, it amounted to only 2 percent of all items; and despite the rise of the Bloc Québécois, national unity as an issue sank almost out of sight, probably because the BQ campaigned on bread-and-butter issues rather than the constitution.

Table 7
OBJECT OF ATTACK
(percentages)

	V.Sun	W.FP	T.Star	M.Gaz	M.LP	H.C-H	G&M
Campbell	8.8	6.7	14.3	10.6	8.7	7.0	9.8
Chrétien	1.9	0.9	3.8	5.2	5.9	2.2	4.4
McLaughlin	0.2	0.5	0.9	1.1	0.6	—	1.7
Manning	1.5	1.8	3.3	2.3	2.2	0.4	4.7
Bouchard	1.9	1.8	2.8	9.2	6.0	1.7	3.7
Other	26.3	27.6	26.5	29.4	14.2	27.0	38.1
No attack	59.4	60.7	48.4	42.2	62.4	61.7	37.6

A majority of all items, 54.6 percent, contained no attack in any form. Where there was an attack it was usually on a party leader or other individual, and might be one leader attacking another, a columnist attacking a leader, even the writer of a letter to the editor attacking a leader or the news media. Most of the items in the "Other" category involved criticism of more than one leader. Nobody will be surprised to learn that there was very little criticism of journalists or pollsters.

It is clear from the analysis that Campbell received more coverage than her opponents, and that more of it was in the form of attacks. A similar pattern appears when coverage of each leader is assessed as "Favourable", "Unfavourable", or "Neutral". Coupled with the fact that, in general, the coverage of Campbell was more unfavourable, we can assume that the average reader would have a declining opinion of her as the campaign went on. This seems to match the trend revealed by the major polls reported in the press; there was a week by week decline in support rather than sharp drops related to particular events. As is usually the case, the NDP leader was attacked less than the other party leaders, but that is probably because NDP leaders are seldom perceived as real threats to the other parties. Setting aside McLaughlin, it is interesting to note that Manning was subject to fewer attacks than his rivals.

TABLE 8
FAVOURABLE OR UNFAVOURABLE COVERAGE OF LEADERS
(percentages of items about each leader, excluding not-applicable items)

	FAVOURABLE	UNFAVOURABLE	NEUTRAL
Campbell	4.9	43.8	51.2
Chrétien	12.0	24.4	63.6
McLaughlin	7.5	16.8	75.7
Manning	16.2	24.5	59.3
Bouchard	9.6	21.7	68.7

This deals only with items in which the party leader was the principal subject. Campbell received more coverage than her rivals and more of it was unfavourable and less of it favourable. All the leaders, however, received more unfavourable than favourable attention. Manning came closest to a balance, while Audrey McLaughlin received the most neutral coverage.

When this coverage is examined by week, the proportion of unfavourable coverage of both Campbell and Chrétien was relatively constant throughout the campaign, undercutting any theory that Campbell was the victim of progressive disenchantment among journalists.

Analyzing unfavourable coverage by type of journalism, 63.5 percent of editorials expressing the opinion of the paper were deemed unfavourable (and only 7.7 percent favourable), 36.7 percent of columns, 5.7 percent of news items, and 4.7 percent of news backgrounders. In other words, there was a clear division between those parts of a paper reserved for opinion and those devoted to news.

COVERING CAMPBELL

We have seen that, from the opening of the campaign, Prime Minister Campbell received more critical coverage than her opponents, and the question to be discussed here is whether this was justified. To put it another way, when and why did she lose the momentum she had when she entered the election and begin the slide to personal and party defeat? Quite possibly on the opening day of the campaign when, in the opinion of the news media, she made the first of several blunders. As *The Globe and Mail* reported on the front page the following day (September 9), "Ms Campbell spoke of a jobless economic recovery, holding out little hope of making major inroads into unemployment in the 1990s. Her priority remains the deficit." Naturally, her opponents leapt to denounce her and to promise jobs now, and she was stuck with the view that reducing the deficit would mean no reduction in unemployment for years to come. As the *Globe* put it on September 10, "Yesterday, Ms. Campbell stuck to her grim assessment – made on Wednesday when she announced the October

25 election – that it would be unrealistic to expect a sharp drop in the unemployment rate in the next few years."

Reality Check, to use the *Globe's* terminology? Did she ever say such a thing? There was no quotation in the original front-page story, but there was one inside the paper: "I would like to see, certainly by the turn of the century, a country where unemployment is way down..." Other papers used the same quote. So she was not saying, at least on this occasion, that unemployment would not drop significantly in the 1990s. In fact, she was saying close to the opposite, in words that could easily have been used by Jean Chrétien or Audrey McLaughlin. Nor was she saying that her priority was the deficit rather than jobs; her view, stated repeatedly, was that reducing the deficit will create jobs. Perhaps the truth of the matter is that Campbell, on this occasion and others, expressed her thoughts clumsily, even ambiguously. The question, then, is whether it is fair game for reporters to put the most dramatic interpretation on her words, or whether they should try to convey what she seemed to be trying to say.

Another example of Campbell's problems with words and reporters occurred later. "PM won't touch key issue," bannered the *Globe* on its front page on September 24. "Social programs called too vital for campaign trail." Other papers and the radio and TV newscasts followed much the same line, and again the opposition leaders expressed their outrage.

Reality Check. This time Ms. Campbell accused the media of misreporting her remarks. In response, the Canadian Press news service distributed the text of what she had said during an impromptu question-and-answer session with reporters. Precision of language is not to be expected in such a situation and the prime minister certainly did not produce rounded thoughts in grammatical sentences. But she did make several clear points: (1) she was "fundamentally committed to preserving quality social programs in this country, to preserving our health-care system;" (2) the programs must be modernized, but the government had no blueprint for reform and did not want to try to generate one during the 47 days of the election campaign; (3) the issues were complex and had to be discussed with the provinces before action was taken; and (4) if she was returned to office, that discussion would probably be after the new parliament met in the fall and before a budget was introduced in February.

Was it fair, then, to report her as saying, as most of the media did, that an election was no time in which to debate the key issue of social policy? Certainly she said that, or something very like it, and it made a shocking headline for a damaging story. But in context, her views were hardly different from those of other party leaders, and in fact the Liberal government is following the scenario for reform she outlined.

Campbell began the campaign by saying that it was her policy to eliminate the deficit in five years, but that she could not say how that would be done. For one thing, the provinces would have to be consulted. She was then subjected to what a *Globe* reporter described as "unrelenting pressure," presumably by journalists, to produce numbers. Numbers make news because they have a certainty about them, wrong though they often are. She gave in and blundered again because her numbers did not seem credible. This time because her forecasts of revenue for the next five years were too generous.

Reality check. The prime minister and the journalists knew perfectly well that short-term forecasts are no better than guestimates and long-term forecasts are worse. Revenues depend on the level of economic activity in Canada, and that depends very largely on what is happening to the global economy of which Canada is a small part. In short, no prime minister can control revenues. Mostly for that reason we have a budget every year, sometimes more than once a year, to take stock of the economic circumstances and of revenues and spending, and to make adjustments. Budgeting five or six years ahead may be useful as a yardstick to keep track of developments, but to suggest that forecasts can be accurate is a game. The prime minister did not want to play, but the media insisted. So who was at fault?

Even if there are grounds for questioning the details of how the press covered Campbell on three occasions which may have been important in changing her public image, the fact remains that, as previous chapters have documented, neither she nor the party were prepared for the election or for legitimate scrutiny by the media. The strategy was to win on her personal appeal as a new type of politician with new policies and a new approach to government. Aggressive media coverage revealed the emptiness of her image – her inexperience, lack of policies, and we dare to say her arrogance in refusing to take advice. Indeed, the whole performance may remind old hands of Prime Minister Pierre Trudeau's campaign in 1972 when he sallied forth with a mindless slogan – The Land is Strong – and proceeded to hold what amounted to policy seminars across the country, refusing to debate issues with his opponents or to provide the media with hard news. It was new, different, and may even have been magnificent, but it wasn't politics as the media and the voters understood it. Having almost lost the election, Trudeau rapidly learned how to play the conventional game of party politics, and won handily in 1974.

Campbell will not have that opportunity, but journalists might well pause to reflect on whether they would really be open to "the new politics" for which they so often call. For example, what if a woman leader – or a man for that matter – brought to political campaigning qualities said to be feminine, such as gentleness, peacemaking, compassion, conciliation, the ability to listen, and comfort? Could traditional news values adjust to report fairly such an eccentric approach to politics?

The Polls

For the first time in several federal elections the opinion polls in 1993 were not a matter of controversy. This was probably because there were fewer polls at the national level, their findings were remarkably consistent, and they were reported better. To be sure there was criticism, especially of the way in which polls were reported in the media, but it was relatively muted. No rogue polls appeared, most polls showed a similar pattern of opinion during the development of the campaign, and some attempted to go beyond the horse-race aspect of the campaign and deal with issues. This was a surprise, since the polls in the years between the elections of 1988 and 1993 had, with one exception, simply rolled out the party and leader standings.

Pre-election polls

All the evidence shows that polls between elections are not good predictors of election outcomes. One could argue that the polls during the second Mulroney government accurately reflected the depth of public disenchantment and thereby suggested its defeat, but this would be simplistic. The Tories dropped to the lowest level of federal party support in Canadian polling history, 11 percent as reported by Gallup in February 1992. The previous lowest had been 15 percent between the elections of 1984 and 1988, after which they recovered and won a majority in the House of Commons. By the beginning of 1993 a Tory recovery was obvious and the final poll taken before Prime Minister Mulroney's resignation showed the party standing at 21 percent, a level that rose to 33 percent after the resignation and to 36 percent after the election of Ms Campbell as party leader. The last poll before the election call was conducted by the Toronto research firm Environics and showed the Tories with 34 percent of the vote, one percentage point above the Liberals, with 19 percent of the electorate undecided.

Polls between elections are, then, somewhat like by-elections. They constitute an expression of opinion, a sort of "free vote," when nothing is at stake, and they should be evaluated as such. For example, on September 8, 1992, before the national referendum that rejected the Charlottetown agreement, the *Toronto Star* reported a poll indicating "The unity deal has 2-1 backing." Clearly any individual poll is of little relevance, but a number of polls taken together give indications of how the various parties are viewed over time. They can also reduce the fixation on the horse-race aspect of politics by providing information that is relevant even between elections and enriches political reporting, such as detailed studies of issues, policy concerns and underlying political values.

The quarterly collaboration between the CBC and *The Globe and Mail* on the most comprehensive media poll ever produced in Canada was an attempt to do this. The first joint poll was released in October 1989. There were three distinct advantages to the scheme. First, because resources were being pooled, better samples, more questions, and more detailed analyses were possible. Second, the newspaper was able to provide specific details about the poll, such as the actual questions asked, after the results had been announced on the CBC. And third, the cost of the enterprise ensured that the partners would make the fullest use in their reports of the information gathered. The results were released on the CBC's *Sunday Report* hosted by Peter Mansbridge, and then in *The Globe* on Monday, with additional reporting on Tuesday. Two *Globe* political reporters were assigned to the poll stories, Hugh Winsor and Chris Waddell, thus ensuring continuity. This approach to media polling is common in the United States, where most major TV networks are affiliated with a newspaper or news magazine in a polling venture and use reporters who are comfortable writing about polls and are knowledgable about the techniques involved. While the experiment worked for a time, although the polls were not always quarterly, the deal fell apart at the time of the referendum. There was disagreement between the partners about who should do the field work (interviewing), when and if referendum polling would be done, and on the deadlines for the release of the results. There was also a feeling among some of the participants that there was little enthusiasm for the venture among senior management in both organizations.[1] This may be understandable given the fact that the field work for each poll cost in the region of $60-70,000, and to this had to be added journalists' time, other research expenses, and consultant costs. Although *The Globe and Mail* decided to continue the regular polling, it has now decided that future polling will be occasional and usually part of an omnibus poll to reduce costs.

ELECTION POLLS

The most important aspect of election polling in 1993 was that there were a lot fewer public polls, 13 major national polls compared to 24 in 1988. This is only partly due to the shorter campaign and the new electoral law that banned the publication of poll results in the last three days of the campaign.

Table 9
National Polls Published

	PC	LIB	NDP	BQ	REF	Other
AR Sept. 11	35	37	8	8	10	2
CQ Sept. 14	36	33	8	10	11	2
AR Sept. 20	35	35	6	11	11	2
Gallup Sept. 25	30	37	8	10	13	2
Environics Sept. 26	31	36	7	11	13	2
LL Sept. 26	28	34	7	12	15	4
Ekos Sept. 30	25	39	6	12	17	1
CP OCT. 2	26	38	8	12	14	2
AR Oct. 8	22	37	8	12	18	3
CQ Oct.16	22	40	7	13	16	2
LL Oct. 19	21	39	6	14	17	3
AR Oct. 22	17	43	7	14	17	2
Gallup Oct. 22	16	44	7	12	19	2
Result Oct. 25	16	41	7	14	19	3

(AR, Angus Reid; CQ, Comquest Research; CP, Compass Research; LL, Leger & Leger).

In addition there were numerous riding, regional, and provincial polls. Notable were the provincial polls in Manitoba, Saskatchewan, and British Columbia conducted for local papers by Angus Reid. In Quebec tracking polls were done by the Quebec polling company SOM for *La Presse.*

Not only were there fewer polls, there were fewer poll stories as a percentage of total newspaper coverage. In 1988 roughly one-quarter of all articles in papers analyzed (see above) identified polls as a primary or secondary topic; in 1993 it was 11.5 percent. The reduction was evident across the board.

Table 10
MEDIA USE OF POLLS
(percentages)

	V. Sun	W.FP	T. Star	M. Gaz.	M.LP	H.C-H	G&M
No Mention	91.0	92.9	88.1	84.5	84.1	96.1	87.1
Main Topic	4.2	3.7	2.7	8.3	6.8	3.0	6.4
Secondary Topic	4.8	3.4	9.2	7.2	9.1	0.9	6.4

Graph 1
Current Federal Vote

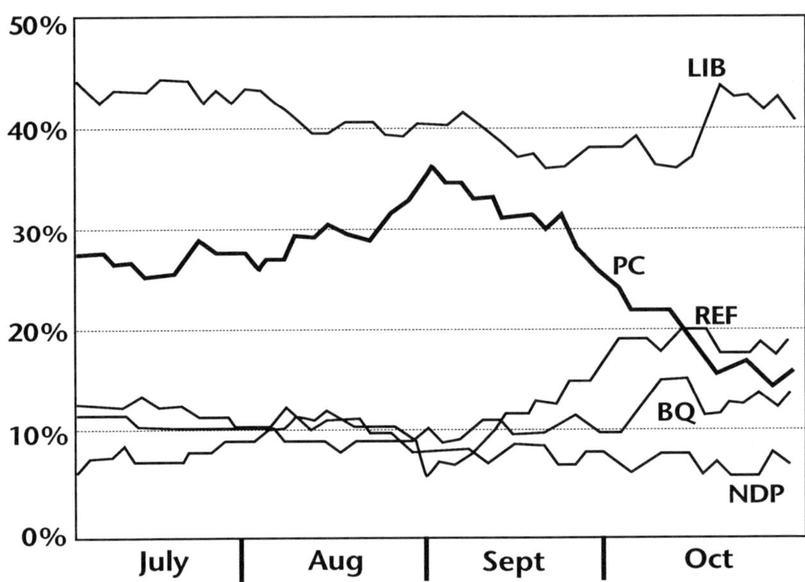

Source: Insight Canada Research

Graph 2
Best Prime Minister

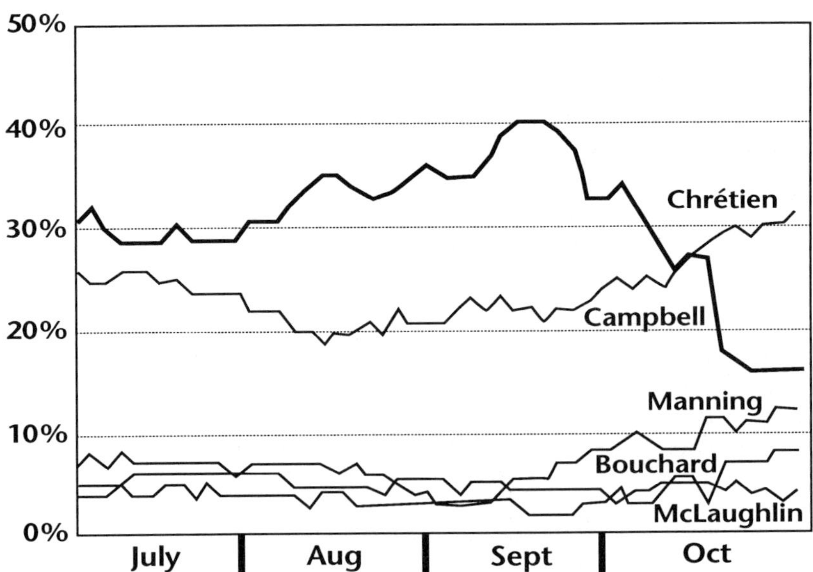

Source: Insight Canada Research

Ottawa remained the main locale of poll stories, despite regional polling. Only 4.7 percent of stories were coded as unfavourable in the content analysis, and 93.8 percent were deemed to be neutral, while the remaining 1.5 percent were coded favourable.

Most poll stories, 70.8 percent, dealt with party or leader standings, as opposed to 3.7 percent which dealt with issues in the campaign.

Although most polls tracked the horse-race, it was evident that rather than an election of dramatic shifts this was one of fairly steady trends. If there was one event that prompted a movement from the Conservatives to the Liberals it was the release on October 14 of the Conservatives' anti-Chrétien television commercial. On the whole, however, the trends over the election period were steady, as the tracking data from the Toronto based Insight Research firm make clear. (Graphs 1 and 2).

The polls assessed levels of party support throughout the campaign, but they did not do very well in explaining the reason for the changes. Such questions as whether voting intentions were "soft" or "hard", what were "positives" and "negatives" for each party, and "likes" and "dislikes" of party leaders were not addressed. True, some polls especially those in the *The Globe and Mail* and from the Angus Reid organization, did relate party support to issues, but that was the extent of the analysis. In our analysis of press coverage, only 3 percent of poll stories dealt with opinions on policy issues.

However, if the polls did not explain as much as they could have, there were fewer examples of the pollster-as-guru phenomenon. Journalists are becoming more accustomed to reporting polling results and are less reliant on the pollsters for interpretation. Such writers as Julian Beltrame of Southam News, Hugh Winsor of the *Globe*, and particularly Denis Lassard and Louis Falardeau of *La Presse* seem to have made poll reporting a speciality. The dean of polling in North American journalism would approve of this distance of the pollster from the final copy. Philip Meyer has argued that "journalism needs a stronger base in scientific methods and that pollsters should stay close to their scientific roots."[2] Pollsters did not, however, completely give up the limelight to concentrate on their numbers. For example, *La Presse* quoted Alain Giguère, President of the Quebec polling firm CROP, and Donna Dasko of Environics as saying that the leaders' debates would have no significant impact on the election outcome although no polling data were reported in support of those conclusions. In the *Toronto Star* John Higgins of Gallup was quoted as saying that the 28 percent undecided in his last campaign poll indicated "a lot of those are just sitting back right now, waiting to decide," but he did not explain why his undecided figure was more than double that in any other poll at the time.[3]

While there was much more straight reporting of the numbers, there were still errors of omission and commission. While most newspapers present much better explanations of the methodology than they did in the past, they rarely make it into secondary reports. And there are still dubious claims being made on the basis of poll results. For example, an article in *The Globe and Mail* on October 19 said that poll results sway voters in strategic voting plans, although there is little evidence that voters do vote strategically. Another danger is reporting more than the numbers warrant. Again in the *Globe*, a poll taken before the election was called suggested, "The inroads the Campbell-led Tories could make on Bloc Québécois supporters is one of the poll's most optimistic implications for the Conservatives since it suggests that they could rebuild much of their Québec base." Predictions of this sort give credence to pollsters' claims that polls should be seen as snapshots of opinion rather than estimates of future behaviour.

The *Globe* was also responsible for the biggest poll blooper of the election when it reported spurious numbers. It gave results attributed to a forthcoming Angus Reid survey which were shown to overestimate Liberal and Reform support when the actual survey was published. The paper also published seat projections based on the false numbers when no such estimates were included in the actual poll. Worse still, the false results were picked up by other newspapers and broadcasters. The figures were supposedly leaked to the *Globe* by a an aide to Liberal leader Chrétien. Reid retorted, "I'm dumbfounded as to who in their right mind would take a piece of gossip from one of the parties and put it out as the top of the news."[4]

In an election with fewer polls and sharply reduced coverage, there was still criticism of the emphasis on poll stories in the media. Columnist Robert Fulford argued that journalists were "so intoxicated by polling that sometimes they prominently display opinion stories that literally mean nothing: the word poll switches on an automatic pilot in editors' brains".[5] His analysis was partly based on a widely quoted article by the Anglo-American journalist Christopher Hitchens, arguing that polls are a threat to democracy as they depoliticize politics through the process which "is very distinctly weighted against the asking of an intelligent question or the recording of a thoughtful answer."[6] He went on: "On their own, one could argue that opinion polls do no more than seek a common denominator among the demographics. But as practiced, polling searches for a confirmation of consensus, this to be exploited and reinforced by professional politicians. In alliance with the new breed of handlers, fundraisers, spin-specialists and courtier journalists it has become both a dangerous tranquilizer and artificial stimulant."[7] Another critic, *Winnipeg Free Press* publisher Maurice Switzer, is less vehement but questions the polls' contribution to the democratic process since such things as margins of error and vague questions can mislead rather than inform.[8]

Even Switzer is not in favour of the recommendation of the Royal Commission on Electoral Reform and Party Financing that the publication of polls be banned during an election. In a research report for the commission Guy, Lachapelle argues that polls do influence the vote, though he presents little evidence. Many other countries ban the publication of polls for at least part of the election campaign. For example, France bans public polls for the final week, and in Belgium the ban lasts two weeks. In his report, Lachapelle says that only journalists oppose the regulation of polls and suggests not only a publication ban but also some sort of commission to scrutinize the methodology of polls.[9]

In fact the law in Canada was changed to ban the publication of polls for the last three days of the federal campaign. Many pollsters would argue that this was exactly the wrong thing to do since it leads to leaking party polls, the use of non-scientific straw polls, and withholds from the voters crucial information in tight elections. When scientific polling results could not be published during provincial elections in British Columbia between 1939 and 1982, so-called hamburger polls appeared, and in some very tight elections, such as the UK general election of 1970, only polls close to election day managed to reflect the actual result. Polls taken several days prior to the election may mislead voters about the true state of public opinion.

Journalists in Quebec appear to be most opposed to the regulation of polls. Louis Falardeau argues that the same arguments in favour of banning publication of polls could be made for banning other election news, and a *La Presse* editorial described the publication ban in strident terms, "Cette loi est bête, incohérente et méprisant.[10]

NOTES

[1] Interviews with CBC and *Globe and Mail* journalists.

[2] Philip Meyer, "Polling as Political Science and Polling as Journalism", *Public Opinion Quarterly* 54 (1990), p.452.

[3] Pollsters define "undecided" in different ways. Gallup probably includes "refusals" and "will not vote" in the undecided category.

[4] The *Vancouver Sun*, October 9, 1993, p.A9.

[5] *The Globe and Mail*, March 24, 1993, p.A3.

[6] *Harper's*, April 1992, p.45.

[7] Ibid., p.49.

[8] *Winnipeg Free Press*, October 1, 1993, p.A6.

[9] Guy Lachapelle, *Les Sondages et les Médias lors des Election au Canada*, Vol. 16. Research Reports, Royal Commission on Electoral Reform and Party Financing.

[10] *La Presse*, October 23, 1993, p.B2.

CHAPTER 8

The Television of Inclusion

LIONEL LUMB

In her summer of goodwill and benign coverage on the barbecue circuit, Prime Minister Campbell promised a different kind of leadership centred on her theme of the "politics of inclusion." It proved to be an ideal she could not deliver, and in fact the news media were more successful at including Canadians in the election. During the campaign they gave ordinary citizens unprecedented presence on page and screen and airwaves. This effort – arguably the most significant change in the way in which the election was reported – delighted media executives almost as much as it dismayed the working journalists. The executives were evangelical in their fervour to raise the media's credibility by inviting the public into the newsrooms, as it were. The journalists viewed the effort either cynically, as a mere public relations exercise, or more seriously as an abdication of their responsibility.

Newspapers promoted vox populi, voters' panels, and special phone numbers through which readers could put questions to local candidates and national leaders, provoking Ottawa's *Hill Times* columnist Claire Hoy to sneer at the "ongoing campaign to replace journalism with stenography." But people enjoyed the opportunity to get involved. When *The Toronto Star* offered readers a chance to call in with their views, almost 13,000 responded within three days. One reader said: "Politicians should be forced to sit down and listen to us about what we think matters." Politicians did sit and listen on television, which perhaps went even further than print in embracing the average Canadian. For instance, the CBC's *Prime Time News* electronic town halls turned private citizens into instant pundits, challenging and discomfiting politicians representing the main parties.[1] There were so many angry ordinary people on television that one was reminded of the famous line from *Network,* Paddy Chayefsky's movie about television: "We're mad as hell, and we're not going to take it any more." Many participants went far beyond asking questions of the captive politicians on the town hall panels, venting open hostility or listing grievances. They were seldom interrupted or even prompted to ask questions by the CBC moderators (either Peter Mansbridge or Pamela Wallin, depending on the night). In fact, the moderator was more likely to interrupt an evasive politician and press for an answer to the question.

This deference to people power, both in print and on television had its critics.

A former senior CBC parliamentary journalist commented:

> A lot of it was allowing automatic and unquestioning access by ordinary citizens to their pages and airtime. They allowed people to say the most egregiously hostile things and then took their side. To simply elicit it and then wash your hands is an abdication. I found the whole thing a very weird process.[2]

Similar views emerged at an election post-mortem held by the Canadian Association of Journalists (CAJ), in Ottawa in November. Speakers, almost all of them journalists, decried the town halls and forums as failures, and boring ones at that. For example, Joan Bryden, parliamentary columnist for Southam News, described the *vox populi* trend as an insult to voters' intelligence. She asked, "What greater public voice can there be than voting results?" The lone politician on the CAJ panel, Rick Anderson, was more careful in criticism – understandably, since he is an adviser to an avowedly grassroots party, Reform. He said it was encouraging to see the town halls attempted, "...but it was done begrudgingly, it was so overstructured that it became boring."

Criticism is unlikely to stop the media's attempts to involve the public directly in political journalism. First, because there's no doubt many of the Canadians who took part, particularly in the TV town halls, enjoyed the opportunity to press politicians on issues that mattered to *them*, rather than to journalists or other politicians. Second, and more profoundly, the public rejection of the Meech Lake and Charlottetown constitutional accords demonstrated that both politicians and journalists were poor readers of the public mood. Journalists were forced to admit that they had been lumped in with the politicians as an elite. As Jim Travers, editor of the *Ottawa Citizen*, told the CAJ post-mortem, the public accused the media of trying to sell the Charlottetown Accord, and the national debate revealed "an insatiable public appetite for information, and more unfiltered information." Readers wanted facts and barebones analysis. All this prompted journalists to distance themselves from the political elite, and the experience with the Citizens' Forum on Canada's Future, chaired by Keith Spicer, offered a model. The Spicer commission toured the country in 1991 seeking the opinion of ordinary Canadians on constitutional issues, and the hearings, in a sense, were an ongoing town hall. Daily news reporting and frequent live television coverage on *CBC Newsworld* worked to assure Canadians their opinions mattered. Media coverage of the election built on this trend.

Travers said that to help voters cast an informed ballot the *Citizen* coverage included more issue-oriented reporting, "voters' voice" features, truth checks (to verify politicians' claims), and reader advisory panels. There were fewer opinion polls and less emphasis on reporting the campaign as a horse race. Many other papers followed the same general pattern, and the story was much the same for the television networks. The executive producer of CBC *Prime Time*

News, Tony Burman, agrees the public felt shut out of the Meech and Charlottetown processes while "the CBC and other media appeared to be on the inside of those meetings...the impression of being part of an elite had to be dealt with."[3] In its coverage, he said, *PTN* had two main objectives: "We wanted to increase our analysis of issues, as opposed to getting locked into the rush of same-day straight news coverage, on the assumption that our viewers would be coming to us to get some sense of what's real and what isn't real, and what's true and what isn't true, to get some useful information which helps them as citizens to make a choice. We would continue the daily coverage of the leaders' tours and yet ensure there was a great amount of analytical debate and discussion. I guess we did turn around the proportions considerably.[4] The second objective related to public involvement in the election, (to deal with) the obvious sense of alienation that many people felt about the political process, and the desire on their part to be integral players as opposed to bystanders. So we set about trying to create formats that would level the playing field." PTN's coverage therefore included:

**The town halls, each of which ran about an hour in *PTN* extended to 90 minutes.

**Voters' Voice – focus groups of selected voters who provided a second-by-second electronic assessment of leaders' speeches and party ads.

**Reality Watch, a check by senior correspondent Brian Stewart on the truth of party statements and positions.

**Campaign Closeup, a series of special reports, with informative graphics, on major issues such as the deficit, crime and punishment, and jobs.

** Profiles of key ridings that illustrated national trends.

**Studio interviews with the party leaders, including the National Party's Mel Hurtig who was excluded from the leaders' debates, ranging from about 10 to 15 minutes.

**CBC punditry in the form of essays by the perceptive chief political correspondent, Joe Schlesinger, and the acerbic writer Rex Murphy.

**Partisan punditry weekly by a lively panel made up of regulars Stephen Lewis (representing the NDP point of view), Hugh Segal (Tory), Heather Reisman (Liberal), Tom Flanagan (Reform), and with appearances for the Bloc Québécois by Daniel Turp, a senior party adviser.

**A challenging but successful attempt – rare on television which is so often condemned by print reviewers as a non-intellectual medium – to present a primer on the Canadian economy: 25 minutes of Mansbridge leading Leigh Anderson, an economist at Carleton University, and Jeffrey Rubin, chief economist for an investment company, through basic concepts such as the debt, deficit, GNP, GDP, and the credibility of campaign promises on issues such as job creation and deficit reduction.[5]

**And, of course, almost daily coverage of the leaders, with occasional references to significant polls.

CTV also reached out to the public but in a less structured and formal way than the CBC. For instance, instead of locking politicians into the bearpit atmosphere of a town hall, *Canada A.M.* devoted two-and-a-half hours a week to an open-line question-and-answer show with the party leaders. Another innovation was a weekly report on CTV News featuring extracts from radio open-line programs from Vancouver, St John's, and a couple of places in between. These reports included interviews with the radio hosts summing up the main interests and views of their callers. CTV chief news editor Henry Kowalski explained: "Talk radio is the lightning rod for public opinion. If we tune into the most popular radio talk show in a different province, once a week, we will get a pretty good cross-section of what people are thinking."[6] CTV also sent veteran news anchor Lloyd Robertson into the field to report on close encounters with voters. This served both to give viewers a feel for the mood of the country, and to expose Robertson to that mood in preparation for election night. Robertson showed up in Richmond, BC, Quebec City, and in the farmers' market at Kitchener, Ontario, where he shucked the anchor's customary suit-and-tie in favour of a comfortable sweater.

Dennis MacIntosh, senior producer of CTV News, explained his network's different approach: "Our coverage was layered with people (reporters) on the buses and planes, and also our (national) bureau people concentrating on doing stuff in the field with local candidates and riding officials. We tried as much as possible to do local issues out in the field....We find that the national picture gets dealt with at the local level as well and sometimes better than if you're always looking at things from a totally national perspective."[7] *CTV National News* coverage also included:

**More frequent and extended use of polls than the CBC, and regular studio punditry from pollster Angus Reid.

**Regular punditry from its outspoken Ottawa bureau chief, Craig Oliver, such as his assessments in field reports of leaders and strategies, and reports on issues such as health care.

**Lloyd Robertson interviews with the party leaders, generally about four minutes (CTV's news slot is 24 minutes after commercials, compared to 53 minutes for *PTN*).

**Fact Check, CTV's version of the truth check.

Both networks' forays into coverage which involves the public are likely to continue and even be enhanced although their motivation may be different. For CTV and its affiliate stations the driving purpose is to stay close to local audiences and milk the community goodwill which they enjoy to a greater extent than the CBC regional stations. Local audience loyalty will become crucial for survival in the age of mega-channel choice. The CBC is committed to becoming more accountable to the public: accountability is the new buzzword at the corporation which even has a vice-president of accountability. So, to the CBC, offering the public greater access is certainly no burden. Besides, the feedback to its election coverage was mostly positive. Tony Burman says: "We were actually quite surprised at the extent to which the town halls garnered attention, in terms of the political community but also in terms of audience response. Even those of us who felt they were frustrating, that there was too much shouting going on – which reflected the mood of the people rather than the format – felt that it was worthwhile, and that it was a real attempt to get public views on to the agenda. (We have) a viewer talk-back line here that virtually exploded with the numbers of calls that flowed in after the four town halls...There was no part of our coverage that generated a response like that. We also had letters and faxes, a huge response." Some of the feedback dealt with the issues, some with the perception of bias on the part of the moderator or the format – "it clearly provokes partisan comment," says Burman.

Many people saw the format as a breakthrough, which surprised Burman since the CBC has been staging town hall meetings since early 1991, including several during the referendum campaign.[8] The ratings were good. The last CBC town hall, on public faith in government, attracted an audience of 1.01 million, just under the 1.2 million viewers of the news segment of the 90-minute program.

THE TV DEBATES

Average Canadians played a part not only in news coverage but even in that most sacrosanct of political encounters, the leaders' debates. A studio audience of about 50 francophones was recruited for the French debate on October 3. The next day the English debate was held in Ottawa and 80 or 90 members of the public were brought in from across the country at considerable expense to the three networks that jointly aired the debate, CTV, Global, and CBC. "It's all part of a different way of looking at things, about who's involved in public discourse," said Arnold Amber of the CBC, who headed the networks' group organizing the debates. "In fact, it's almost bringing political debate back to its roots."[9] Both Amber and Michael Robinson, the Liberals' chief debates negotiator, pointed to the US experience in the 1992 presidential election where, said Amber,"the voice of the population is much more involved." Robinson said the presence of the studio audience in the US debates had an enormous effect on the style of the leaders' arguments. For instance, George Bush ran into trouble with the American audience when he tried to attack Bill Clinton's character.[10]

In Ottawa, the average Canadians forming the audience were sequestered from the media, fed and housed in hotels, transported in buses to the National Arts Centre for the debate, and finally allowed their shots at the party leaders on the stage in the last 45 minutes of the two-and-a-half hour production. Meanwhile viewers at home might well have wondered what had happened to the audience or why they were there at all. After all, the English debate's broadcast began with video pictures of the average Canadians filing into the National Arts Centre. Their importance to the proceedings was then underlined when some were asked what they expected to hear from the leaders. In her preamble to the event, TV moderator Medina raised expectations even further when she said the debate would be unique because there were five leaders instead of the usual three, and added, "Also unique, tonight we have an audience, an audience chosen from all regions of the country, an audience that will be asking questions." In fact, after the opening interviews, viewers saw nothing of them until an hour and three quarters into the program. Then, the average Canadians were briefly visible, poorly lit and out-of-focus, in the background as three sharp-focus, well-groomed journalists[11] questioned the brilliantly lit leaders. Unwittingly, the producers thereby achieved the opposite of what they intended – the perfect image of two elites playing to each other with the Canadian people on the sidelines. But there was worse to come. The network news producers had ordered that the studio audience – the voices of the people – were not to applaud or otherwise react to the leaders' theatrics. This was unnatural for any audience but in the mild-mannered Canadian way these average citizens accepted the stricture until some got carried away and started to applaud, whereupon the producers rushed in a "NO APPLAUSE" sign.

When the members of the audience were finally allowed to ask questions the control continued. Questioners were selected and introduced by the three journalists who had been quizzing the leaders and now held the portable microphones. The leader to whom a question was addressed was given a minute to answer, and moderator Medina cut off any who went longer. At one point she interrupted Campbell, saying "And that's the only part of the answer we're going to hear." To a later question Campbell responded with one word, "Yes." Only twice did the audience break loose from the straitjacket fitted by the producers. There was modest applause when a woman asked about support for single-parent families, and laughter which united audience, leaders, and journalists – and probably the viewers – when another woman asked if the Blue Jays were going to win the World Series. To glorify this event as bringing "political discourse back to its roots" is risible. Significantly, most journalists who reported on the debate ignored the presence of the audience, whereas the audiences' behaviour in the US debates was widely commented upon. This is somewhat understandable in view of the small part played by the Canadian audience, but it may also reflect the attitude of Canadian journalists to the *vox populi* trend.

COVERING THE HORSE-RACE

After winning the Conservative leadership, Campbell spent the summer touring Canada and enjoying favourable media coverage. The National Media Archive of the Fraser Institute kept tabs on how she and other leaders scored on the main CBC and CTV newscasts between June 13 and August 16. Campbell outshot Chrétien by five to one in the percentage of mentions.(It's intriguing in the light of how many seats Reform won on October 25 that Manning was almost ignored during this period, getting fewer mentions than Bouchard.)

	CBC %	CTV %
Campbell	75	70
Chrétien	14	14
McLaughlin	8	9
Bouchard	2	6
Manning	1	1

Perhaps this coverage lulled Campbell and her strategists into overconfidence: after all, at one point in August she was the most popular politician in 30 years. They probably thought that a young, energetic, photo-smart and articulate baby-boomer who could even joke about the spreading "prime ministerial bottom" could overwhelm Chrétien, who began the campaign under the cloud of poor publicity. There were numerous media references to the contempt in which Chrétien was held in Quebec, and the polls showed that Canadians by a wide margin thought that Campbell would make the better prime minister. Logically, her campaign was planned to play the Tories' best card – Campbell herself. But the media had their plans, too. It was almost as if journalists said to themselves: "Okay, now we've got to get serious. Campbell's had her free ride all summer, now she's going to have to earn favourable coverage." And, of course, an election is a serious matter, and much is expected of a prime minister. CBC anchor Pamela Wallin seemed to set the new tone when she introduced the first *Prime Time News* report of the campaign with these words: "As Prime Minister, Kim Campbell started things off this morning. She's prime minister only because Conservatives chose her, and now all Canadians will have a vote." Clearly, Campbell was going to have to prove her mettle during the campaign, and the analysts' consensus was she got off to a bad start. Viewers saw Campbell announcing the election by reading a statement in a lacklustre style, and then came the fateful reply to a reporter's question about unemployment: "I think, realistically, all the developing and industrialized countries are expecting what I consider to be an unacceptable level of unemployment for the next few...three or four years." The CBC reporter, Denise Harrington, said Campbell refused to set targets for job creation, and Campbell continued with her unhopeful message, delivered with an unfeeling shrug: "I mean I could say how many jobs I would like to create but — I'm sorry, that's old policy." (In her answer, Campbell also said, "I would like to see, certainly by the turn of the century, a country where unemployment is way down and we're paying down our national debt, and there is a whole new vision of Canada opening up for Canadians," but it was not in the CBC report.) Campbell continued her chosen campaign on Day One when she visited a school and talked to children about the importance of reading and learning. On Day Two she took part in a town hall meeting. She pushed her "politics-of-inclusion," taking notes, cultivating the image of a leader who listened to the people. Journalists were cold-shouldered, and also puzzled by the absence of hard news – policy pronouncements, fiery speeches, and mass rallies. On Day Three viewers saw and heard her heckled by construction workers over jobs. Her strategists must then have made contact because CTV's Lesley Jones reported Campbell was trying to portray the Tories as the party of hope, fine-tuning her comments about unemployment and the year 2000. And on Day Four, the last day of the first week, Harrington on the CBC was telling viewers that Campbell was refusing to answer questions from reporters because her handlers feared she might get into trouble.

The Liberals chose a different and more conventional style of campaigning. On the morning the election was called, Chrétien's message, and the theme of the party's television ads, was, "I have the team, we have the plan, and we can make the difference." But by that evening, realizing the gift handed him by Campbell in her comments on unemployment, Chrétien had embraced jobs as the Liberal issue of the campaign. Finger stabbing for emphasis, voice rising in a rallying cry, he declaimed: "They want to create jobs for the year 2000. For us the priority is to create jobs in 1993 — right now – and we'll start in November." Day Two saw him fighting the "yesterday's man" tag by looking vigorous and energetic, and talking about job creation. On Day Three he promised to create 120,000 jobs, and on Day Four he was showing the Liberal flag in Quebec. In the second week, the Liberals unveiled their election platform – live on *CBC Newsworld*. Media reporter Chris Cobb wrote: "The skill and precision with which the Liberals organized their Big Event illustrates just how difficult it is for news media to avoid being used....The show went like clockwork...Liberal organizers spent thousands of dollars, organized to the nth degree and executed the event brilliantly. Wednesday night television newscasts and Thursday morning's front pages testified to that."[12] From then on Chrétien was seldom seen without the Liberal "Red Book" – "we have a plan" for all to see – waving it aloft at every opportunity, and assuring voters they could challenge him on its promises after electing him to power.

The pattern was set: the contrast in speaking styles, the content of the messages, even to some extent the reporting of the two campaigns, continued more or less as they had begun on September 8. The National Media Archive says that by the end of the second week of the campaign the Liberals and the Conservatives had received equal amounts of coverage on the CBC, while CTV gave slightly more attention to the Liberals. But, says the Archive, two-thirds of the evaluations of the Conservatives on the CBC were negative. By contrast, the Liberals received slightly more favourable than unfavourable assessments. On CTV, the Conservatives received almost twice as many negative as positive evaluations, while only slightly more negative than positive evaluations were heard about the Liberals.[13] But what does the Right-leaning Archive mean by negative coverage? At the CAJ post-mortem journalists asked themselves if they had set Campbell up over the summer only to knock her down during the campaign. The feeling was, no, that Campbell chose her own "tough love" message, and harped on the deficit and debt control without offering hope over jobs; and she was hampered by a disastrous campaign and a team with no discernible strategy. Part of the problem was the record of the Mulroney government and Campbell's reluctance to distance herself from its policies. For example, on that first day in what should have been only a cute photo opportunity at a school she was asked questions about her predecessor's policies. On Day Two she voiced a thought that would compound into real trouble later: "Many people realize that cuts to social programs are inevitable." When Chrétien unveiled his Red Book, Campbell and the other leaders were seen on the newscasts that night criticizing the plan, but Campbell had nothing with which to fight back. The next day she was shown in Calgary praising business for doing many things better than government, and repeating her promise to eliminate the deficit – but, as CTV's Jones pointed out, she didn't say how. Campbell waffled over the government's book-keeping methods, and the next day (September 17) Chrétien jumped on this as evidence her government's books were in a mess. At the post-mortem Joan Bryden said: "Reporters could see the pattern of things going wrong, and could see Campbell becoming a problem." From the journalists' point of view, they were covering a horse-race,[14] and that entailed constant evaluation of gains and losses in public support, campaign and backroom strategy, leaders' performance and gaffes – or handling of gaffes – and, of course, policy statements and how these compared with previous party policies.

The Tories and Campbell were far less successful at getting across their message than the Liberals and Chrétien. The Tory message was confused and defensive at best, and it was given the news frame the journalists considered appropriate. A frame allows both the journalists and their readers or viewers to understand the context of the event – how facts add up to make an unfolding story. In the early days, the frame was the exuberant new Tory leader against the tired old Liberal pro. But soon it became the Campbell campaign and whether she would be able to keep her job as prime minister on election day. Later the frame broadened to include the rise of Reform and the Bloc Québécois, and the collapse of the NDP. But for the most part the frame of the story was the tracking of the self-inflicted Tory wounds as the race gathered steam.

At the start the polls suggested a hung parliament. After nine days, (September 17) CTV released an Angus Reid poll which showed the Bloc Québécois at a record 43 percent in Quebec, followed by an Allen Fryer report in which Bouchard told Quebeckers it was obvious that federalism does not work. Later, on September 20, CTV ran a special edition featuring its Reid-Southam poll predicting a Liberal minority government. The NDP vote was shifting to the Liberals[15] and Reform was picking up rural votes. Lesley Jones reported Campbell's personal popularity was still high, but Craig Oliver pinpointed the fact that Chrétien was running on the right issue — job creation. Anchor Lloyd Robertson interlaced the news reports with poll information and two interviews with pollster Angus Reid, so anyone watching CTV that night certainly discovered the state of the race.

As if inspired by the poll's bad news, Campbell came out with her strongest criticism to that point of the Liberal platform: the difference between the Liberals and the Conservatives, she said, "was the difference between hype and hope." Her handlers must have felt encouraged by the way she looked and sounded, confident and convincing, especially when she totted up the cost of the Liberal plan in tax increases and inflation. But her surge was soon arrested by the major gaffe of the campaign. She was asked about a report of a federal study suggesting the government could save billions by revamping social programs. Campbell waffled: she was unaware of the study, she said, and she supported social programs. But under the pressure of more questions she felt compelled to add: "(Social programs are) a very important issue — the issue is too complex to generate some kind of blueprint in the 47 days of an election campaign...that's the worst possible time because it takes more than 47 days to settle anything that is that serious." The media swooped and so did Chrétien. Both CTV and CBC reported him suggesting Campbell had a secret agenda. McLaughlin said: "It's arrogant, elitist and condescending in the extreme for the prime minister to suggest to Canadians that social programs cannot be discussed because, somehow, they could not understand the issues."[16] The next day (September 24) Campbell blamed the media for "spinning" her remarks and missing the real point about eliminating the deficit. To underline her criticism of the reporting she read from a prepared statement because "I don't want there to be any doubt about what I said." She restated her firm commitment to "our cherished social programs" but said these needed reforms because they were outdated. The prepared statement may have served not only as a broadside against the media, but also as a way for her handlers to keep Campbell on track. They lived in fear of her unscripted remarks and lecture-hall persona on television which provoked analysts to cast her as arrogant, going her own way, and believing she had the answers and could best gauge the public's mood.[17] Edward Greenspon and Jeff Sallot quoted senior aide Patrick Kinsella as saying that, despite briefings and notes, Campbell left those around her "not knowing what she was going to say...we never know until she speaks."[18]

Chrétien also had his tense moments. CBC viewers on September 20 heard him speak about a Danish program that requires people to work for welfare. Reporters seized on this as a new idea, and possibly one with tough, Tory-like overtones. Chrétien showed his discomfort and tried to recover by saying he was just thinking aloud about an interesting concept. Not satisfied, CBC reporter Keith Boag raised this "work-fare" issue again the next day. Once again Chrétien put up a weak defence but this time New Brunswick Premier Frank McKenna came to his aid, and in his open, matter-of-fact way talked about a similar plan in his province. The issue died, never rising to the status of gaffe.

Campbell was beset with questions for days after she said she didn't want to talk about social programs, but Chrétien received much less attention when he said something similar on October 7 on CBC: "If you ask me, 'Will you never pass a piece of legislation on any of the (social) programs?' I can't say that. Who can say that?" The Liberal plan was to keep the social safety net in place and ensure that health care would be accessible to all. But he would not say how this was to be done until after the election: "Let me win the election, and after that you come and ask me questions about how you (I) run the government." In her on-camera summary of the report, Harrington said it was likely that Chrétien would come under increasing pressure to be more specific, but this never seems to have happened. Chrétien also refused to discuss specific plans for replacing the goods and services tax, with a similar lack of journalistic follow-up.

The nearest Chrétien came to disaster was on October 5. After a lead story on CBC about Campbell taking hard shots at Reform and the Bloc Québécois, and a report on new negative Tory advertising, Wallin introduced a story about Chrétien, who she said was buoyed by being undamaged in the debates and was now running an upbeat campaign. Harrington's report showed pictures of a confident, smiling Chrétien striding the streets of Toronto like a winner. Later he took a shot at the Tory platform, which Campbell had "written on the back of an envelope, you know, one night in the plane." He also criticized the Tory plan to privatize Toronto's Pearson airport: "He would not call it patronage, just made it sound like that," said Harrington. Then Harrington reported that Chrétien had left Toronto for a fund-raising party in Montreal. Harmless enough, on the face of it, but lying in wait for Chrétien was a Radio-Canada reporter and TV crew. Chrétien was obviously chagrined at being videotaped and although viewers didn't hear his exchange with the reporter, his body language said it all as he waved one hand peevishly and shrugged dismissively. Most media reported his aides as saying he was at a private dinner, although obviously Radio-Canada and some others knew otherwise. In fact, he was attending a reception at the exclusive Laurier Club to meet supporters who had paid $1,000 each for an invitation. Although the CBC did not make more of the event that night, the following night Wallin introduced the newscast's lead story: "Jean Chrétien has had the roughest day of this election campaign. For 28 days things have been rolling along fairly smoothly, and the Liberals have surged to the top of the polls and avoided any controversy. But now on Day 29, Chrétien has a problem." Peter Mansbridge then intoned: "The Liberals sent a letter to wealthy supporters in Montreal outlining the advantages they can expect when they contribute a thousand dollars to the party. Chrétien was left to answer questions about the relationship between money and influence." Harrington's report picked up the theme: "Today Chrétien was on the spot." Then she showed a beleaguered Chrétien fending off question after question by saying, "The Liberals have raised money in that way for years," and "To have access to Jean Chrétien is free for anyone." He even tried humour: "My wife is a member of the (Laurier) Club, and she is the only one who has privileged access to me." Harrington summed up the day: "Chrétien had hoped to capitalize on the Conservatives' dwindling support in Quebec. The exclusive fund-raiser has overshadowed all that and put Chrétien on the defensive on one of his central campaign promises: that a Liberal government would put the interests of all Canadians ahead of the interests of the party's friends." A banner headline in *The Toronto Star* said: "Well-heeled voters can buy Chrétien — for $1,000." *The Globe and Mail* headline read: "Liberal campaign hits a bump," and in smaller type: "Grits accused of selling access to leader at $1,000-a-person affair." But again Chrétien got away with this "bump in his campaign." *Canadian Press* reporter Bob Cox described it as "a classic bit of damage control." Chrétien's aides, rather than react defensively, called the stories fair and apologized for not advising reporters of the fund-raiser, he wrote.[19] Then Chrétien offered juicier news by announcing a Liberal government would review the controversial Conservative plan to privatize Pearson airport and cancel it if need be. Reporters lost interest in the fund-raiser, and soon CBC was reporting about Chrétien and aboriginal issues while CTV's Ken Ernhofer was evaluating the Liberal strategy on jobs. Ernhofer noted that critics of the Liberal plan were emerging, and aides were starting to shield Chrétien from the media.

But the big news that day (October 9) was a new Angus Reid poll. Both CTV and CBC led with it, showing that the Tories "had dropped like a stone" (CBC's words). The Liberals were at 37 percent, the Tories at 22 percent, Reform had surged to 18 percent, the Bloc had 12 percent in the country overall, and the NDP trailed with 8 percent. CBC's Schlesinger said the "big slide" showed the Tories had lost one-third of their voters in just three weeks.[20] In Quebec the Tory slide was even steeper, and Reform had doubled its popularity in Ontario to 19 percent.

Preston Manning led a charmed life for most of the campaign. The National Media Archive[21] says that while television reporters judged the merits of the Conservatives and Liberals on their campaigns, Reform was judged on its policies. While Campbell was consistently questioned on campaign strategies, or had to explain a gaffe, Manning was shown presenting Reform's vision of Canada. "By the second week of the campaign, they received more attention than the traditional Canadian third party, the NDP," the Archive reported. In the first three weeks, assessments of Reform were three times more likely to be favourable than unfavourable. But after the debates, and as the polls showed the party climbing, TV paid more attention and there was more unfavourable coverage. Even so, overall the assessments were balanced. Manning's campaign did hit one major bump, providing a genuine defining moment on television – the John Beck affair. Critics had accused Manning of "speaking in code," of cloaking contentious policies on, say, immigration in language that disguised his real meaning, which was nevertheless recognizable to the party faithful and likely recruits. On October 12 Pamela Wallin interviewed Manning for about 15 minutes on *Prime Time News*. She tried more than once to press Manning on the business of coded language, toward Quebec, for instance, or on Reform's religious underpinnings, raising the question of intolerance. But Manning was both plausible and imperturbable. But in the next couple of days he lost some of his celebrated cool after students at Ontario's York University confronted Manning with racist remarks made by Reform's York Centre candidate, John Beck, and reported in their student newspaper, *The Excalibur*. Beck had said, "Immigrants will overwhelm us," and they bring "death and destruction." Television reports of Manning's response to the student question showed him pausing uncharacteristically for a couple of seconds before trotting out his standard line: "The tenor of those statements is not compatible with the Reform Party's positions...I urge you to go to source, to go to our source document." The CBC's legislative reporter in Ontario, Havard Gould, and producer Bob Weiers tracked Beck down and interviewed him on camera. The result was a dramatic report that played on the CBC's local stations in Toronto and Ottawa, on other regional news programs, on *CBC Newsworld,* and in an updated version by Paul

Adams on *Prime Time News*. It is worth describing Gould's report in some detail.The opening titles began with a voice-over by anchor Bill Cameron: "Tonight, race and Reform." Then Beck's image appeared in a graphic box and he said: "I can see the transition of the people in Toronto, going from the WASP into different types of people. I don't even know where they come from." Gould interjects: "Are you against that?" Beck: "I'm against it now. I think we have to stop it." Cut to the studio with both Cameron and Gould at the anchor desk. After an introduction, Gould presented his "explosive" story. He said Beck stood by his comments as quoted in the student newspaper, and then "went further...much further." The report included the following exchange:

> Beck: I feel that if an immigrant comes into Canada and gets a job for $150,000, he is taking jobs away from us.
>
> Gould: Who's us?
>
> Beck: Us, the gentile people.
>
> Gould: White people?
>
> Beck: The white people...(and later)...
>
> Beck: Immigrants are going to overwhelm us. Well they are — they already have.

There it was, not words printed in quotation marks but spoken by a flesh-and-blood Reformer with all the veracity and immediacy of television, complete with inflection, tone, emphasis — language stripped of code. It could not be denied. To his credit Manning bounced Beck immediately (though it was too late to remove his name from the ballot), but the next day he continued to look rattled. He said he wanted to discover how things had gone wrong, and if Reform's screening process for candidates had failed, or if, Beck was "just one bad apple in the barrel."

It is interesting to speculate about what Reform might have achieved if there had been no Beck incident. The party had gone from single digits to 19 percent in the polls in just a few weeks, a strong rising trend which flattened out after Beck. Michael Marzolini, chairman of Insight Canada Research, the Liberal party's pollster, says its tracking polls show that Manning was not personally touched by the affair, which had an impact only in Ontario, especially in the Metro Toronto area. Reform fell three points the day after the Beck story broke on TV, then climbed back again: "The growth of Reform was limited, hampered; it didn't go on in the same manner." Without the setback it's conceivable that Reform would have won more than its single seat in Ontario and therefore become the official opposition. A defining moment, indeed. Another factor worked to Reform's advantage and drew media attention away when, the day after the Beck affair, the Tories made their final, and near-fatal error: the ads attacking Chrétien.

The Advertising War

Television advertisements are the politicians' best way of speaking directly to the people without journalistic filtering and contextualizing. But while ads can get a party's message across, they also reveal much about its strategies, state of confidence, and attitudes toward voters. For instance, the bullying Yes side ads during the Charlottetown Accord referendum campaign offered disturbing insights into establishment attitudes and served to fortify many Canadians' resolve not to be pushed around by the claim that those who opposed the accord were enemies of Canada. On the other hand, negative advertising worked for the Conservatives in the 1988 election campaign after Liberal leader John Turner had won the debate with Mulroney on free trade. Conservative strategist Allan Gregg devised a "bomb the bridge" strategy which attacked Turner's credibility – the bridge linking Liberals and anti-free trade voters – and has been credited with turning around the election. Gregg was also the adviser behind the referendum ads in 1992 but he seems to have learned little about changes in public mood from this failure because when the Tories' situation became desperate in mid-October of 1993 he reached back to his tactics of 1988. It was an incredible miscalculation.

The first wave of Tory campaign advertising released on September 26 was bland and inoffensive. Seven out of eight ads featured Campbell looking off-camera at an unseen interviewer and explaining various policy issues. The ads ended with the ambiguous slogan: "It's time," and suggested the Tory strategists were still counting on Campbell as their election winner. The Liberal ads were tougher, featuring Chrétien talking directly to camera, blaming the Campbell-Mulroney Conservatives for the 1.6 million unemployed, and 300,000 bankruptcies, with black-and-white pictures of recession-ravaged streets, closed stores, and a montage of headlines about lay-offs. Instead of harping on the deficit, Chrétien held out the hope of job creation: "I have the team, we have the plan, and we can make the difference." The New Democrats had the rawest ads, also in black and white, and so full of crackling anger and emotion they seemed to leap off the screen at viewers. It was as if the NDP wanted voters to see themselves as victims of the Tories, victims of free trade, unemployment, patronage, of policies that favoured the rich, and tried to distil all that anger into a minute of explosive television. But while the ads tossed problems at viewers like so many hand-grenades, they offered no hope or solutions.

The day after the English debate, Campbell displayed an aggressive new style in her speeches, taking hard shots at the two parties eating into Conservative support, Reform and the Bloc Québécois. That night the CBC also reviewed unexpected new Tory ads that Wallin described as "the political equivalent of heat-seeking missiles." Schlesinger reported the ads dispensed with Campbell and instead mounted an attack on Chrétien and the cost of his policies. A grimy worker pushed a wheelbarrow of $1 coins into a close-up on camera and shovelled the coins into a muddy pit. Another ad poked fun at Preston Manning, showing a magician sawing a woman in half while a voice said: "Governing is an easy trick, just pick a spot and start cutting." The Conservatives' campaign chair, John Tory, told the CBC his party was just catching up: "We were the very last party of any of the major parties to engage in advertising that criticized our opponents at all." Nine days later, October 14, the Tories went further down the booby-trapped path of negative advertising, no doubt driven by their collapse in the polls. Mesley reported on *Prime Time News* that the Conservatives had started a new television ad campaign that took a swing not at Chrétien's policies but at the man himself. One of the two ads aired (apparently four were produced) combined close-up photographs of Chrétien focused on the partially paralysed left side of his face (the result of a childhood illness), while off-screen voices described his job-creation policy as a joke, suggested he wasn't with it, had lost touch with reality and so on. The last voice on this ad said: "I personally would be very embarrassed if he were to become prime minister of Canada." The second ad began with a close-up photo of Chrétien's contorted face and a voice that asked: "Is this a prime minister?" Then other voices over more unflattering close-ups asked why Chrétien didn't answer questions and wondered whether he understood them. Mesley's report used the key clips from the two ads and included an interview with a media consultant, Peter Swain, who said the pictures were there "to appeal to a very base instinct...'Gee, we want a statesman to represent Canada.'" Swain also said this kind of portrayal "is the nuclear fuel of the advertising world. It can work, it can be incredibly effective, but it can be extremely dangerous."

Swain was prophetic. The ads ignited a firestorm of revulsion that showed how badly the Conservatives had misread the mood of the public. Party headquarters in Ottawa and campaign offices across Canada were bombarded with calls of protest. On radio talk-shows caller after caller proclaimed disgust with what some described as American-style tactics. The *Canadian Press* reported that Tory candidates and ministers called and faxed media outlets to dissociate themselves from the ads which they denounced as "mean-spirited" and "offensive." Others sent personal notes of apology to Chrétien and suggested that Campbell too should apologize. Both CTV and CBC led their newscasts on October 15 with reports about the Tories' day of torment. At first, party insiders tried to defend the ads, to play down the personal-attack angle. But by late afternoon Campbell, who had not been shown the ads in advance, viewed them and ordered them off the air. "I think the tone is inconsistent with the message I'm trying to deliver," she said. Campbell initially did not offer Chrétien an apology and actually started moving away from the journalists' microphones but was brought back by questions. Then she said: "I would apologize to Jean

Chrétien and anyone else who found them offensive." The news reports also showed a dignified Chrétien delivering these moving words: "They tried to make fun of the way I look. God gave me a physical defect. I've accepted that since I was a kid." The next morning a *Globe* poll (taken before the ad controversy broke) showed the Liberals at 40 percent nationally and the Tories trailing in every region of the country. That night on CTV Oliver predicted the largest defeat of a government in 70 years. That the Tories were going down to defeat was certain before the Gregg gaffe, but the ads made the last nine days of the campaign almost irrelevant.

There's one curious footnote to the ads. By her action and her words when she pulled them, Campbell dissociated herself from them. But just a few days earlier she had received minimal coverage when she took a jocular yet strangely similar personal swipe at Chrétien's deformity. While campaigning in Hamilton, Toronto's CITY-TV captured this scene in a doughnut shop: Campbell fondled a pumpkin and, ever one for a fast quip, said, "What a face I can put on that. I think I'll carve it to look like Mr Chrétien." She delivered this tasteless line in her breezy fashion without venom, though clearly without much thought. But it showed that the Tory leader was similar to Gregg and her other strategists in their ability to regard Chrétien as a caricature, easy to poke fun at. Chrétien's revenge was to win big by using his experience to gauge the temper of the times. "Yesterday's man" knew most Canadians wanted a return to policies and values of "yesterday's Canada," pre-Mulroney.

Notes

1 Mel Hurtig of the National party made it on to one town hall panel. Otherwise, politicians from the Tory, Liberal, NDP, Reform and Bloc Québécois faced off against sixty voters.

2 Elly Alboim, CBC parliamentary bureau chief until July, 1993, in an interview in *The Globe and Mail*, November 4, 1993.

3 Interview with Lionel Lumb.

4 This claim of Burman's runs counter to a detailed content analysis done by the National Media Archive of the Fraser Institute in Vancouver. It says both CBC's *Prime Time News* and the *CTV National News* gave the substantive issues — such as jobs, free trade, health care — less attention in 1993 than in the 1988 election. CBC's issue reporting fell slightly from 38 percent in 1988 to 35 percent. On CTV the drop was more dramatic: from 38 percent to 27 percent. Free trade, the dominant theme of the 1988 election campaign, was barely mentioned in the first week of the campaign (2 percent of CBC's coverage, 4 percent of CTV's), despite the fact that side agreements to NAFTA were signed by President Clinton and Prime Minister Campbell during the period. The NMA also says the CBC "nearly doubled the proportion of its attention to the horserace (i.e., gains and losses in public support) from 1988."

5 This effort won high praise from the Fraser Institute's National Media Archive.

6 *Canadian Press* interview, September 14, 1993.

7 Interview with Lionel Lumb.

8 Many commentators mistakenly speak of the electronic town hall as an innovation of the 1992 presidential race in the United States.

9 The *Globe and Mail*, September 6, 1993.

10 Ibid.

11 Lesley Jones, CTV; Peter Kent, Global; Joe Schlesinger, CBC.

12 The *Ottawa Citizen*, September 17, 1993.

13 Press release.

14 Joan Bryden told the CAJ post-mortem: "What is it (an election) if it is not a horserace?" Elly Alboim, veteran of countless federal and provincial elections, was quoted in *The Globe and Mail* (November 4, 1993) as saying that the media's self-flagellation over their coverage of campaigns is just plain silly. "This dichotomy between the horserace and real issues has been driving me crazy for 20 years. Objectively, there *was* a horserace out there. And people voting for someone want to know if they are going to win or not. It's like going to a basketball game and saying: 'You're concentrating too much on points.'"

15 The NDP seems to have sensed this earlier. On September 11 and 12, Audrey McLaughlin indicated the New Democrats would support a minority Liberal government — if NAFTA was killed.

[16] *The Toronto Star*, September 24, 1993.

[17] On October 3 Joe Sornberger, national bureau chief of *The Ottawa Citizen*, wrote: "In the space of a 40-minute interview (Campbell) figuratively clamped my jaw shut with her fist and coldly told me that the people who write about politics 'haven't the foggiest clue what's happening out there in the country,' that we 'don't really understand the government process' and that the Canadian people 'are a million miles ahead of the commentary.'"

[18] *The Globe and Mail*, October 27, 1993.

[19] October 7, 1993.

[20] The pollster Allan Gregg — who functioned as top strategist, ad designer, debates coach, and policy chief for Kim Campbell — has since blamed this on the Tory leader's gaffe about social programs. Edward Greenspon and Jeff Sallot (*Globe and Mail*, October 27, 1993) wrote that, according to Gregg, prior to Campbell's comments the Tories were trailing the Liberals by three points. Over the next week they dropped a staggering 12 points.

[21] In its report, *On Balance* (Volume 6, No.9) published in December 1993, compiled and written by the NMA's director, Lydia Miljan, with data research by Mark Canofari and Erica Meiners.

CHAPTER 9

The Leaders' Debates: Critical Event or Non-event?

LAWRENCE LEDUC

The televised debates between the five party leaders on October 3 and 4 were a centerpiece of the 1993 campaign. Although they occurred three weeks before election day, debates have assumed such prominence in elections that it sometimes appears as if nothing else matters. "The final result of an exhausting 47 day election campaign could be decided in 4 1/2 hours of televised debates," suggested *The Globe and Mail* in a front page article the day before the first debate.[1] The extensive preparation by the party leaders likewise underscored the importance of the debates. Several factors are responsible for the increased emphasis placed on debates: the central role played by party leaders, the role of television, the influence of American presidential politics, and the precedent of previous debates, to mention only a few. Although they are more directly associated with the style of American presidential politics, televised debates between the party leaders now approach the point of becoming institutionalized in Canadian election campaigns. Indeed, it has been proposed that provision for such debates be incorporated into the Canada Elections Act.[2] This chapter examines not only the significance of the 1993 debates but also the role of televised leader debates more generally.

The first televised debate in Canada was in 1968. But until at least the early 1980s the decision by a party or leader to accept or reject a challenge to debate was largely a matter of strategy. Unless all the major contenders were convinced of the strategic value of debates (or of the strategic cost of a refusal to take part), they were unlikely to occur. Thus proposed debates in the 1972 and 1974 elections were killed.[3] The next debate in 1979 was very nearly vetoed when hesitancy and uncertainty by one or more of the participants combined to produce a single unilingual debate only a week before election day.[4] Largely for the same reasons, there was no debate in 1980, but the 1984 debates established new norms, and the repetition of a similar sequence of decisions in 1988 solidified the idea that debates were a normal and necessary component of an election campaign. Following the election call in 1993, there was never any doubt that debates, both in French and English, would be a major part of the campaign. It was clear that precedents set in the two previous elections had changed the thinking about the role of debates in irreversible ways.

Because they have been part of the North American political landscape for more than 30 years, much is known about the nature of debates as campaign events, the strategic interest of parties in them, and their actual and potential effects on attitudes and behaviour.[5] Still, each case is sufficiently different to induce caution in generalizing about debates. Each election has produced new developments. For example, the 1992 Bush-Clinton-Perot US debates were different in significant ways from the Reagan-Mondale debates only eight years earlier. And those in turn had been far different from the Kennedy-Nixon debates of 1960 that ushered in the era of televised debates.[6] Thus, while there are similarities among the five Canadian campaigns that have featured leader debates – 1968, 1979, 1984, 1988, 1993 – each debate has changed thinking by practitioners, scholars and observers about the role of debates in election campaigns.

THE STRATEGIC CONTEXT

John F. Kennedy and Richard Nixon entered a series of televised debates during the 1960 presidential campaign without much strategic consideration, although there is evidence that at least some of Nixon's advisers were opposed.[7] Thereafter, until 1976, incumbent presidents generally refused to debate their opponents because the format, by its very nature, tends to favour the challenger by placing him or her on an equal footing with the incumbent, often providing much-needed exposure to a less well-known figure. But after Gerald Ford debated Jimmy Carter in 1976, and Carter (as president) debated Ronald Reagan in 1980, this unwritten rule lapsed. When Reagan (also as president) debated Walter Mondale in 1984, a new era was established in which debates were taken almost for granted.

A similar evolution occurred in Canada. Pierre Trudeau, as a new prime minister agreed in 1968 to debate other party leaders. But with Trudeau as an established prime minister there were no debates in the subsequent elections of 1972 or 1974. Then in 1979, with his party seriously behind in the polls and sensing that his principal opponent, Joe Clark, was vulnerable, Trudeau actively sought a debate. Less than a year later however, Trudeau, feeling that he was all but assured of victory in the 1980 election, once again would not debate. Debates took place in 1984 under circumstances similar to those of 1968, where both major party leaders were new. But the pattern changed in 1988 when Brian Mulroney as prime minister agreed to debates similar to those in 1984. Graham Fraser notes that the 1988 election date itself (November 21) was selected by Mulroney "with the date of the television debates in mind."[8] Thus Canada, like the US, had come to a position where incumbency and electoral advantage were no longer the principal considerations determining whether debates would take place. The expectations of both media and public that debates are a normal part of a political campaign had altered the strategic landscape.

The 1984 debates ushered in a new era in Canada, much as the Carter-Reagan and Reagan-Mondale debates had done in the US. This was the first election in which two debates took place, one in French and one in English.[9] These debates took place early in the campaign, largely at the insistence of the Liberals who saw debates occurring too close to election day as a greater risk. This represented a significant departure from 1979, when the single debate in English was only nine days before election day. The 1984 debates were memorable for their dramatic impact on the campaign. Mulroney, at ease in French and confident of his overall strategy, was effective in the French debate. But the English debate the following night is more widely remembered for the "no option" exchange between Mulroney and Prime Minister John Turner regarding patronage appointments. Whether the debates in themselves accounted for the Liberal disaster in 1984 is doubtful.[10] Although there are reasons to believe that the Liberals were headed for defeat anyway, the debates in which Turner performed poorly illustrated the political potential of the forum.

By the 1988 election, many of the norms established in 1984 were widely accepted. Both the Liberals and NDP were anxious as opposition parties to debate, but the terms were largely dictated by the Conservatives as the governing party and front runner in the early polls: two three-hour debates, one in French, one in English, one month before the election to allow time to recover from any negative fallout. The Conservatives thus pursued exactly the same strategy as the Liberals had in 1984. But in contrast to 1984, the Tories, despite pressure, declined to participate in a separate women's debate, and agreed instead that an additional hour on each of the debates should be devoted to women's issues. The format of the French and English debates was identical, and differed only slightly in length and structure from those of 1984. Questions were posed by three panelists, all television journalists. Both debates permitted introductory and concluding remarks, and included three rounds of debate between the pairings of leaders. Rounds one and three were devoted to issues of general interest, while round two in both the French and English debates was designated for issues of particular interest to women. The potential advantages and disadvantages accruing to each of the three parties under these arrangements were well known to all concerned.

All three leaders prepared extensively, but the most detailed and elaborate preparations were undertaken by Turner and his advisers.[11] The result was impressive. There can be little doubt that Turner's performance in the two debates turned the campaign around, at least temporarily. The most dramatic segment, later used in Liberal campaign spots, occurred near the end of the second hour of the English debate, when Turner lectured Mulroney on the Canada-US Free Trade Agreement, saying, "I happen to believe that you've sold us out..." Well-coached and confident, Turner appeared prime ministerial, while Mulroney, attempting to project a statesman-like image, came across as weak and ineffectual. The NDP leader, Ed Broadbent, was relegated to the sidelines, particularly in the French debate where his lack of fluency was less well received than in 1984. Had the election taken place within a week of the debates, as in 1979, the Liberals might have been able to ride the subsequent surge in support to victory. But they were unable to sustain the momentum. Although the debates created a period of disruption and uncertainty in the middle of the campaign, they seemed to have had little effect on the result. The Conservative share of the total vote was about where most polls had placed it at the beginning of the campaign.[12]

WHY ARE DEBATES IMPORTANT?

A crucial observation about the impact of debates on election campaigns is that they draw very large audiences. Consistently, between half and two-thirds of the Canadian adult population watches some part of a debate, a figure roughly comparable to that found in the US.[13] Prior to 1984, the fact that debates were in English reduced the audience.[14] For 1993, data available suggests an audience comparable to, but probably no greater than, that found in previous elections.

Table 1
Percentages of national samples who saw all or part of at least one debate, 1968-93

	Total sample	Anglophones	Francophones
1993[a]	57	55	61
1988[b]	63	63	64
1984[c]	60	61	57
1979[d]	51	61	26
1968[e]	61	64	50

a Insight Canada Post-Election Study (N=1200)
b 1988 Canadian National Election Study. Post election wave (N=2922).
c 1984 CNES. Excluding the Womens' Debate (N=3359).
d 1979 " Random half-sample (N=1296).
e 1968 " (N=2767).

Table 2
Correlations between exposure to debates and selected political participation items (Pearson r)

Watched other political programs on television	.33
Discuss politics with friends or family	.24
Reads about politics in the newspapers	.23
Attended a political meeting	.20
Voted in the election	.19
Contributed money to a party or candidate	.14

Source: 1984 Canadian National Election Study (N=3359).

The opportunity to reach such massive audiences explains why the parties and leaders attach such importance to televised debates.

As might be expected, watching debates is related to other participatory acts, particularly those of a relatively passive nature such as watching other political programs on television or engaging in political discussion. Table 2 shows the relationship between such activities and watching debates. Thus people who watch other political programs on television are more likely to watch debates, as are those who engage in other types of political activity.

Watching debates is related also to sociodemographic variables such as education, age, and socioeconomic status.[16] The 1993 debates were somewhat more likely to be watched by those living in urban areas, with higher income and education, and by older respondents – as was the case in all previous debates studied. Men (59 percent) were slightly more likely than women (54 percent) to report having watched. However, sociodemographic variables explain little about the audiences. It is more accurate to say that debates tend to be seen by a broad cross-section of the public, and that the extent to which some watch and others do not is related to other factors that explain attentiveness to election campaigns, particularly through the medium of television. This point is important since those who are the most likely viewers of the debates are also the most likely to be exposed to other political programs, political advertising, news programs, news specials, and commentary preceding or following the debates. Among campaign strategists, "spin" is now an important part of the total event, as parties seek to encourage and build on favourable commentary in the media in the hours and days following the debates. The use of "bites" from the program in political advertising and on news programs also assures wider exposure, and has the effect of making the debates and their content an even more critical part of the total campaign effect. In the process, however, it also confounds attempts to isolate the effects of debates from those of other short term forces associated with campaigns, and/or the images the public holds of the party leaders.

While debates can sometimes act merely to reinforce existing attitudes toward parties and leaders, viewers often form new and distinct impressions of the leaders. Turner's strong performance in the 1988 debates was widely recognized and attitudes toward him became significantly more positive following the debates. Fraser notes that "the next day, candidates across the country could feel the effects of the debates."[17] The National Election Study likewise found in their rolling cross-section samples a significant shift in public attitudes following the debates.[18] In another study the same panel of respondents gave Turner a low rating in the 1984 debates and a higher one in 1988.[19]

Such findings do not necessarily imply that the debates directly influenced the outcome of the election. It is entirely possible that while recognizing Turner's strong performance voters nevertheless continued to feel that he would make a poor prime minister, and were no more prepared to vote for his party after the debates than before. Intuitively, it would seem that debates with a wide audience and clear perceptions of the participants' performances *should* have made some difference. Yet in 1988 Mulroney went on to win the election in spite of the debates, just as Clark had done in 1979. Likewise, Broadbent's relatively poor performance in the 1988 debates did not prevent the NDP from winning a record high 43 seats in that election. So, while debates can affect public perceptions of political leaders, this does not always translate into votes. In part, this is because the effects of debates on public opinion can in fact be surprisingly short-lived. When a leader has succeeded in gaining an advantage over his opponents in a debate, it is not an easy matter to sustain that advantage through an additional three or four weeks of a campaign.[20] Both the campaign itself, and the attention of the public, soon move on to other matters.

Debates may have a particularly important, if somewhat more subtle, influence on public opinion when several of the leaders are new faces, as in 1993. Without preconceptions, voters may more easily develop "first impressions" of leaders which are not as quickly dispelled by subsequent campaign events. There is some evidence that Mulroney in 1984 may have benefitted from such an effect. As a relatively unknown political figure at the time, his performance in the debates significantly strengthened his image with many voters. The negative characteristics that later became dominant were not evident until well after he became prime minister.[21] In the 1993 contest, Kim Campbell, Audrey McLaughlin, Lucien Bouchard, and Preston Manning were all new leaders, relatively unknown to the public at large. For them, the debates represented a crucial opportunity to establish a positive image with the public rather than to dispel or reinforce an existing one. And even for Jean Chrétien, fighting his first election campaign as Liberal leader, the debates presented the best single opportunity of the campaign to impress a favourable image on a large cross section of the electorate.

THE 1993 DEBATES

Considering the vast differences in political circumstances from the previous two elections, together with the perceived importance of these debates, agreement on their timing, structure, and format was surprisingly simple. None of the parties sought to avoid or postpone the debates, so ingrained have such events become in the structure of modern election campaigns. Neither was any serious attempt made to exclude Reform or the Bloc Québécois from participating. An early date seemed acceptable to all concerned. Agreement was reached just prior to the election call that the debates would take place in early October, in both English and French, and that five party leaders would be invited to participate. It was agreed that Preston Manning, who does not speak French, would read a prepared statement in English (with simultaneous translation) at the beginning of the French debate, but would not fully participate. Lucien Bouchard would be a full participant in both the French and English debates. Immediately after the election call, these arrangements were finalized for October 3 and 4.

The role that the debates would play in the strategies of all parties was clear from the beginning. The Tory campaign, heavily centred on Kim Campbell, would use them to showcase her leadership qualities and to draw a contrast with the "old politics" of Jean Chrétien. For the Liberals, the debates afforded the best opportunity to address the most serious potential weakness of their campaign – the suitability of their leader for the job of prime minister. While both the Liberal and Conservative strategies needed the debates, the events nevertheless posed risks. Campbell, as a new prime minister and relatively inexperienced party leader, had already stumbled badly in the first days of the campaign: a serious mistake in a debate seen by millions might prove fatal. For Chrétien likewise, a poor performance could reinforce doubts about his leadership and reinvigorate the Tory campaign. The other three parties, however, could only benefit from participating in an event which provided more or less equal time to all, regardless of party size, campaign budgets, and electoral potential.

The French debate on the evening of October 3 lasted two hours, with the final 30 minutes given to questions posed by members of the studio audience. Moderated by Madeleine Poulin, during the main section questions were posed to the leaders by three Radio Canada journalists – Denise Bombardier, Daniel

Lessard, and Marie-Helene Poirier. With five leaders (or four excluding Manning) participating, the format did not allow for the one-on-one types of exchanges that had been the highlight of the 1984 and 1988 debates. But there were nevertheless a number of lively exchanges directly between the leaders, as well as with the journalists. Campbell was quickly on the attack, seeking particularly to confront Bouchard whenever possible, and often intervening in exchanges between the other leaders. Chrétien, appearing calm and low key, never interrupting, tried to stick to his basic message of "jobs and the economy." Bouchard, wanting to appear as a "national" leader, emphasized broad economic issues rather than purely regional ones. And McLaughlin gave a balanced performance in reasonably competent French, varying little from her basic partisan message. But the debate did have its moments. Campbell, challenging Bouchard's legitimacy in federal politics, gave him the opening that he sought when he reminded her that sovereigntists were taxpayers also and entitled to representation. And Chrétien, eventually drawn out from his basic themes, gained points when he poignantly described himself in an exchange with Bouchard as a "proud Quebecker, a proud francophone, and a proud Canadian." The questions from the audience to which each leader responded individually fell somewhat flat. The closing statements, including one in translation by Manning, reinforced each leader's basic themes.

Few would have been prepared to declare a winner in the French debate, and indeed reviews in most newspapers the following day were restrained. But it was clear that Campbell, although she had given a strong performance in more than competent French, did not achieve the breakthrough that many felt was necessary to restore the momentum to her party's campaign. Bouchard, seemingly on the defensive in many of the exchanges with the other leaders, had nevertheless preserved the substantial lead that his party had built up in Quebec, and may well have enhanced his stature. And Chrétien, benefiting from low expectations on the part of many Quebeckers, improved his position at least slightly. For the two front runners (Bouchard and the Bloc in Quebec, and Chrétien and the Liberals in much of the rest of Canada), the French debate might be seen as at least a strategic success.

In all but minor ways, the English debate was similar in structure to the French debate. Because both Manning and Bouchard participated fully, the English debate was 30 minutes longer, with the segment at the end involving questions from a pre-selected studio audience extended to 45 minutes. Moderated by CBC journalist Ann Medina, the debate seemed less disciplined, with the leaders often interrupting and attempting to talk over each other. Questions were posed by Peter Kent of Global TV, Leslie Jones of CTV, and Joseph Schlesinger of the CBC. For the most part, the leaders stuck to strategies similar to those revealed in the French debate. But Chrétien's low key style was initially not as effective in the frequent free-for-alls that erupted, and he was often forced to join the fray simply to avoid not being heard. Campbell, again quickly on the attack, found herself having to confront Manning, Bouchard, and Chrétien at different times. McLaughlin, seeking to save her party's seats in the West, targeted Manning from the beginning, and emphasized health care in addition to fundamental economic issues. There were few memorable moments in these exchanges. Perhaps the most noteworthy was one that occurred between Campbell and Bouchard, when he challenged her to give the finance department's forecast of the deficit. Avoiding the question, Campbell stuck to her own themes. But Bouchard persisted. "I had a question. It is a simple figure. What is the real deficit?" he demanded. Campbell forged on. "I have a plan to eliminate the deficit." Bouchard: "You are hiding the truth, madam. You don't answer the question." "What is the alternative?" continued Campbell, not acknowledging Bouchard's interventions. "There is no alternative to the truth," Bouchard shot back. By comparison, the final segment, involving audience questions to individual leaders, was painfully dull.

As with the French debate, few commentators were prepared to declare winners and losers.[23] Certainly, none of the leaders had made the big mistake that is often feared in such events. But the strategic implications for each of the leaders were clear. Campbell had not succeeded in scoring the big success that she needed, and had perhaps been slightly damaged in the encounter with Bouchard. Chrétien had got through the debates without serious incident, thus fulfilling one of the Liberals' most important goals. Reform benefited simply from full participation in such a debate, and Manning conceded no ground to what he consistently referred to as "the old line parties." Bouchard, whose party had no candidates running outside Quebec, had little to gain in the debate except perhaps enhanced stature as a national figure, and certainly nothing to lose. And McLauglin's generally strong performance in the debates seemed almost not to matter, given the problems which her party faced more generally in the election.

Only 9 percent of the respondents in the Insight Canada study felt that Campbell had given the best performance, placing her fourth among the five leaders in this sample of viewers. Chrétien gave the best performance according to 36 percent, while 20 percent were not impressed with any of the five leaders. In this sample, demographic differences were not much evident in the evaluation of the leaders' performances. Among francophones, Bouchard was rated above Chrétien, but by a surprisingly small margin. Westerners, older viewers, and those in higher income groups were somewhat more favourably impressed by Manning, but Chrétien also scored well in all of these groups. In spite of the novelty of two women participating for the first time as party leaders, neither

Table 3
Leader seen as having given the best overall performance in the debates

	Campbell	Chrétien	McLaughlin	Manning	Bouchard	DK/None
Total sample	9 %	36	7	16	13	20
Francophones	7 %	30	2	4	38	19
Anglophones	9 %	37	9	20	5	20
Ontario	9 %	40	8	19	3	21
Western provinces	12 %	33	12	21	3	19
Union members	8 %	37	6	14	18	18
Youngest age group	12 %	51	9	5	12	12
Oldest age group	8 %	35	10	15	8	25
Lowest income group	11 %	39	5	13	10	23
Highest income group	7 %	33	6	21	19	15
Women	8 %	39	10	12	10	22
Men	9 %	33	5	19	16	19

Source: Insight Canada Post-Election Study. Viewers only (N=680).

Campbell nor McLaughlin were rated particularly well among women. Considering this evidence alone, one might consider Chrétien the clear winner of the debates, and Campbell the largest overall loser. Further evidence suggesting that Chrétien may have gained from the debates at Campbell's expense is found in a comparison of two polls showing attitudes toward the party leaders before and after the segment of the campaign in which the debates took place.

Table 4
Rating of party leaders as "best prime minister"

	Total Canada		Quebec only	
	Sept.	Oct.	Sept.	Oct.
Chrétien	19 %	31 %	13 %	20 %
Campbell	39	24	44	19
Manning	7	10	1	2
Bouchard	4	7	14	28
McLaughlin	4	5	3	3
Other	1	2	1	1
DK/None	25	23	25	27

Source: Globe/ComQuest polls, Sept. 15th and October 16th, 1993. As reported in *The Globe and Mail*, October 16, 1993. N=1504. Field work for the first poll reported was conducted between September 8 and 14 (the week following the election call, and for the second poll between October 11 and 14 (about a week after the debates). The question was: "Which leader do you think would make the best prime minister of Canada?"

In early September, Campbell was considered the leader who would make "the best prime minister" by 39 percent of the sample, compared to 19 percent for Chrétien. A week after the debates, these positions had shifted, with 31 percent feeling that Chrétien would make the best prime minister compared to 24 percent mentioning Campbell. The turnaround was even greater in Quebec, with Campbell dropping from 44 percent to 19 percent, and Chrétien rising from 13 percent to 20 percent. In the Quebec sample, Bouchard's position strengthened significantly also, rising from 14 percent to 28 percent.

While these data suggest that the debates may have played a role in shaping or reshaping the images of the leaders, one should not conclude that the debates determined the outcome of the election. Various polls taken at different times during the campaign show that the Conservatives had already entered a steep slide in public support well before the debates took place, and that the Liberals had held a solid lead in vote intention throughout most of the campaign. Polls taken immediately before and after the debates show little change in the Conservative vote, which in percentage terms had already declined to the low 20s. And, while the Liberals gained ground in the period afterwards, the largest apparent shift in the Liberal vote took place later in the campaign. Likewise, both Reform and the Bloc showed steady gains over the course of the entire campaign, not the sort of sudden surge that might seem attributable to an effect generated specifically by the debates. A comparison of voting behaviour between viewers and non-viewers of the debates likewise suggests little direct effect. (Table 5)

Table 5
Voting behaviour in the election, by exposure to the debates

	Watched	Did not watch
Liberal	45 %	45 %
PC	13	16
NDP	8	8
Reform	19	19
Bloc	12	11
Other	3	2
	N= (496)	(335)

Source: Insight Canada Post-Election Study. Voters only.

Differences between the two groups were not statistically significant, and in fact the percentage of Liberal supporters was identical among viewers and non-viewers. One might therefore argue that the debates had some effects on the images of the party leaders, particularly Campbell and Chrétien, but little if any on voting behaviour. Such a finding would be consistent with most of the evidence regarding debates in other elections, both in Canada and elsewhere.

Nevertheless, the debates represented a lost opportunity for Campbell and the Conservatives, one that could not be recaptured in the three weeks remaining in the campaign. For the Liberals, the debates represented perhaps the largest single element of strategic uncertainty in a generally well-planned and well executed campaign.

CONCLUSION

Debates stimulate interest in elections and may have some positive effects on participation. But they are only one event of the campaign, albeit a major one. Abolishing the boxing ring vocabulary beloved by many who write about campaign debates would improve our understanding of these events. The language of tennis or football might serve us better. Debates are the second set or the third quarter in a long match. What comes both before and after matters, and there can be no knockout punch.

Debates are now a permanent fixture of Canadian election campaigns, and some of the innovations in 1993 are likely to be carried forward into future elections, just as the debates of 1984 and 1988 helped to determine the structure in 1993. As debates come close to being institutionalized, the risks associated with them are increasingly being limited, with all parties and leaders planning a strategy for the debates well in advance of the election. So while it is now difficult to imagine a future election in which televised debates, in French and English, will not play an important role, it is equally difficult to imagine a situation in which the outcome of the election itself hinges entirely on these events.

Notes

1 Ross Howard, "Leaders Hoping Effort Won't Go Down the Tube," *The Globe and Mail*, October 2, 1993.

2 Studies conducted for the Royal Commission on Electoral Reform made a number of recommendations concerning the organization and conduct of debates. See Cathy Widdis Barr, "The Importance and Potential of Televised Leaders Debates," in Frederick Fletcher, ed., *Media, Elections and Democracy* (Toronto: Research Studies of the Royal Commission on Electoral Reform, Dundurn Press, 1992).

3 See Lawrence LeDuc, "Party Strategies and the Use of Televised Campaign Debates," *European Journal of Political Research* 18 (1990), pp. 121-41; and John H. Kessell, *Presidential Campaign Politics* (Homewood, Ill., Dorsey, 1984). For an examination of debates from the perspective of a campaign strategist, see Myles Martel, *Political Campaign Debates: Images, Strategies, Tactics* (NY, Longmans, 1983).

4 For an analysis of the 1979 debates, see Lawrence LeDuc and Richard Price, "Great Debates: the Televised Leadership Debates of 1979," *Canadian Journal of Political Science* 18 (1985), pp. 135-53. See also Frederick Fletcher, "Playing the Game: the Mass Media and the 1979 Campaign," in Howard Penniman, ed., *Canada at the Polls: 1979* (Washington: American Enterprise Institute, 1981), pp.285-87.

5 For a review of some of the US literature on debates, see Kathleen Jamieson and David Birdsell, *Presidential Debates* (NY, Oxford University Press, 1988); and Richard Joslyn, *Mass Media and Elections* (Reading, Mass., Addison-Wesley, 1984). Reference to debates is also found in studies of particular presidential elections. See, for example, Paul Abramson, John Aldrich, and David Rohde, *Change and Continuity in the 1984 Elections* (Washington, CQ Press, 1986), pp. 57-60. Analyses of the 1984 and 1988 Canadian debates may be found in David J. Lanoue, "Debates that Mattered: Voters' Reactions to the 1984 Canadian Leadership Debates," *Canadian Journal of Political Science* 24 (1991), pp. 51-65; and in Denis Moniere, "Analyse lexicographique de debat des chefs en francais dans l'election federale canadienne de 1988," *Canadian Journal of Political Science* 24 (1991), pp. 29-50. Analyses of these events may also be found in Harold D. Clarke, Lawrence LeDuc, Jane Jenson, and Jon H. Pammett, *Absent Mandate*, 2nd ed. (Toronto: Gage, 1991), pp. 101-104; and in Richard Johnston, Henry Brady, Andre Blais, and Jean Crete, *Letting the People Decide* (Montreal, McGill-Queen's Press, 1992), pp. 168-96.

6 Evron M. Kirkpatrick, "Presidential Campaign Debates: What Can We Learn From 1960?" in Austin Ranney, ed., *The Past and Future of Presidential Debates* (Washington: American Enterprise Institute, 1979). A number of analyses of the 1960 Kennedy-Nixon debates may also be found in Sidney Kraus, ed., *The Great Debates* (Indiana: Indiana University Press, 1962).

7 Kirkpatrick, "Presidential Campaign Debates...," op. cit., pp. 7-8.

8 Graham Fraser, *Playing for Keeps* (Toronto: McLelland and Stewart, 1989), p. 264. See also the discussion of the role of the debates in the 1988 campaign in Allan Frizzell, Jon

Pammett, and Anthony Westell, *The Canadian Federal Election of 1988* (Ottawa: Carleton University Press, 1989).

[9] A third debate, fully bilingual and focusing specifically on women's issues, also took place during the 1984 campaign, but lacked the impact of the previous two encounters. About 38 percent of the 1984 NES sample reported having seen this debate.

[10] But see Lanoue, "Debates that Mattered...," op. cit., pp. 58-62. See also LeDuc, "Party Strategies and the Use of Televised Campaign Debates," and Barr, "The Importance and Potential of Leaders' Debates," for further analyses of the 1984 events.

[11] These are described in some detail in Fraser, *Playing for Keeps*, op. cit., pp. 267-276.

[12] Further analyses of the 1988 debates may be found in Clarke et al, *Absent Mandate*, op. cit., pp. 101-104; and in Johnston et al., *Letting the People Decide*, op. cit., pp. 180-191.

[13] The audience for debates in the United States has generally been estimated to be in the range of 60-75 percent of the voting age population. See Joslyn, *Mass Media and Elections*, op. cit., pp. 200-205.

[14] In 1979, the single unilingual (English) debate reportedly was watched by 61 percent of anglophone respondents and 26 percent of francophones. In 1968, when a similar unilingual (English) debate was also broadcast in translation, an estimated 64 percent of anglophone and 50 percent of francophone respondents reported having watched the debate. LeDuc and Price, "Great Debates...," op. cit., pp. 140-142.

[15] The relationships shown in Table 2 are very similar to those reported for a comparable analysis of data from the 1979 National Election Study. See LeDuc and Price, "Great Debates...," op. cit., pp. 140-44.

[16] The correlations between exposure to the 1984 debates and indices of political efficacy and political interest were .15 and .35 respectively. With regard to sociodemographic variables, all relationships were fairly weak. The correlation between watching the debates and a composite measure of occupation and income was .09, while those with education and age were only slightly stronger (.13 and .17 respectively). These patterns were similar to those found in the 1979 study, although the unilingual format of the 1979 debates limited the analysis to anglophone respondents in that instance. LeDuc and Price, "Great Debates...," op. cit., pp. 142-143.

[17] *Playing for Keeps*, op. cit., p. 295.

[18] *Letting the People Decide*, op. cit., pp. 180-182.

[19] *Absent Mandate*, op. cit., pp. 102-104.

[20] See, for example, the discussion of the 1984 Reagan-Mondale debates and the role they played in the US presidential campaign of that year in Paul Abramson, John Aldrich, and David Rohde, *Change and Continuity in the 1984 Elections* (Washington, CQ Press, 1986), pp. 57-60. Polls at the time showed that the damage inflicted by Reagan's poor performance in the first debate with Mondale dissipated rapidly, even before the second debate which took place two weeks later.

[21] *Absent Mandate*, op. cit., pp. 97-99. See also *Letting the People Decide*, op. cit., pp. 168-80.

[22] Angus Reid poll, September 8-9.

[23] See, for example, Carol Goar, "Kim Campbell Didn't Win — Or Lose," *Toronto Star*, October 5, 1993.

CHAPTER 10

TRACKING THE VOTES

BY JON H. PAMMETT

The 1993 election produced one of the most dramatic results in Canadian electoral history. The destruction of the Progressive Conservative Party, while at times offhandedly predicted during the interelection period when the popularity of the Conservative government dipped to new lows, was in the end a surprise even to seasoned political observers. The story of the decline and fall of the Conservatives has been told in previous chapters detailing their disastrous campaign and the way in which other parties succeeded or failed to take advantage of it. But the background to the campaign was the public's dissatisfaction with the efforts of politicians to solve economic problems and the constitutional impasse.[1] This was demonstrated in the voting on the 1992 referendum on the Charlottetown agreement, and by the fact that since 1988 two new political parties had come to prominence - the Reform Party and the Bloc Québécois. While their support was regionally concentrated, these parties structured a lot of the general campaign debate, forcing the other parties to take positions on the rate of deficit reduction and on the future of Quebec. Their existence also allowed the Liberal Party to emphasize in their campaign the desirability of a majority government, an argument which had stood them in good stead in several past campaigns.[2]

Partisan ties in Canada are flexible for a majority of the electorate, and those voters make up their minds *de novo* at each election which party to support.[3] This means that voting decisions are largely determined by the short-term images and issues which are formed and discussed during and immediately prior to the campaign. Thus movement toward the new parties was not inhibited by long term loyalties to existing parties. This chapter examines voting behaviour empirically,utilizing a survey conducted in the days immediately following the election by Insight Canada Research. This study consisted of telephone interviews with a sample of 1200 Canadians from all provinces and territories about the reasons for their voting decisions. Although a number of questions in this survey were specially commissioned for this analysis, we wish to thank Insight for providing the complete dataset,and for their cooperation throughout.

THE FLOW OF THE VOTE

Table 1 shows the behaviour of the total electorate in two elections,1988 and 1993. For example, the first column shows that 18.1 percent of the 1993 electorate voted Liberal in both elections, while 9.4 percent had voted PC in 1988 but voted Liberal this time. The last row shows that,because there were five years between elections, more than 10 percent of 1993 voters had not been eligible in 1988. Still others had been eligible but had chosen not to vote in 1988. On the other hand, an even larger group of people voted in 1988 but decided not to vote in 1993. The overall turn out was lower in 1993 than in 1988, but it remains for future research to determine to what extent this was the result of administrative disenfranchisement and of lower interest in the election.

Table 1
CANADIAN ELECTORAL BEHAVIOUR, 1988-1993

	1993						
	LIB	PC	NDP	REFORM	BQ	OTHER	Did Not Vote
1988							
LIB	18.1	1.3	.7	2.1	1.5	.3	1.8
PC	9.4	7.8	1.2	8.5	4.9	.4	3.6
NDP	4.2	1.3	4.1	2.2	.9	.7	2.1
REFORM	–	.1	–	.9	–	–	–
OTHER	–	.1	.1	.2	.5	.3	.1
Did Not Vote	1.9	.5	–	1.4	.5	.1	5.1
Not Eligible	3.5	.6	.3	1.1	.9	.1	4.2
							100%
						N=934	

SUMMARY

VOTED SAME PARTY	SWITCHED VOTE	PREVIOUS VOTERS NOT VOTING	PREVIOUS NON-VOTERS VOTING	NOT VOTING EITHER TIME	NEW VOTERS
30.9%	40.6%	7.6%	4.4%	5.1%	10.7%

Note: The entire table adds to 100%.

Source: Insight Canada Research post-election survey

An electoral victory, such as that of the Liberals in 1993, is made up of a number of components, all of which are illustrated in Table 1. Five of these are: the retention of past supporters from the 1988 election; gains from vote-switching by previous supporters of other parties; the loss of previous voters choosing not to vote this time; gains from previous non-voters moving into the electorate; and the attraction of the party to newly eligible voters, most of whom are from the youngest age group in the electorate.

Retention of past supporters played a major part in the Liberal success, as attested by the fact that the largest cell in Table 1 is at the top left corner, representing the proportion of the electorate which remained Liberal in the two elections. But while large when compared with the other factors shown in this table, the 18.1 percent of Canadians who remained Liberal in two elections is low by comparison with the retention rates of other parties in previous pairs of elections. For example, the comparable table in the previous volume in this series, *The Canadian General Election of 1988*, shows the Conservatives retained over 30 percent of the total electorate from 1984.[4] Nevertheless, the Liberal party was more successful than other parties in retaining supporters.

Table 1 also illustrates the flow of votes to the Liberals through conversion from other parties: 9.4 percent of the electorate was composed of PC voters who switched to the Liberals, while only 1.3 percent went the other way. There was a similar imbalance in NDP support; 4.2 percent of the electorate switched to the Liberals, while Liberal-NDP switching was only 0.7 percent. In fact, the table documents massive switching over the whole electorate. As the summary indicates, over 40 percent of the total electorate, which includes new voters, changed their vote from 1988 to 1993. If we consider only those people who voted in both elections, the proportion of switchers rises to over half. Much of this switching consisted of people abandoning the Conservatives and the New Democratic Party. Fewer Conservatives stayed with their party from 1988 to 1993 than switched to the Liberals or Reform. A further substantial percentage changed from the Conservatives to the Bloc Québécois. The NDP lost slightly more of their 1988 voters to the Liberals than they retained for themselves, and a further substantial group to the Reform Party. Overall, the presence of the Reform and Bloc Québécois meant that the proportion of people changing their behaviour between 1988 and 1993 was likely the largest between any pair of elections in Canadian history.

The reduced voting turnout in 1993 is reflected in the figures in Table 1. The largest components of the 1993 nonvoting column (last on the right of the table) are those who did not vote in 1988 either,and those newly eligible in 1993 who decided not to cast a ballot. In looking at the Liberal victory, however, it is important to note that 1988 Conservative and NDP voters who decided not to vote in 1993 were more numerous than Liberal voters who did the same. Of the three major parties who contested both elections, only the Liberals achieved an approximate equivalence between 1988 voters who decided not to vote this time, and previous nonvoters deciding to vote for the party. Thus, the Liberals were able to neutralize the turnout factor. Finally, the liberals gained substantially from the voting choices made by newly eligible, mostly young, voters in 1993. More new voters went to the Liberals than to all the other parties combined.

The patterns seen in the aggregate in Table 1 are arranged in Table 2 to show what happened to various groups of 1988 voters and nonvoters.

Table 2
WHERE THE 1988 VOTE WENT

	1988					
	PC	LIB	NDP	OTHER	Did Not Vote	Not Yet Eligible
1993 BEHAVIOUR	%	%	%	%	%	%
PC	22	5	8	9	6	6
LIB	26	70	27	–	20	33
NDP	3	3	26	5	–	3
REFORM	24	8	14	45	14	11
BLOC	14	6	6	23	5	10
OTHER	1	1	5	14	1	1
Did Not Vote	10	7	14	5	54	36

N=930
Source: Insight Canada Research post-election survey

Most striking is the fact that the Conservatives retained less than a quarter (22 percent) of their 1988 voters, the NDP just over a quarter (26 percent) and the Liberals a full 70 percent. Relatively small percentages of 1988 Liberals changed to support the Conservatives, NDP, Reform and the Bloc. The columns for the 1988 Conservatives and NDP look dramatically different, as large proportions shifted to the other parties. The contribution to the Liberal vote of 1988 non-voters and newly eligible voters is also evident here.

Table 3
WHERE THE 1993 PARTY VOTE CAME FROM

	LIB	PC	NDP	REFORM	BLOC
PREVIOUSLY	%	%	%	%	%
LIB	49	11	12	13	16
PC	25	66	18	52	53
NDP	11	11	63	14	9
OTHER	–	2	2	7	6
NON VOTERS	5	5	–	8	5
NEW VOTER	10	5	5	7	11

N=757
Source: Insight Canada Research post-election survey

The contributions of various groups of voters to each party's support in 1993 is displayed in Table 3. Just over half of Reform Party and Bloc Québécois support came from former Conservative voters, and one-quarter of Liberal voters had cast their previous ballot for the PCs. Almost two-thirds of PC and NDP voters in 1993 were repeating their 1988 behaviour, an indication of the failure of these two parties to make conversions with their 1993 campaigns. However, the Liberals fell short of retaining all their previous support. Former Liberals made up portions (ranging from 11 percent to 16 percent) of the groups voting for all the other parties. New voters were most important to the Liberals and the Bloc Québécois.

Despite the dramatic support for two new parties and the equally dramatic decreases for two old ones, the overall picture of the 1993 vote is in some ways familiar.The coalitions put together by the successful parties are usually new ones, and the winning Liberals this time had to attract more than half of their vote from people who had not voted for them in 1988. As it had in many past victories, the party attracted substantial support from new voters and previous nonvoters, as well as through conversion. The campaign itself played an important part in voter decision-making, and as we shall shortly see, people's reasons for voting choices were similar to those cited in the past.

Factors in the Vote Decision

Beginning with the National Election Study of 1974 a sequence of questions has been asked of national samples of Canadians to determine the relative importance of factors in the vote decision. First, there is an inquiry as to whether the respondent found the party leaders, local candidates, or the party taken as a whole to be the most important factor in their own voting decision. Second, there is a question about whether an issue was the basis for the first choice. Thus, people who said that party leaders were most important to them are asked, "When you say that the leader was most important to you are you thinking of this person's personal qualities or this person's stand on certain issues?" Similar follow-up questions are asked of those citing local candidates or parties as a whole as the most important factor.

This set of questions has consistently found that "party as a whole" has been the most important factor in voting decisions. Originally, however, the gap between the importance of party and that of party leader was not large. For example,in the election of 1974 party was cited as most important by 40 percent of Canadians, and leader by 33 percent.In the following election in 1979, these factors were even closer, with party still at 40 percent and leader up to 37 percent. In the 1980 election, leader stayed at 36 percent, while party rose to 44 percent. These results reflected the preeminence of Pierre Trudeau in the politics of this period; love him or hate him, people could not ignore him when making their voting decisions. Since Trudeau left the stage, party leaders have become much less important in conditioning the voting decisions of the public. The figures for the last three elections are presented in Table 4.

Table 4
MOST IMPORTANT FACTORS IN VOTING

1993 ELECTION

PARTY LEADERS		LOCAL CANDIDATES		PARTY AS A WHOLE	
22%		21%		57%	
Issues Stood For	Personal Qualities	Issues Stood For	Personal Qualities	Issues Stood For	General Approach
62%	38%	52%	48%	54%	46%

1988 ELECTION

PARTY LEADERS		LOCAL CANDIDATES		PARTY AS A WHOLE	
20%		27%		53%	
Issues Stood For	Personal Qualities	Issues Stood For	Personal Qualities	Issues Stood For	General Approach
71%	29%	57%	43%	57%	43%

1984 ELECTION

PARTY LEADERS		LOCAL CANDIDATES		PARTY AS A WHOLE	
30%		21%		49%	
Issues Stood For	Personal Qualities	Issues Stood For	Personal Qualities	Issues Stood For	General Approach
56%	44%	46%	54%	37%	63%

Source: 1993 – Insight Canada Research post-election survey; 1984 National Election Study and 1988 reinterview of 1984 National Election Study sample. Population weights applied.

In 1984, when Brian Mulroney emerged to lead the Conservatives to a massive majority in parliament, only 30 percent of the public thought leader was the most important factor in their voting decisions. And that election represented the zenith of Mulroney's popularity. In 1988,the proportion picking leaders had plummeted to 20 percent, reflecting not only the public's declining enthusiasm for Mulroney but the negative verdict on John Turner, the Liberal leader. In that election, the proportion citing party as the most important factor rose above half the voting population, and there was also a leap in those picking local candidates as most important.

The 1993 results continue these trends. The proportion picking party leaders as most important was 22 percent, second only to 1988 as a low figure. Local candidates declined to the level of just over 21 percent where they had been in most past elections. Party was the most important factor for 57 percent,a record high. Despite the fact, then, that the election campaigns centre around the leaders,with their pronouncements reported daily,the general question of party competence to govern was most important to voters. In 1988, the public judgement was that, despite a lack of enthusiasm for the Conservatives and their Free Trade Agreement, this was the party seen as most competent to form a government. In 1993, the judgement on the Conservatives was harsh; the second Mulroney government's image of incompetence was reinforced by the blunder-filled campaign run by the Campbell team. This time, the Liberal Party was the only one which could be trusted to form an administration. Jean Chrétien performed well during the campaign, particularly in the debates, but his personality was not in itself a major factor in attracting Liberal votes.

Table 4 indicates that in 1993, as in previous years, people were more likely than not to have issues in mind when selecting the most important factor in their voting decision. This tendency was most common with leader-oriented voters, reinforcing the comments above about the lack of direct influence of leaders on the voting. Only 38 percent of these voters made up their minds because of the personal qualities of leaders; much more important were the issues the leaders stood for. Since the party campaigns all featured the leaders as the major spokespersons for issues, this connection of issues and leaders is understandable. However, the proportion of the population citing an issue basis for their focus on leaders has increased from the Trudeau years to the present. In 1979 and 1980, majorities of leader-oriented voters cited the personal qualities of the leader as important.

Another indication of the importance of various factors in the 1993 vote can be obtained from open-ended questions in the survey which asked respondents to state the single most important major reason for their vote. Also, those who switched their votes between 1988 and 1993 were asked what was the single most important reason. Table 5 shows the reasons for voting, and Table 6 the reasons for vote-switching, coded into identical categories.

Table 5
Reasons for Voting, 1993
(all voters)

	LIB %	PC %	NDP %	REF %	BLOC %	OTHER %
ECONOMIC ISSUES	23	17	8	15	6	10
OTHER ISSUES	4	3	16	11	45	19
LEADERSHIP – POSITIVE	8	9	5	3	3	5
LEADERSHIP – NEGATIVE	6	1	–	3	9	10
LOCAL CANDIDATE	7	20	21	2	5	14
PARTY – POSITIVE	41	32	43	54	25	29
PARTY – NEGATIVE	11	18	7	14	8	14

N=791
Source: Insight Canada Research post-election survey

For supporters of all parties except the Bloc Québécois,positive aspects of the party were the largest set of reasons offered for voting choices. Also important were a variety of economic and noneconomic issues, which will be investigated in the next section of this chapter. For the Conservatives and the NDP, local candidates were cited as important reasons for voting, suggesting that some voters who decided to remain with these parties did so because of local factors.

Table 5 shows that negative opinions of a party or a leader were reasons for some in deciding how to vote. Prominent were derogatory comments about the Conservatives and Mulroney, but unflattering views were expressed about other politicians and parties. Table 6 shows that among vote-switchers negative opinions were a much more important factor. For those people who switched to the Liberals, for example, more cited negative views of other parties as a reason than positive qualities of the Liberals. The same is true for the small numbers of voters who switched to the PCs and the NDP. For those who switched to the Liberals,the Reform Party, and the Bloc Québécois, negative comments on party leaders were quite important. The Mulroney legacy to the Conservative Party was to motivate many voters to abandon it in 1993.

Table 6
Reasons for Vote Switch, 1988-93
(switchers only)

SWITCH TO:	LIB %	PC %	NDP %	REF %	BLOC %	OTHER %
REASON:						
ECONOMIC ISSUES	23	8	17	16	6	–
OTHER ISSUES	3	8	–	7	34	8
LEADERSHIP – POSITIVE	6	8	6	7	2	–
LEADERSHIP – NEGATIVE	23	–	11	17	14	42
LOCAL CANDIDATE	3	28	17	1	3	–
PARTY – POSITIVE	21	20	17	40	25	17
PARTY – NEGATIVE	22	28	33	12	17	33

N=369
Source: Insight Canada Research post-election survey

Negative reasons for electoral change are a consistent theme in Canadian politics. In *Political Choice in Canada,* the authors found after extensive investigation during the 1974 election that most reasons given for leaving one party and adopting another were repulsion from the old party rather than attraction to the new.[5] Since the tie to the new party is not based on real affection, the implication of findings now is that it would not take much to make such voters change again in a future election. People were willing in 1993 to take a chance on a new party because they were repelled by Conservative policies and leaders. The operative attitude was "why not try something new," and the operative behaviour was a different choice on the ballot.

The Issues

Economic issues have dominated the campaign rhetoric throughout the 1970s and 1980s, and the first federal election of the 1990s provided no exception to this picture. Table 7 shows the responses given by survey respondents during the last three elections to the open-ended question, "What, in your opinion, was the most important issue in the election?" The 1988 campaign centred around the Free Trade Agreement with the United States,and the issue agenda in the 1993 election bears considerable similarity to that of 1984. Since both elections occurred during economic recessions, unemployment and job creation pushed to the fore as primary concerns. This time these issues were mentioned even more frequently than in 1984 – the campaign in which Mulroney promised "jobs, jobs, jobs."The discussion of job creation was also more specific, centring around the Liberals' proposal to spend $6 billion on short-term job creation "to kick start the economy".

Table 7
Most Important Election Issues, 1984-93 (%)

ECONOMIC ISSUES	1984	1988	1993
economy in general	17	2	9
inflation, cost of living	2	–	–
taxes	3	4	1
govt spending, deficit	12	7	20
unemployment, jobs	36	2	49
free trade	–	88	2
CONFEDERATION ISSUES			
national unity, constitution	2	6	4
bilingualism, language	1	2	–
Quebec independance	2	–	1
RESOURCE ISSUES			
environment	1	9	0.3
SOCIAL ISSUES	11	14	5
OTHER ISSUES			
foreign & defence policy	3	1	1
leadership	8	5	2
change	14	1	4
trust, patronage, in govt.	4	1	1
all others	4	3	2

Sources: 1993 Insight Canada Research post-election survey; 1984 National Election Study and 1988 reinterview of 1984 National Election Study sample. Population weights applied. Two mentions possible in 1984 and 1988; one in 1993.

Running a rather distant but still substantial second in mentions of important issues was that of reducing the budget deficit,and the necessity of controlling government spending. All parties accepted the necessity of dealing with these issues, but they were top priority for the Reform and Conservative parties.

Another group of voters expressed their concern for the state of the economy in general terms, not specifically related to job creation or deficit reduction but simply as a problem. The tendency to talk of the economy in such general terms is common in Canadian elections, but the number of people doing so varies with the specificity of economic policies defined by the parties. The number of people in this category was significantly greater in 1984 than it was in 1993, reflecting the sharpened policy focus in the most recent election.

Voters mentioning important election issues (Table 7) were asked, "Which party is closest to you on this issue?," and the results are shown in Table 8.

Table 8
PARTY CLOSEST ON MOST IMPORTANT ISSUES, 1993

	LIB	PC	NDP	REF	BQ	OTHER	NONE
ECONOMIC ISSUES							
economy generally	51%	6	1	14	10	–	18
taxes	46%	18	18	9	–	–	9
deficit	24%	21	4	29	4	1	17
unemployment	61%	7	4	7	5	*	16
free trade	50%	13	–	1	–	16	1
CONFED. ISSUES							
national unity	50%	8	3	13	11	3	13
Quebec sovereignty	17%	–	–	25	33	8	17
RESOURCE ISSUES	–	–	–	–	–	100%	–
SOCIAL ISSUES	40%	8	21	9	4	4	15
OTHER ISSUES							
foreign, def. policy	17%	17	–	17	–	–	50
leadership	60%	5	–	10	–	5	20
change	50%	–	5	7	12	2	24
trust	60%	–	–	–	20	20	–
other	37%	–	–	16	16	–	32
total	48%	9	4	13	6	2	18

* – less than 1%
N=1083
Source: Insight Canada Research post-election survey

On several economic issues voters felt closest to the Liberal party. This is particularly true for unemployment where 61 percent of those identifying it as the key issue in the election felt the Liberals closest. The Liberals had the edge also with those identifying the economy in general as an issue,and this is true as well for the much smaller groups of people who felt that taxes (including the

GST) and free trade (this time it was NAFTA) were the most important issues. The only exception to this pattern among economic issues was with those mentioning deficit reduction as most important: although 24% did feel that the Liberal "gradualist" position was the most desirable method of attacking the deficit, a somewhat larger proportion (29%) felt the Reform Party's "big cuts now" approach was best. The Conservatives fared worse than the Liberals on the deficit issue, despite the fact that it was emphasized in their campaign. Evidently, the budget hardliners felt that Reform was more likely to actually come across with the cuts. On this issue, as with several other economic issues, significant numbers of people felt that no party was close to their position, but what measures they would have favoured are not known.

Other kinds of issues were cited as most important, but not by large numbers. However, as Table 8 shows,such issues did have connections with the parties. The general category of "Confederation issues" had two dimensions. The first was "national unity", a desire to preserve the Canadian federation, a position predominantly associated with the Liberal Party. The second was the question of sovereignty for Quebec, a position associated on one side with the Bloc Québécois and on the other with the Reform Party, and with the Liberal Party in Quebec. It is interesting to note that Quebec sovereignty was identified by only 1% (Table 7) as the most important issue, despite the fact (seen in Table 5) that such issues were important reasons for the choice of the Bloc Québécois by Quebec voters. Table 7 reflects a more general public assessment of the campaign, and a less personal account of motivation. Nevertheless, it is reasonable to conclude that the judgment of most Bloc Québécois voters matched that of the rest of the electorate when it came to characterizing the 1993 election – it was mainly about economics.

Table 7 also displays some of the more general subjects mentioned as most important issues. Among those, the most prominent was the necessity for change, often expressed simply in the statement, "It's time for a change." Table 8 shows that this sentiment was most often associated with support for the Liberals, though a quarter of the population felt that no party was likely to give them a real change. It is surprising that more voters did not cite this as the important election issue; in 1984, the last time there was a substantial change in government, many more people did so. However, the surveys used in the previous elections allowed respondents to name a second important issue, a procedure not used in this survey. Had respondents been given the opportunity, it is likely that more mentions of the need for change, leadership and a majority government would have been present.

Table 9 explores connections between issues and the result of the election. It identifies people we may call "issue voters" – those for whom issues were the most important factor in choosing a leader, candidate or party to vote for –

classifies them by issue, and groups them into those who switched parties, remained with the party they supported in 1988, or entered the electorate in 1993 either for the first time or because they had abstained from voting in 1988.

Table 9
EFFECTS OF ISSUES
(% of those voting and citing issues as most important factor in vote decision)

VOTING	LIB	PC	NDP	REF	BLOC	OTHER
All Economic Issues						
switch to	5.9	1.5	.6	7.1	3.5	.9
remain	8.2	3.6	1.9	.3	–	–
1988 nonvote	3.0	.9	.1	1.0	.5	–
	17.1	6.0	2.6	8.4	4.0	.9
Unemployment						
switch to	3.9	.6	.4	3.0	2.4	.5
remain	6.0	1.4	1.5	–	–	–
1988 nonvote	1.9	.4	.1	.5	.1	–
	11.8	2.4	2.0	3.5	2.5	.5
Deficit						
switch to	.9	.6	.3	3.1	.4	.1
remain	1.7	1.8	.1	.3	–	–
1988 nonvote	.5	.3	–	.5	–	–
	3.1	2.7	.4	3.9	.4	.1
All Other Issues						
switch to	1.8	–	.5	1.2	1.0	–
remain	1.2	.5	.4	.1	–	.3
1988 nonvote	.5	–	–	.3	.1	.1
	3.5	.5	.9	1.6	1.1	.4

Source: Insight Canada Research post-election survey

A substantial proportion of "issue voters" cited unemployment or job creation as the most important issue in the election (Table 9.) The proportion of the electorate who did so, and who chose the Liberal Party to vote for was 11.8 percent. The total of the electorate with the same priorities who chose to vote for all the other parties combined was 10.9 percent. However, the fact that this non-Liberal vote was spread among several other parties, and the fact that the Liberals succeeded in establishing their policy on job creation as a specific distinct policy position during the campaign argues for considering unemployment as an effective issue for the Liberal party. It is reasonable to consider, as well, that the Liberal job creation plan received a mandate in the 1993 election.

This was a salient issue to the public, in that it was the focus of much electoral discussion and heavily cited as important. The plan was clearly identified with the Liberal Party, and was also generally approved by the public. The pattern of voting on the issue, while not heavily in favour of the Liberals overall, definitely favoured that party over any other alternative.

The other specific important issue for "issue voters" was deficit reduction. Voting on this issue looks quite different than that motivated by concern for unemployment. By a small margin, voters in this category were most likely to choose the Reform Party – 3.9 percent of the total electorate as opposed to 3.1 percent for the Liberals and 2.7 percent for the PCs. Therefore, it cannot really be said that Canadian voters endorsed the Reform Party's views, or indeed any party's views on the right way to accomplish deficit reduction. The concept of mandate makes sense only when applied to the winner of an election, who is in a position to put specific campaign ideas into practice. In this connection, the first panel of Table 9 indicates that when all economic issues are lumped together, the public's verdict on the Liberals was much more mixed than when unemployment alone is considered. Not only are substantially more people favourable to other parties than to the Liberals (21.9 percent to 17.1 percent), but this category contains a large number of people who simply expressed general views on the need for economic improvement rather than specific ideas. Thus, the Liberal mandate was a very constrained one, limited to unemployment reduction and their job creation plan.

CONCLUSION

In 1993, the electorate opted massively for change, but the parties which gained support represented different types of change. The Liberals were prepared to change the management of government, the faces in (and in some cases, the faces of) the ministries, and some of the short term policies, particularly those relating to the stimulation of the economy, expenditures on military equipment, methods of taxation and privatization. The Reform Party wanted to bring about a more fundamental change in the scope of government activity, one which would curtail spending of all sorts in order to reduce the extent of government borrowing requirements. The governing Conservatives, caught between the gradualist and cut-now visions of change offered by the challengers, tried to have it both ways, arguing that the Liberals were too timid about the economy and that Reform was too radical. The problems for the Tories in representing themselves as a party of change were the unspecific nature of their proposals and the legacy of years in government. To the extent that the Mulroney government had brought about economic change, it was not seen by the public as a change for the better.

TABLE 10
ATTITUDE TOWARDS QUEBEC INDEPENDENCE BY 1993 VOTE

ATTITUDE TOWARDS QUEBEC INDEPENDENCE

A. IN QUEBEC

	FAVOUR	OPPOSE	DON'T KNOW
LIBERAL	6%	87	8
PC	36%	59	5
BQ	76%	19	5

N=192

B. REST OF CANADA

	FAVOUR	OPPOSE	DON'T KNOW
LIBERAL	11%	79	11
PC	14%	83	3
NDP	22%	74	3
REFORM	24%	67	9
OTHER	21%	58	21

N=831
Source: Insight Canada Research post-election survey

The Bloc Québécois intended the most radical change of all, sovereignty for Quebec. While many of the votes for the BQ were ostensibly motivated by economics,no one in the Quebec electorate was unaware of the potential change the party represented. Table 10 shows that just over three-quarters (76 percent) of Bloc Québécois voters in 1993 supported the independence of Quebec. While this is certainly a large majority, it does indicate that the correspondence between sovereigntist opinion and the BQ is not perfect, a situation which is also true for the vote for the Parti Québecois provincially. A number of votes were cast for the BQ for strategic reasons, perhaps by people simply looking to defeat a rival candidate by the time-honoured practice of voting for the strongest opposition figure. However, the contrast between the independentist views of BQ voters and the opposition to independence among Quebec Liberals is a striking indication of the polarization in attitudes toward change in that province. The majority of the remaining Quebec Conservatives are also opposed to independence, but by less of a margin than the Liberals. Voters for all of the parties outside of Quebec were opposed to independence for that province, 'though Reform and NDP voters were more likely to take a "let them go" position than were Liberals and Conservatives. Thus the 1993 election played a role in crystallizing opinion about the coming electoral battle in Quebec, and perhaps a referendum. The parties have staked out their positions, and very few Canadians answer "don't know" when asked their opinion about Quebec independence.

Sociodemographic correlates with the 1993 voting were small and weak. An incipient gender gap which had been noted in 1984, and which seemed to deepen in 1988, disappeared in 1993: females were just as likely as males to vote for the Conservatives,perhaps because of the selection of Kim Campbell as leader. Social class differentiated little between the parties. Multiple regression analyses performed on the vote for each of the parties shows that most of the variance explained came from variables measuring the closeness of the party to respondents on issues of most importance, and vote in the previous election – not from any sociodemographic characteristics of the respondents.

In many ways, the decision to opt for the Liberals in 1993 was the safe choice. The party demonstrated calmness, confidence and competence for much of its period in opposition, and during the campaign. It proposed to tackle economic problems in a measured, gradualist manner rather than with radical surgery. History also gave some support to the Liberals. Their association with the implementation of many of the social welfare programs valued by Canadians gave confidence that these would not be ruthlessly attacked in the name of budget cutting. Their promotion of bilingualism made them credible as a national party in the face of regional challengers. And they had been in power in previous periods of national prosperity. However, the new government has created a high level of public expectation based on their past record and campaign promises. Canadians have been quick in recent years to judge whether government performance has been adequate or not.

Notes

[1] For a discussion of voting behaviour in the 1992 referendum, see Lawrence LeDuc and Jon Pammett, "Referendum Voting: Attitudes and Behaviour in the 1992 Constitutional Referendum," *Canadian Journal of Political Science*, forthcoming.

[2] Lawrence LeDuc, "Political Behaviour and the Issue of Majority Government in Two Federal Elections," *Canadian Journal of Political Science* vol 10 (1977) pp 311-40.

[3] See Harold D. Clarke, Jane Jenson, Lawrence LeDuc and Jon H. Pammett, *Absent Mandate: Interpreting Change in Canadian Elections* (Toronto: Gage, 1991) and, by the same authors, *Political Choice in Canada* (Toronto: McGraw-Hill Ryerson, 1979).

[4] Alan Frizzell, Jon H. Pammett and Anthony Westell, *The Canadian General Election of 1988* (Ottawa: Carleton University Press, 1989), p 116.

[5] *Political Choice in Canada*, op cit, p 150.

APPENDIX

The Election Results

Nationally

Federal Election Results
(X = less than 1%)

	Liberal		PC		NDP*		SC		BQ		Reform		Other		%	Total
	vote %	seats	vote %	seats	vote %	seats	vote %	seats	vote %	seats	vote %	seats	vote %	seats	Turn-out	No. of seats
1945	41	**125**	27	**67**	16	**28**	4	**13**	–	–	–	–	12	12	75	245
1949	49.5	**193**	30	**41**	13	**13**	4	**10**	–	–	–	–	4	5	74	262
1953	49	**171**	31	**51**	11	**23**	5	**15**	–	–	–	–	3	5	67.5	265
1957	41	**105**	39	**112**	11	**25**	7	**19**	–	–	–	–	3	4	74	265
1958	34	**49**	54	**208**	9.5	**8**	3	**0**	–	–	–	–	X	0	79	265
1962	37	**100**	37	**116**	13	**19**	12	**30**	–	–	–	–	1	0	79	265
1963	41	**129**	33	**95**	14	**17**	12	**24**	–	–	–	–	X	0	79	265
1965	40	**131**	32	**97**	18	**21**	8	**5**	–	–	–	–	2	11	75	265
1968	46	**155**	31	**72**	17	**23**	4	**14**	–	–	–	–	2	1	76	264
1972	39	**109**	35	**107**	18	**31**	8	**15**	–	–	–	–	X	2	77	264
1974	43	**141**	35	**95**	15	**16**	5	**11**	–	–	–	–	2	1	71	264
1979	40	**114**	36	**136**	18	**26**	5	**6**	–	–	–	–	1	0	76	282
1980	44	**147**	33	**103**	20	**32**	2	0	–	–	–	–	1	0	69	282
1984	28	**40**	50	**211**	18	**30**	1	**0**	–	–	–	–	3	1	76	282
1988	32	**83**	43	**169**	20	**43**	X	**0**	–	–	–	–	5	0	75	295
1993	41	**177**	16	**2**	7	**9**	–	–	13.5	**54**	19	**52**	3.5	1	69	295

* CCF before 1962

BY CONSTITUENCY

KEY

PC	Progressive Conservative Party
LIBERAL	Liberal Party
NDP	New Democratic Party
REFORM	Reform Party
BQ	Bloc Québécois
NLP	Natural Law Party
GREEN	Green Party
CONFED RWP	Confederation of Regions Western Party
CHP	Christian Heritage Party
LIBERTARIAN	Libertarian Party
RHINO	Rhinoceros Party
COMMONWEALTH	Party for Commonwealth of Canada
COMMUNIST	Communist Party
SC	Social Credit Party
M-L	Marxist Leninist
NAT	National Party
INDEPENDENT	Independent
ABOLITION	Abolition Party
CP	Canada Party

NEWFOUNDLAND

	1988	1993
	%	%
BONAVISTA-TRINITY-CONCEPTION		
PC	42.9	21.3
LIBERAL	51.3	74.8
NDP	5.7	1.1
REFORM	–	2.9
TOTAL	*41,471*	*35,082*

NEWFOUNDLAND

	1988	1993
	%	%
BURIN-ST. GEORGE'S		
PC	45.6	15.9
LIBERAL	48.4	80.3
NDP	6.0	2.4
NLP	–	1.4
TOTAL	*38,314*	*31,022*

NEWFOUNDLAND

	1988	1993
	%	%
GANDER-GRAND FALLS		
PC	31.5	19.6
LIBERAL	55.8	78.1
NDP	12.7	1.7
NLP	–	0.7
TOTAL	*36,410*	*30,995*
HUMBER-ST.BARBE-BAIE VERTE		
PC	29.4	15.8
LIBERAL	66.9	82.2
NDP	3.7	2.0
TOTAL	*39,392*	*35,844*
LABRADOR		
PC	33.0	18.9
LIBERAL	53.5	77.1
NDP	11.3	3.9
INDEPENDENT	2.1	–
TOTAL	*13,320*	*11,305*
ST.JOHN'S EAST		
PC	44.1	42.1
LIBERAL	19.1	44.2
NDP	35.3	6.4
REFORM	–	3.0
NAT	–	2.7
CHP	1.6	0.8
NLP	–	0.9
TOTAL	*48,725*	*45,862*
ST.JOHN'S WEST		
PC	61.5	37.6
LIBERAL	32.5	55.1
NDP	6.0	4.0
REFORM	–	2.4
NLP	–	1.0
TOTAL	*39,314*	*43,627*

PRINCE EDWARD ISLAND

	1988	1993
	%	%
CARDIGAN		
PC	43.9	32.7
LIBERAL	51.6	61.7
NDP	4.5	5.7
TOTAL	*18,066*	*16,492*
EGMONT		
PC	39.4	37.6
LIBERAL	53.1	57.6
NDP	7.5	4.8
TOTAL	*19,134*	*18,550*
HILLSBOROUGH		
PC	42.4	26.7
LIBERAL	43.7	60.6
NDP	9.7	5.8
REFORM	–	3.8
NAT	–	1.8
INDEPENDENT	2.8	–
CHP	1.3	0.8
NLP	–	0.6
TOTAL	*20,361*	*19,772*
MAPLEQUE		
PC	40.2	31.6
LIBERAL	51.9	60.8
NDP	7.9	4.4
CHP	–	1.8
GREEN	–	1.4
TOTAL	*18,075*	*17,408*

NOVA SCOTIA

	1988	1993
	%	%
ANNAPOLIS VALLEY-HANTS		
PC	44.2	20.3
LIBERAL	40.0	39.4
NDP	12.5	5.0
REFORM	–	12.8
INDEPENDENT	0.4	19.4
CHP	2.8	1.3
NAT	–	1.1
NLP	–	0.7
TOTAL	*47,007*	*46,246*
CAPE BRETON-EAST RICHMOND		
PC	20.8	8.4
LIBERAL	66.2	78.3
NDP	13.0	5.6
REFORM	–	5.5
NAT	–	1.4
NLP	–	0.5
TOTAL	*34,441*	*31,910*
CAPE BRETON-HIGHLANDS-CANSO		
PC	44.0	22.3
LIBERAL	50.9	64.4
NDP	5.1	3.9
REFORM	–	8.4
NLP	–	1.0
TOTAL	*39,911*	*35,280*
CAPE BRETON-THE SYDNEYS		
PC	28.8	11.2
LIBERAL	63.2	75.8
NDP	7.9	6.4
REFORM	–	5.7
NLP	–	0.8
TOTAL	*37,831*	*33,232*
CENTRAL NOVA		
PC	48.6	32.2
LIBERAL	38.4	43.5
NDP	13.0	6.5
REFORM	–	15.7
NAT	–	1.4
NLP	–	0.7
TOTAL	*39,241*	*37,524*

NOVA SCOTIA

	1988	1993
	%	%
CUMBERLAND-COLCHESTER		
PC	46.2	36.6
LIBERAL	41.6	42.6
NDP	9.3	5.6
REFORM	–	13.2
CHP	2.5	1.4
INDEPENDENT	0.5	–
NLP	–	0.7
TOTAL	*44,134*	*42,844*
DARTMOUTH		
PC	41.8	23.5
LIBERAL	46.2	50.8
NDP	10.9	7.2
REFORM	–	15.7
NAT	–	1.8
NLP	–	1.1
LIBERTARIAN	0.9	–
NO AFFILIATION	0.2	–
TOTAL	*47,539*	*46,172*
HALIFAX		
PC	38.0	20.7
LIBERAL	43.0	45.9
NDP	17.7	13.4
REFORM	–	14.5
NAT	–	3.0
NLP	–	1.0
GREEN	–	0.7
INDEPENDENT	0.3	0.8
LIBERTARIAN	0.6	–
COMMUNIST	0.3	–
COMMONWEALTH	0.2	–
M-L	–	0.2
TOTAL	*52,250*	*46,455*
HALIFAX WEST		
PC	44.8	23.5
LIBERAL	38.6	46.0
NDP	16.3	8.5
REFORM	–	19.4
NAT	–	1.8
NLP	–	0.8
COMMONWEALTH	0.4	–
TOTAL	*55,452*	*58,889*

NOVA SCOTIA

	1988	1993
	%	%
SOUTH SHORE		
PC	46.4	32.6
LIBERAL	42.6	46.9
NDP	10.2	5.0
REFORM	–	13.5
NAT	–	1.1
NLP	–	0.8
LIBERTARIAN	0.8	–
TOTAL	*39,923*	*36,965*
SOUTHWEST NOVA		
PC	41.5	22.7
LIBERAL	50.0	54.8
NDP	5.7	5.6
REFORM	–	15.6
CHP	2.8	–
NLP	–	1.4
TOTAL	*42,113*	*37,877*

NEW BRUNSWICK

	1988	1993
	%	%
ACADIE-BATHURST		
PC	–	27.6
LIBERAL	–	66.4
NDP	–	6.0
TOTAL	–	*40,418*
BEAUSÉJOUR		
PC	27.2	15.2
LIBERAL	58.6	76.2
NDP	10.2	5.7
CONFED RWP	3.9	–
NAT	–	1.9
CHP	–	1.1
TOTAL	*38,644*	*39,550*
CARLETON-CHARLOTTE		
PC	47.2	40.6
LIBERAL	41.6	43.1
NDP	7.7	3.1
REFORM	–	11.8
CONFED RWP	3.5	–
NAT	–	1.3
TOTAL	*33,921*	*32,407*
FREDERICTON		
PC	43.0	29.2
LIBERAL	39.7	46.6
NDP	10.3	5.0
REFORM	–	17.1
CONFED RWP	5.8	–
NLP	–	0.8
CP	–	0.8
RHINO	0.7	–
INDEPENDENT	0.5	0.5
TOTAL	*47,680*	*46,703*
FUNDY-ROYAL		
PC	46.7	28.3
LIBERAL	36.3	46.5
NDP	11.0	4.8
REFORM	–	17.7
CONFED RWP	6.1	–
INDEPENDENT	–	2.7
TOTAL	*45,261*	*46,844*

NEW BRUNSWICK

	1988	1993
	%	%
GLOUCESTER		
PC	42.7	–
LIBERAL	51.7	–
NDP	5.5	–
TOTAL	*39,135*	–
MADAWASKA-VICTORIA		
PC	48.2	45.7
LIBERAL	43.8	48.8
NDP	8.0	2.6
REFORM	–	2.9
TOTAL	*30,573*	*32,910*
MIRAMICHI		
PC	32.4	22.8
LIBERAL	50.8	61.1
NDP	6.1	5.1
REFORM	–	9.9
CONFED RWP	10.7	–
CP	–	1.0
TOTAL	*27,696*	*30,817*
MONCTON		
PC	34.0	14.3
LIBERAL	46.9	66.3
NDP	9.7	4.9
REFORM	–	12.4
CONFED RWP	7.3	–
CHP	1.8	1.1
NLP	–	1.0
NO AFFILIATION	0.3	–
TOTAL	*50,779*	*50,759*
RESTIGOUCHE-CHALEUR		
PC	40.0	19.9
LIBERAL	49.4	70.5
NDP	10.6	6.9
NLP	–	2.7
TOTAL	*30,890*	*29,871*

NEW BRUNSWICK

	1988	1993
	%	%
SAINT JOHN		
PC	43.1	43.3
LIBERAL	38.6	33.6
NDP	12.5	4.1
REFORM	–	–
CONFED RWP	4.6	–
CP	–	1.0
LIBERTARIAN	0.7	–
NLP	–	0.7
INDEPENDENT	0.4	10.6
NAT	–	0.4
TOTAL	*39,006*	*34,910*

QUEBEC

	1988	1993
	%	%
ABITIBI		
PC	57.6	35.3
LIBERAL	16.2	16.2
NDP	26.3	2.3
BQ	–	46.2
TOTAL	*38,666*	*41,274*
ARGENTEUIL-PAPINEAU		
PC	56.4	22.2
LIBERAL	27.1	28.8
NDP	14.1	1.8
BQ	–	47.3
RHINO	2.3	–
TOTAL	*40,895*	*49,441*
BEAUCE		
PC	68.7	8.2
LIBERAL	25.9	14.5
NDP	5.4	0.7
BQ	–	36.2
INDEPENDENT	–	40.5
TOTAL	*52,709*	*50,290*
BEAUHARNOIS-SALABERRY		
PC	58.4	15.1
LIBERAL	26.7	31.5
NDP	11.9	2.0
BQ	–	51.4
GREEN	1.5	–
RHINO	1.5	–
TOTAL	*49,937*	*50,337*
BELLECHASSE		
PC	65.0	37.9
LIBERAL	26.2	20.0
NDP	6.5	1.4
BQ	–	40.7
GREEN	2.4	–
TOTAL	*42,513*	*41,779*

QUEBEC

	1988	1993
	%	%
BERTHIER-MONTCALM		
PC	56.3	8.9
LIBERAL	25.9	27.4
NDP	11.3	1.0
BQ	–	60.9
GREEN	4.0	–
NO AFFILIATION	2.5	–
NLP	–	1.4
NAT	–	0.5
TOTAL	*52,153*	*59,059*
BLAINVILLE-DEUX MONTAGNES		
PC	62.0	14.6
LIBERAL	21.0	23.1
NDP	14.1	1.1
BQ	–	59.4
RHINO	2.7	–
NLP	–	1.2
COMMONWEALTH	0.2	0.1
LIBERTARIAN	–	0.5
TOTAL	*65,772*	*81,154*
BONAVENTURE-ILES-DE-LA-MADELEINE		
PC	58.6	21.5
LIBERAL	35.6	43.6
NDP	5.8	1.3
BQ	–	33.5
TOTAL	*26,435*	*27,543*
BROME-MISSISQUOI		
PC	54.0	17.2
LIBERAL	32.9	36.7
NDP	13.1	1.3
BQ	–	40.8
ABOLITION	–	1.7
NLP	–	1.3
INDEPENDENT	–	0.9
NAT	–	0.4
TOTAL	*41,762*	*43,754*

QUEBEC

	1988	1993
	%	%
CHAMBLY		
PC	47.0	7.8
LIBERAL	19.9	29.1
NDP	31.6	2.9
BQ	–	59.7
RHINO	1.4	–
COMMONWEALTH	0.1	0.5
TOTAL	*54,780*	*59,325*
CHAMPLAIN		
PC	64.7	27.0
LIBERAL	16.2	23.2
NDP	19.1	0.9
BQ	–	48.8
TOTAL	*46,051*	*48,436*
CHARLESBOURG		
PC	60.1	12.6
LIBERAL	26.6	23.4
NDP	13.4	1.9
BQ	–	59.4
NLP	–	2.3
ABOLITION	–	0.5
TOTAL	*59,190*	*64,958*
CHARLEVOIX		
PC	80.0	17.8
LIBERAL	14.2	18.8
NDP	4.3	1.4
BQ	–	62.0
RHINO	1.4	–
TOTAL	*42,143*	*38,110*
CHATEAUGUAY		
PC	44.8	9.7
LIBERAL	32.8	30.3
NDP	16.5	1.4
BQ	–	58.0
NO AFFILIATION	3.4	–
RHINO	2.5	–
COMMONWEALTH	–	0.5
TOTAL	*50,117*	*59,730*

QUEBEC

	1988	1993
	%	%
CHICOUTIMI		
PC	70.4	24.1
LIBERAL	18.4	10.8
NDP	11.2	1.2
BQ	–	63.9
TOTAL	*43,616*	*46,185*
DRUMMOND		
PC	53.5	19.8
LIBERAL	34.7	24.1
NDP	11.7	1.3
BQ	–	54.9
TOTAL	*44,523*	*45,423*
FRONTENAC		
PC	73.6	16.3
LIBERAL	19.9	22.5
NDP	5.1	1.0
BQ	–	58.4
GREEN	1.5	1.1
ABOLITION	–	0.6
TOTAL	*35,146*	*33,258*
GASPÉ		
PC	57.7	18.5
LIBERAL	34.6	34.6
NDP	5.2	0.7
BQ	–	45.2
GREEN	–	1.0
RHINO	1.8	–
INDEPENDENT	0.6	–
TOTAL	*28,424*	*29,277*
GATINEAU-LA LIEVRE		
PC	39.4	6.3
LIBERAL	43.3	55.5
NDP	15.4	1.6
BQ	–	35.3
RHINO	1.2	–
NLP	–	1.0
OTHER	0.7	0.3
TOTAL	*54,302*	*70,798*

QUEBEC

	1988	1993
	%	%
HULL-AYLMER		
PC	31.9	6.2
LIBERAL	49.8	53.3
NDP	15.4	2.6
BQ	–	27.2
RHINO	1.2	–
NO AFFILIATION	1.5	8.7
GREEN	–	0.9
NLP	–	0.8
M-L	–	0.3
ABOLITION	–	0.1
TOTAL	*46,591*	*52,548*
JOLIETTE		
PC	55.1	14.2
LIBERAL	24.8	16.3
NDP	14.3	1.2
BQ	–	66.3
GREEN	4.5	–
NLP	–	2.1
NO AFFILIATION	1.0	–
COMMONWEALTH	0.3	–
TOTAL	*50,661*	*61,983*
JONQUIERE		
PC	63.6	17.9
LIBERAL	15.6	12.2
NDP	20.8	1.1
BQ	–	67.6
NLP	–	1.2
TOTAL	*33,816*	*37,159*
KAMOURASKA-RIVIERE-DU-LOUP		
PC	58.5	23.0
LIBERAL	29.7	21.4
NDP	9.3	1.3
BQ	–	52.9
GREEN	2.0	–
NO AFFILIATION	0.6	1.5
TOTAL	*34,875*	*35,014*

QUEBEC

	1988	1993
	%	%
LAC-SAINT-JEAN		
PC	66.3	8.9
LIBERAL	15.4	14.3
NDP	18.2	1.2
BQ	–	75.6
TOTAL	*34,843*	*36,074*
LANGELIER		
PC	46.6	–
LIBERAL	28.2	–
NDP	20.1	–
BQ	–	–
GREEN	3.6	–
NO AFFILIATION	O.8	–
INDEPENDENT	O.6	–
TOTAL	*52,638*	–
LA PRAIRIE		
PC	53.0	12.1
LIBERAL	33.5	42.3
NDP	10.7	1.1
BQ	–	43.1
RHINO	2.4	–
NLP	–	1.1
COMMONWEALTH	0.3	0.3
TOTAL	*58,123*	*63,860*
LAURENTIDES		
PC	55.2	10.4
LIBERAL	28.0	27.1
NDP	13.8	1.2
BQ	–	60.7
RHINO	2.5	–
COMMONWEALTH	0.4	0.7
TOTAL	*56,164*	*68,926*
LÉVIS		
PC	57.4	14.0
LIBERAL	22.2	21.7
NDP	19.6	1.8
BQ	–	61.5
ABOLITION	–	1.0
SC	0.8	–
TOTAL	*58,621*	*65,809*

QUEBEC

	1988	1993
	%	%
LONGUEUIL		
PC	53.3	7.7
LIBERAL	22.6	24.2
NDP	19.6	1.7
BQ	–	66.0
RHINO	3.8	–
NO AFFILIATION	0.4	–
COMMONWEALTH	0.3	0.4
TOTAL	*54,539*	*58,955*
LOUIS-HÉBERT		
PC	59.8	15.3
LIBERAL	24.8	25.8
NDP	13.0	1.3
BQ	–	55.7
RHINO	2.4	–
NLP	–	1.5
ABOLITION	–	0.3
COMMONWEALTH	–	0.2
TOTAL	*62,452*	*60,844*
MANICOUAGAN		
PC	61.6	22.2
LIBERAL	22.9	21.1
NDP	14.4	1.7
BQ	–	55.0
COMMONWEALTH	1.0	–
TOTAL	*27,770*	*27,028*
MATAPÉDIA-MATANE		
PC	50.2	7.7
LIBERAL	36.4	32.6
NDP	13.4	0.7
BQ	–	57.3
NLP	–	1.8
TOTAL	*31,799*	*31,977*
MEGANTIC-COMPTON-STANSTEAD		
PC	60.3	15.7
LIBERAL	30.0	35.3
NDP	8.3	1.3
BQ	–	44.7
SC	1.4	–
NLP	–	2.0
ABOLITION	–	0.6
NAT	–	0.5
TOTAL	*38,557*	*38,495*

QUEBEC

	1988	1993
	%	%
MONTMORENCY-ORLEANS		
PC	60.5	23.1
LIBERAL	22.9	14.4
NDP	15.2	2.1
BQ	–	57.7
NLP	–	2.1
NO AFFILIATION	1.3	–
ABOLITION	–	0.5
TOTAL	*48,868*	*54,866*
PONTIAC-GATINEAU-LABELLE		
PC	53.6	21.9
LIBERAL	30.2	40.3
NDP	16.2	1.6
BQ	–	33.7
NAT	–	1.7
INDEPENDENT	–	0.9
TOTAL	*38,318*	*42,997*
PORTNEUF		
PC	57.4	14.8
LIBERAL	26.5	23.1
NDP	12.2	1.4
BQ	–	53.6
INDEPENDENT	–	5.1
GREEN	3.9	–
NLP	–	2.0
TOTAL	*38,328*	*44,871*
QUEBEC		
PC	–	13.7
LIBERAL	–	27.0
NDP	–	2.0
BQ	–	53.8
NLP	–	1.7
GREEN	–	1.5
ABOLITION	–	0.3
TOTAL	–	*51,620*

QUEBEC

	1988	1993
	%	%
QUEBEC-EST		
PC	55.7	11.3
LIBERAL	25.9	24.4
NDP	14.3	1.7
BQ	–	59.6
RHINO	1.9	–
GREEN	1.7	–
ABOLITION	–	0.6
OTHER	0.4	0.5
TOTAL	*52,931*	*58,051*
RICHELIEU		
PC	68.9	9.4
LIBERAL	19.3	23.1
NDP	6.8	0.7
BQ	–	66.5
GREEN	4.1	–
RHINO	1.0	–
COMMONWEALTH	–	0.3
TOTAL	*46,590*	*47,440*
RICHMOND-WOLFE		
PC	47.5	23.5
LIBERAL	41.0	21.5
NDP	9.6	1.1
BQ	–	52.3
RHINO	1.9	–
NLP	–	1.6
TOTAL	*40,972*	*42,553*
RIMOUSKI-TEMISCOUATA		
PC	62.6	12.0
LIBERAL	27.8	24.7
NDP	6.4	0.9
BQ	–	59.9
INDEPENDENT	3.2	1.6
NLP	–	1.0
TOTAL	*37,977*	*38,444*
ROBERVAL		
PC	76.4	18.1
LIBERAL	12.1	20.5
NDP	9.5	1.5
BQ	–	60.0
RHINO	2.1	–
TOTAL	*34,977*	*33,537*

QUEBEC

	1988	1993
	%	%
SAINT-HUBERT		
PC	48.9	7.4
LIBERAL	29.1	31.9
NDP	18.0	1.5
BQ	–	56.9
RHINO	2.3	–
GREEN	1.4	–
NLP	–	1.4
NAT	–	0.6
COMMONWEALTH	–	0.4
TOTAL	*52,289*	*61,444*
SAINT-HYACINTHE-BAGOT		
PC	52.6	20.1
LIBERAL	33.9	20.7
NDP	13.4	1.7
BQ	–	57.4
TOTAL	*47,993*	*48,820*
SAINT-JEAN		
PC	56.3	14.6
LIBERAL	29.8	26.9
NDP	11.8	0.9
BQ	–	55.9
RHINO	2.2	–
NLP	–	1.5
COMMONWEALTH	–	0.2
TOTAL	*49,198*	*53,246*
SAINT-MAURICE		
PC	45.3	4.1
LIBERAL	24.6	54.1
NDP	30.1	0.5
BQ	–	40.5
NLP	–	0.8
TOTAL	*41,372*	*46,613*
SHEFFORD		
PC	43.2	12.0
LIBERAL	48.2	29.1
NDP	8.5	1.2
BQ	–	55.7
NLP	–	1.6
ABOLITION	–	0.5
TOTAL	*49,630*	*48,704*

QUEBEC

	1988	1993
	%	%
SHERBROOKE		
PC	63.3	52.4
LIBERAL	22.6	7.9
NDP	11.7	0.8
BQ	–	37.9
RHINO	1.9	–
NO AFFILIATION	0.3	–
COMMUNIST	0.3	–
NLP	–	0.9
ABOLITION	–	0.2
TOTAL	*54,556*	*56,819*
TÉMISCAMINGUE		
PC	46.3	19.3
LIBERAL	14.2	22.9
NDP	37.8	–
BQ	–	55.7
RHINO	1.7	–
NLP	–	1.3
ABOLITION	–	0.7
TOTAL	*41,284*	*40,435*
TERREBONNE		
PC	52.8	11.7
LIBERAL	18.5	17.9
NDP	10.7	1.1
BQ	–	68.9
INDEPENDENT	15.5	–
RHINO	2.5	–
COMMONWEALTH	–	0.5
TOTAL	*66,998*	*84,260*

QUEBEC

	1988	1993
	%	%
TROIS-RIVIERES		
PC	68.9	23.5
LIBERAL	15.8	21.2
NDP	12.8	0.8
BQ	–	53.4
RHINO	1.9	–
NLP	–	1.1
NO AFFILIATION	0.6	–
TOTAL	*42,642*	*46,651*
VERCHERES		
PC	66.0	9.2
LIBERAL	17.3	21.1
NDP	13.8	1.2
BQ	–	67.3
RHINO	2.6	–
CHP	–	0.8
COMMONWEALTH	0.2	0.3
TOTAL	*48,931*	*57,393*

QUEBEC (Island of Montreal)

	1988	1993
	%	%
ILE JESUS AHUNTSIC		
PC	42.4	8.8
LIBERAL	41.1	41.8
NDP	11.0	1.3
BQ	–	45.1
GREEN	2.2	–
RHINO	2.0	–
NLP	–	1.0
NO AFFILIATION	0.7	1.1
COMMUNIST	0.4	–
ABOLITION	–	0.7
COMMONWEALTH	0.2	0.3
TOTAL	*51,161*	*50,345*
ANJOU-RIVIERE-DES-PRAIRIES		
PC	51.5	11.6
LIBERAL	32.7	42.2
NDP	12.6	1.6
BQ	–	43.1
GREEN	2.3	–
NLP	–	1.2
OTHER	0.9	0.2
TOTAL	*53,529*	*60,704*
BOURASSA		
PC	43.3	12.0
LIBERAL	41.5	41.9
NDP	11.0	2.4
BQ	–	42.0
RHINO	2.0	–
NLP	–	1.1
GREEN	0.9	–
ABOLITION	–	0.5
SC	0.4	–
COMMUNIST	0.4	–
NO AFFILIATION	0.3	–
COMMONWEALTH	0.2	0.2
TOTAL	*43,782*	*43,431*

QUEBEC (Island of Montreal)

	1988	1993
	%	%
DUVERNAY		
PC	60.7	–
LIBERAL	22.9	–
NDP	14.8	–
SC	0.9	–
COMMONWEALTH	0.7	–
TOTAL	*55,028*	–
HOCHELAGA-MAISONNEUVE		
PC	39.1	8.7
LIBERAL	34.2	25.0
NDP	20.6	2.5
BQ	–	61.4
RHINO	3.0	–
GREEN	1.9	–
NLP	–	1.4
NO AFFILIATION	0.7	–
COMMONWEALTH	0.3	0.4
COMMUNIST	0.3	–
M-L	–	0.6
TOTAL	*41,570*	*42,645*
LACHINE-LAC-SAINT-LOUIS		
PC	45.4	8.0
LIBERAL	44.1	67.5
NDP	7.9	1.4
BQ	–	20.4
GREEN	1.5	–
NO AFFILIATION	–	1.1
NLP	–	1.0
LIBERTARIAN	0.6	0.3
COMMONWEALTH	0.2	0.3
OTHER	0.4	0.1
TOTAL	*57,036*	*58,903*
LASALLE-EMARD		
PC	42.7	4.6
LIBERAL	45.5	59.5
NDP	10.6	1.4
BQ	–	33.3
NLP	–	0.8
NO AFFILIATION	0.6	–
COMMUNIST	0.4	–
COMMONWEALTH	0.2	0.3
ABOLITION	–	0.1
TOTAL	*51,465*	*51,874*

QUEBEC (Island of Montreal)

	1988	1993
	%	%
LAURIER-SAINTE-MARIE		
PC	29.7	5.3
LIBERAL	39.1	24.5
NDP	21.6	3.1
BQ	–	61.8
RHINO	5.2	–
GREEN	3.5	2.6
NLP	–	1.6
M-L	–	0.5
COMMUNIST	0.4	–
NO AFFILIATION	0.3	0.3
COMMONWEALTH	0.2	0.3
TOTAL	*54,691*	*40,558*
LAVAL CENTRE		
PC	–	8.0
LIBERAL	–	33.4
NDP	–	1.1
BQ	–	55.2
NLP	–	1.2
COMMONWEALTH	–	0.4
NAT	–	0.4
ABOLITION	–	0.3
TOTAL	–	*57,003*
MERCIER		
PC	54.8	4.2
LIBERAL	23.0	20.1
NDP	18.2	1.2
BQ	–	58.9
RHINO	2.9	–
COMMUNIST	0.5	–
ABOLITION	–	0.4
NO AFFILIATION	0.3	15.2
COMMONWEALTH	0.2	0.2
TOTAL	*56,192*	*58,885*

QUEBEC (Island of Montreal)

	1988	1993
	%	%
MOUNT ROYAL		
PC	32.0	5.8
LIBERAL	59.9	82.9
NDP	5.4	1.7
BQ	–	7.0
RHINO	1.1	–
NO AFFILIATION	–	1.1
GREEN	1.0	–
NLP	–	0.7
NAT	–	0.6
COMMONWEALTH	0.2	0.2
OTHER	0.1	0.1
TOTAL	*45,699*	*47,743*
NOTRE-DAME-DE-GRACE		
PC	27.9	6.5
LIBERAL	54.6	70.7
NDP	12.3	3.5
BQ	–	14.2
GREEN	2.0	–
RHINO	1.6	–
NAT	–	1.6
NLP	–	1.1
CHP	0.9	–
LIBERTARIAN	0.5	0.6
INDEPENDENT	–	0.4
NO AFFILIATION	0.2	1.3
ABOLITION	–	0.2
COMMONWEALTH	0.1	0.1
TOTAL	*42,014*	*40,508*
OUTREMONT		
PC	38.4	8.7
LIBERAL	34.7	47.1
NDP	20.5	4.5
BQ	–	37.4
GREEN	2.9	–
RHINO	2.4	–
NLP	–	1.5
COMMUNIST	0.4	–
NO AFFILIATION	0.4	–
M-L	–	0.4
ABOLITION	–	0.3
COMMONWEALTH	0.3	0.2
TOTAL	*45,790*	*46,115*

QUEBEC (Island of Montreal)

	1988	1993
	%	%
PAPINEAU-SAINT-MICHEL		
PC	33.2	4.4
LIBERAL	46.0	52.0
NDP	15.1	1.8
BQ	–	39.2
RHINO	2.5	–
GREEN	1.2	–
NLP	–	1.8
NO AFFILIATION	0.9	–
COMMUNIST	0.6	–
M-L	–	0.4
COMMONWEALTH	0.4	0.2
ABOLITION	–	0.3
TOTAL	*39,400*	*38,601*
PIERREFONDS-DOLLARD		
PC	49.8	13.2
LIBERAL	40.2	65.0
NDP	7.0	1.4
BQ	–	17.4
RHINO	1.5	–
INDEPENDENT	0.8	0.6
NLP	–	0.8
NAT	–	0.8
LIBERTARIAN	0.5	0.7
COMMONWEALTH	0.1	0.2
TOTAL	*55,317*	*61,514*
ROSEMONT		
PC	37.8	5.4
LIBERAL	29.2	27.5
NDP	20.2	2.2
BQ	–	63.0
NO AFFILIATION	5.2	–
RHINO	3.7	–
GREEN	3.1	–
NLP	–	1.4
M-L	–	0.4
SC	0.3	–
COMMUNIST	0.3	–
COMMONWEALTH	0.3	0.2
TOTAL	*45,259*	*46,724*

QUEBEC (Island of Montreal)

	1988	1993
	%	%
SAINT-DENIS		
PC	30.4	5.3
LIBERAL	47.2	52.4
NDP	14.7	2.3
BQ	–	36.6
RHINO	2.8	–
GREEN	2.6	–
INDEPENDENT	0.8	1.0
NLP	–	1.0
SC	0.6	–
COMMUNIST	0.5	–
COMMONWEALTH	0.5	0.4
ABOLITION	–	0.6
M-L	–	0.5
TOTAL	*42,249*	*41,757*
SAINT-HENRI-WESTMOUNT		
PC	39.3	10.7
LIBERAL	41.6	61.7
NDP	13.1	4.0
BQ	–	18.9
GREEN	2.3	–
RHINO	1.7	–
NO AFFILIATION	1.6	0.3
NAT	–	1.4
NLP	–	1.3
INDEPENDENT	–	0.6
LIBERTARIAN	0.4	–
COMMONWEALTH	–	0.3
CHP	–	0.3
M-L	–	0.3
ABOLITION	–	0.2
TOTAL	*39,887*	*42,029*
SAINT-LAURENT		
PC	41.5	7.4
LIBERAL	46.3	70.1
NDP	9.6	2.0
BQ	–	18.4
GREEN	1.7	–
NLP	–	0.8
NO AFFILIATION	0.7	–
NAT	–	0.6
COMMONWEALTH	0.3	0.5
ABOLITION	–	0.2
TOTAL	*44,114*	*45,955*

QUEBEC (Island of Montreal)

	1988	1993
	%	%
SAINT-LÉONARD		
PC	37.2	8.5
LIBERAL	50.3	61.2
NDP	10.2	1.2
BQ	–	27.4
GREEN	1.8	–
NLP	–	1.1
NO AFFILIATION	0.5	–
M-L	–	0.3
ABOLITION	–	0.2
COMMONWEALTH	–	0.2
TOTAL	*45,796*	*47,090*
VAUDREUIL		
PC	55.7	9.9
LIBERAL	30.0	47.8
NDP	11.3	1.7
BQ	–	38.6
GREEN	1.7	–
RHINO	1.2	–
NLP	–	1.1
LIBERTARIAN	–	0.7
COMMONWEALTH	0.1	0.3
TOTAL	*54,596*	*65,217*
VERDUN-SAINT-PAUL		
PC	45.3	8.6
LIBERAL	34.3	43.7
NDP	14.8	1.9
BQ	–	42.5
GREEN	3.0	1.3
RHINO	2.0	–
NLP	–	1.0
ABOLITION	–	0.3
NAT	–	0.3
COMMONWEALTH	0.3	0.2
NO AFFILIATION	0.2	0.3
TOTAL	*44,380*	*44,966*

ONTARIO

	1988	1993
	%	%
ALGOMA		
PC	23.5	11.5
LIBERAL	53.2	58.1
NDP	23.3	8.6
REFORM	–	21.1
NLP	–	0.8
TOTAL	*31,940*	*31,385*
BRAMALEA-GORE-MALTON		
PC	51.6	19.2
LIBERAL	24.6	43.3
NDP	18.0	5.1
REFORM	–	29.1
NAT	–	1.2
NLP	–	0.7
INDEPENDENT	–	0.7
GREEN	–	0.6
M-L	–	0.2
TOTAL		*40,858*
BRAMPTON		
PC	41.5	17.8
LIBERAL	34.4	51.7
NDP	22.5	2.8
REFORM	–	26.7
NLP	–	0.7
M-L	–	0.4
CHP	4.7	–
LIBERTARIAN	1.0	–
TOTAL	*57,095*	*68,158*
BRANT		
PC	29.7	12.2
LIBERAL	24.2	51.5
NDP	41.5	6.9
REFORM	–	24.7
NLP	–	0.4
LIBERTARIAN	0.2	0.5
NAT	–	2.6
GREEN	0.6	1.0
NO AFFILIATION	–	0.2
CHP	3.8	–
COMMONWEALTH	0.1	–
TOTAL	*47,351*	*47,968*

ONTARIO

	1988	1993
	%	%
BRUCE-GREY		
PC	40.9	18.8
LIBERAL	38.9	49.1
NDP	19.0	4.3
REFORM	–	24.7
NLP	–	0.3
LIBERTARIAN	–	0.3
NAT	–	1.9
GREEN	0.7	0.6
COMMONWEALTH	0.5	–
TOTAL	*48,311*	*52,349*
BURLINGTON		
PC	51.6	26.3
LIBERAL	27.1	44.3
NDP	16.1	2.9
REFORM	–	23.3
NLP	–	0.6
LIBERTARIAN	4.5	–
NAT	–	1.0
INDEPENDENT	–	1.7
CHP	0.6	–
TOTAL	*50,496*	*51,700*
CAMBRIDGE		
PC	40.4	17.3
LIBERAL	26.8	39.3
NDP	28.1	5.3
REFORM	–	33.5
NLP	–	0.7
NAT	–	3.2
INDEPENDENT	0.3	–
CHP	4.5	0.7
TOTAL	*50,961*	*56,345*
CARLETON-GLOUCESTER		
PC	37.3	15.7
LIBERAL	48.1	61.6
NDP	9.7	3.7
REFORM	0.7	16.4
NLP	–	0.7
NAT	–	1.1
GREEN	–	0.5
CHP	4.2	0.3
ABOLITION	–	0.1
TOTAL	*64,269*	*76,025*

ONTARIO

	1988	1993
	%	%
COCHRANE-SUPERIOR		
PC	23.6	9.1
LIBERAL	40.1	72.2
NDP	36.4	9.0
REFORM	–	9.6
TOTAL	*29,839*	*27,012*
DURHAM		
PC	59.3	24.5
LIBERAL	20.8	36.8
NDP	18.6	4.2
REFORM	–	30.5
NLP	–	0.5
NAT	–	1.9
GREEN	–	0.6
CHP	–	1.2
TOTAL		*60,892*
ELGIN-NORFOLK		
PC	38.6	27.5
LIBERAL	34.3	43.1
NDP	20.8	5.3
REFORM	–	20.5
NLP	–	0.6
CHP	6.2	2.9
ABOLITION	–	0.1
TOTAL	*40,623*	*40,510*
ERIE		
PC	38.5	14.5
LIBERAL	36.5	48.7
NDP	20.9	4.5
REFORM	–	28.9
NLP	–	0.5
NAT	–	1.4
CHP	4.1	1.5
TOTAL	*39,116*	*40,665*
ESSEX-KENT		
PC	32.3	13.4
LIBERAL	49.4	62.1
NDP	18.4	5.7
REFORM	–	18.1
NLP	–	0.6
TOTAL	*37,750*	*35,363*

ONTARIO

	1988	1993
	%	%
ESSEX-WINDSOR		
PC	14.3	3.3
LIBERAL	41.3	55.1
NDP	44.1	27.7
REFORM	–	13.2
NAT	–	0.4
M-L	–	0.2
COMMONWEALTH	–	0.2
NO AFFILIATION	0.2	–
TOTAL	*42,893*	*45,725*
GLENGARRY-PRESCOTT-RUSSELL		
PC	19.1	8.2
LIBERAL	70.7	80.2
NDP	9.1	2.3
REFORM	–	8.0
NLP	–	0.8
LIBERTARIAN	0.7	0.4
COMMONWEALTH	0.4	–
TOTAL	*49,868*	*55,815*
GUELPH-WELLINGTON		
PC	43.2	20.7
LIBERAL	31.9	39.2
NDP	19.5	4.7
REFORM	0.4	24.9
NLP	–	0.4
LIBERTARIAN	0.5	0.4
NAT	–	3.3
GREEN	1.0	0.5
INDEPENDENT	–	5.7
CP	3.3	0.2
ABOLITION	–	0.0
NO AFFILIATION	0.1	–
TOTAL	*59,523*	*62,080*
HALDIMAND-NORFOLK		
PC	37.6	16.2
LIBERAL	38.0	53.8
NDP	15.1	3.7
REFORM	–	23.5
LIBERTARIAN	0.4	–
NAT	–	2.8
CHP	8.9	–
TOTAL	*44,500*	*44,966*

ONTARIO

	1988	1993
	%	%
HALTON-PEEL		
PC	54.6	30.5
LIBERAL	31.6	37.0
NDP	13.0	2.4
REFORM	–	28.0
LIBERTARIAN	0.9	0.7
NAT	–	0.9
CHP	–	0.5
TOTAL	*52,223*	*60,203*
HAMILTON EAST		
PC	21.4	6.8
LIBERAL	49.8	67.3
NDP	28.0	6.6
REFORM	–	17.0
NAT	–	1.2
INDEPENDENT	–	0.6
COMMUNIST	0.4	–
M-L	–	0.2
COMMONWEALTH	–	0.2
NO AFFILIATION	0.4	–
TOTAL	*37,416*	*34,175*
HAMILTON-MOUNTAIN		
PC	30.5	11.5
LIBERAL	32.9	57.3
NDP	32.8	7.6
REFORM	–	21.7
NLP	–	0.7
NAT	–	1.2
CHP	3.5	–
COMMONWEALTH	0.2	–
NO AFFILIATION	0.1	–
TOTAL	*51,492*	*47,509*
HAMILTON-WENTWORTH		
PC	41.9	22.4
LIBERAL	34.0	45.8
NDP	15.8	3.9
REFORM	1.2	25.5
NLP	–	0.5
NAT	–	1.0
CHP	7.2	0.7
TOTAL	*57,013*	*64,819*

ONTARIO

	1988	1993
	%	%
HAMILTON-WEST		
PC	33.9	15.0
LIBERAL	37.8	58.7
NDP	25.5	8.2
REFORM	1.2	15.2
NLP	–	1.0
NAT	–	1.6
NO AFFILIATION	–	0.4
CHP	2.1	–
INDEPENDENT	0.4	–
COMMUNIST	0.2	–
TOTAL	*43,860*	*38,517*
HASTINGS-FRONTENAC-LENNOX AND ADDINGTON		
PC	40.0	22.8
LIBERAL	38.0	50.1
NDP	17.3	4.2
REFORM	–	18.4
NAT	–	2.1
CHP	3.7	–
INDEPENDENT	1.1	2.5
TOTAL	*43,158*	*48,070*
HURON-BRUCE		
PC	42.6	28.0
LIBERAL	35.3	44.1
NDP	16.5	4.2
REFORM	–	21.1
NLP	–	0.5
LIBERTARIAN	–	0.6
CHP	5.6	1.6
TOTAL	*47,050*	*49,522*
KENORA-RAINY RIVER		
PC	21.6	6.0
LIBERAL	38.3	64.8
NDP	34.8	6.4
REFORM	1.1	20.6
NAT	–	1.8
CHP	4.2	–
INDEPENDENT	–	0.5
TOTAL	*34,782*	*34,559*

ONTARIO

	1988	1993
	%	%
KENT		
PC	35.0	13.8
LIBERAL	40.0	63.8
NDP	20.1	3.8
REFORM	–	15.5
NLP	–	0.4
NAT	–	2.8
CHP	4.9	–
TOTAL	*39,560*	*36,338*
KINGSTON AND THE ISLANDS		
PC	35.8	19.1
LIBERAL	40.6	56.5
NDP	20.1	7.1
REFORM	–	12.5
NLP	–	0.7
LIBERTARIAN	0.5	–
CHP	2.9	1.2
NAT	–	3.1
TOTAL	*56,919*	*57,340*
KITCHENER		
PC	41.8	19.8
LIBERAL	36.1	50.5
NDP	21.6	4.5
REFORM	–	23.2
NLP	–	0.8
LIBERTARIAN	0.4	0.3
CHP	–	0.9
NO AFFILIATION	0.2	–
TOTAL	*53,640*	*52,694*
LAMBTON-MIDDLESEX		
PC	40.4	22.5
LIBERAL	41.5	48.6
NDP	12.1	3.6
REFORM	–	19.4
NLP	–	0.4
NAT	–	1.1
CHP	5.9	3.8
INDEPENDENT	–	0.6
TOTAL	*41,699*	*41,776*

ONTARIO

	1988	1993
	%	%
LANARK-CARLETON		
PC	48.0	23.6
LIBERAL	35.6	49.4
NDP	14.7	2.4
REFORM	–	22.2
NLP	–	0.4
NAT	–	1.3
LIBERTARIAN	–	0.1
GREEN	–	0.5
ABOLITION	–	0.1
CONFED RWP	1.7	–
TOTAL	*56,999*	*70,833*
LEEDS-GRENVILLE		
PC	38.9	26.9
LIBERAL	43.4	52.6
NDP	11.1	2.0
REFORM	–	16.0
NLP	–	0.4
NAT	–	0.9
GREEN	–	1.1
CHP	3.4	–
ABOLITION	–	0.1
CONFED RWP	3.2	–
TOTAL	*46,416*	*50,539*
LINCOLN		
PC	38.6	15.7
LIBERAL	37.7	52.2
NDP	17.5	3.9
REFORM	–	25.7
NLP	–	0.6
NAT	–	1.7
CHP	5.3	–
INDEPENDENT	0.8	0.6
NO AFFILIATION	0.1	–
TOTAL	*51,702*	*55,656*

ONTARIO

	1988	1993
	%	%
LONDON EAST		
PC	37.5	18.2
LIBERAL	37.7	55.8
NDP	24.4	5.2
REFORM	–	17.2
NLP	–	0.6
NAT	–	1.6
GREEN	–	1.1
CP	–	0.2
COMMONWEALTH	–	0.1
NO AFFILIATION	0.4	–
TOTAL	*51,860*	*50,652*
LONDON-MIDDLESEX		
PC	38.3	18.1
LIBERAL	38.3	53.9
NDP	23.0	5.3
REFORM	–	19.4
NLP	–	0.5
NAT	–	1.1
GREEN	–	0.5
M-L	–	0.1
CP	–	0.1
CHP	–	1.0
ABOLITION	–	0.1
NO AFFILIATION	0.4	–
TOTAL	*48,354*	*50,553*
LONDON WEST		
PC	45.7	23.6
LIBERAL	37.5	48.3
NDP	16.1	4.0
REFORM	–	20.1
NLP	–	0.6
NAT	–	1.9
GREEN	–	0.6
CP	–	0.3
CHP	–	0.5
INDEPENDENT	–	0.2
LIBERTARIAN	0.7	–
ABOLITION	–	0.1
TOTAL	*62,155*	*64,339*

ONTARIO

	1988	1993
	%	%
MARKHAM-WHITCHURCH-STOUFFVILLE		
PC	53.1	25.5
LIBERAL	31.8	46.5
NDP	9.0	2.2
REFORM	–	23.2
NLP	–	0.6
NAT	–	1.3
LIBERTARIAN	0.8	–
ABOLITION	–	0.1
NO AFFILIATION	5.3	0.6
TOTAL	*69,066*	*77,218*
MISSISSAUGA EAST		
PC	41.5	12.8
LIBERAL	45.6	63.8
NDP	11.2	2.7
REFORM	–	18.8
NLP	–	0.6
LIBERTARIAN	0.7	–
NAT	–	0.8
CONFED RWP	0.5	–
INDEPENDENT	0.4	0.3
COMMONWEALTH	0.2	–
M-L	–	0.1
TOTAL	*50,564*	*50,386*
MISSISSAUGA SOUTH		
PC	51.9	23.4
LIBERAL	34.7	46.6
NDP	12.0	2.1
REFORM	–	25.1
NLP	–	0.5
LIBERTARIAN	0.6	0.9
NAT	–	1.0
INDEPENDENT	–	0.3
M-L	–	0.1
TOTAL		*46,102*

ONTARIO

	1988	1993
	%	%
MISSISSAUGA WEST		
PC	48.2	19.4
LIBERAL	41.5	55.9
NDP	9.7	2.3
NLP	–	0.5
LIBERTARIAN	0.7	–
GREEN	–	0.5
ABOLITION	–	0.2
M-L	–	0.1
TOTAL	*68,516*	*95,879*
NEPEAN		
PC	41.5	17.8
LIBERAL	47.2	59.6
NDP	10.8	3.4
REFORM	–	16.1
NLP	–	0.4
LIBERTARIAN	–	0.2
NAT	–	1.5
GREEN	–	0.8
COMMONWEALTH	0.5	0.1
ABOLITION	–	0.1
TOTAL	*56,442*	*60,706*
NIAGARA FALLS		
PC	39.5	22.2
LIBERAL	35.0	47.1
NDP	21.3	3.4
REFORM	–	25.0
NLP	–	0.4
NAT	–	1.2
GREEN	–	0.6
CHP	4.0	–
COMMONWEALTH	0.2	–
ABOLITION	–	0.2
TOTAL	*43,257*	*43,664*

ONTARIO

	1988	1993
	%	%
NICKEL BELT		
PC	20.8	5.4
LIBERAL	23.5	57.2
NDP	44.8	23.1
REFORM	–	12.7
NLP	–	0.4
NAT	–	0.8
INDEPENDENT	–	0.3
CONFED RWP	10.5	–
RHINO	0.5	–
ABOLITION	–	0.1
TOTAL	*38,898*	*44,127*
NIPISSING		
PC	39.8	16.3
LIBERAL	41.1	62.8
NDP	17.2	3.3
REFORM	–	16.9
NLP	–	0.5
CONFED RWP	1.4	–
INDEPENDENT	0.5	–
ABOLITION	–	0.2
TOTAL	*37,679*	*40,446*
NORTHUMBERLAND		
PC	41.0	21.1
LIBERAL	24.7	49.5
NDP	12.0	3.4
REFORM	–	23.8
NLP	–	0.5
LIBERTARIAN	0.4	0.3
CHP	–	0.7
RHINO	0.4	–
NAT	–	0.6
CONFED RWP	0.2	–
TOTAL	*45,288*	*48,413*
OAKVILLE-MILTON		
PC	54.0	26.2
LIBERAL	35.1	46.6
NDP	8.7	2.2
REFORM	–	23.7
NLP	–	0.7
CHP	1.7	–
LIBERTARIAN	0.5	–
OTHER	–	0.6
TOTAL	*64,873*	*73,285*

ONTARIO

	1988	1993
	%	%
ONTARIO		
PC	48.9	18.9
LIBERAL	32.3	43.4
NDP	17.9	3.1
REFORM	–	31.5
NLP	–	0.4
NAT	–	1.0
INDEPENDENT	–	0.8
LIBERTARIAN	0.7	0.5
GREEN	–	0.5
COMMONWEALTH	0.2	0.1
ABOLITION	–	0.1
TOTAL	*71,443*	*89,231*
OSHAWA		
PC	33.8	15.0
LIBERAL	20.5	38.3
NDP	44.3	14.9
REFORM	–	28.9
NAT	–	1.0
CHP	–	0.9
NLP	–	0.6
COMMONWEALTH	0.3	0.2
OTHER	0.1	0.2
TOTAL	*41,534*	*40,893*
OTTAWA CENTRE		
PC	26.5	12.3
LIBERAL	36.5	51.9
NDP	34.9	22.5
REFORM	–	9.4
NLP	–	0.7
NAT	–	1.6
GREEN	0.6	1.2
RHINO	0.6	–
INDEPENDENT	0.5	–
M-L	–	0.2
NO AFFILIATION	–	0.2
OTHER	0.4	0.2
TOTAL	*49,638*	*50,009*

ONTARIO

	1988	1993
	%	%
OTTAWA SOUTH		
PC	35.1	12.6
LIBERAL	50.8	65.9
NDP	13.5	3.9
REFORM	–	14.5
NAT	–	1.9
GREEN	–	0.7
NLP	–	0.5
LIBERTARIAN	0.3	–
COMMONWEALTH	0.2	–
M-L	–	0.1
OTHER	0.1	–
TOTAL	*54,576*	*55,358*
OTTAWA-VANIER		
PC	23.2	10.5
LIBERAL	59.2	70.5
NDP	16.0	6.5
REFORM	–	7.9
GREEN	–	1.3
NAT	–	1.1
RHINO	1.0	–
INDEPENDENT	–	0.9
NLP	–	0.9
M-L	–	0.3
OTHER	0.6	0.1
TOTAL	*48,265*	*48,564*
OTTAWA WEST		
PC	38.7	14.1
LIBERAL	49.4	63.4
NDP	11.2	4.1
REFORM	–	14.2
NAT	–	2.4
GREEN	–	0.8
NLP	–	0.5
LIBERTARIAN	–	0.4
COMMUNIST	0.3	–
OTHER	0.3	0.2
TOTAL	*47,376*	*44,856*

ONTARIO

	1988	1993
	%	%
OXFORD		
PC	39.7	22.7
LIBERAL	37.0	41.1
NDP	16.0	5.0
REFORM	–	26.5
CHP	6.5	2.0
INDEPENDENT	–	1.0
NAT	–	0.9
LIBERTARIAN	0.4	0.5
NLP	–	O.5
COMMONWEALTH	0.3	–
TOTAL	*48,715*	*47,826*
PARRY SOUND-MUSKOKA		
PC	43.3	20.6
LIBERAL	31.1	44.2
NDP	25.7	4.7
REFORM	–	28.2
NAT	–	1.3
NLP	–	0.6
INDEPENDENT	–	0.4
ABOLITION	–	0.1
TOTAL	*39,753*	*46,193*
PERTH-WELLINGTON-WATERLOO		
PC	39.1	23.3
LIBERAL	37.0	43.3
NDP	19.0	4.1
REFORM	–	26.2
CHP	4.4	1.4
NAT	–	1.0
NLP	–	0.4
LIBERTARIAN	0.5	0.3
TOTAL	*45,972*	*46,523*
PETERBOROUGH		
PC	40.7	20.1
LIBERAL	30.3	47.6
NDP	27.6	5.3
REFORM	–	23.2
NAT	–	3.2
NLP	–	0.6
LIBERTARIAN	0.5	–
RHINO	0.4	–
GREEN	0.4	–
TOTAL	*55,056*	*57,930*

ONTARIO

	1988	1993
	%	%
PRINCE EDWARD-HASTINGS		
PC	36.2	17.8
LIBERAL	43.1	57.1
NDP	14.5	2.8
REFORM	–	19.4
CHP	4.5	1.2
NAT	–	1.4
CONFED RWP	1.2	–
LIBERTARIAN	0.5	–
NLP	–	0.4
TOTAL	*45,345*	*46,394*
RENFREW		
PC	32.1	–
LIBERAL	54.3	–
NDP	12.5	–
CONFED RWP	1.1	–
TOTAL	*47,038*	–
RENFREW-NIPISSING-PEMBROKE		
PC	45.0	13.8
LIBERAL	54.3	50.6
NDP	12.5	2.7
REFORM	–	12.2
INDEPENDENT	–	20.2
ABOLITION	–	0.3
NLP	–	0.3
TOTAL	*45,345*	*50,895*
ST. CATHARINES		
PC	40.7	15.3
LIBERAL	33.3	49.0
NDP	25.5	5.7
REFORM	–	28.7
CHP	–	1.2
COMMUNIST	0.5%	–
ABOLITION	–	0.2
TOTAL	*48,167*	*48,840*

ONTARIO

	1988	1993
	%	%
SARNIA-LAMBTON		
PC	45.0	22.6
LIBERAL	31.8	47.6
NDP	22.2	6.2
REFORM	–	21.2
CHP	–	1.4
RHINO	1.0	–
INDEPENDENT	–	0.6
NLP	–	0.4
TOTAL	*42,861*	*42,743*
SAULT STE. MARIE		
PC	32.7	7.8
LIBERAL	32.0	53.0
NDP	35.3	22.2
REFORM	–	16.3
NAT	–	0.5
NLP	–	0.4
TOTAL	*41,385*	*40,459*
SIMCOE CENTRE		
PC	45.4	17.4
LIBERAL	33.3	37.6
NDP	16.2	2.8
REFORM	–	37.9
CHP	4.3	0.6
NAT	–	2.0
INDEPENDENT	–	1.2
CONFED RWP	0.8	–
NLP	–	0.5
ABOLITION	–	0.1
TOTAL	*51,802*	*67,122*
SIMCOE NORTH		
PC	44.1	23.1
LIBERAL	37.8	40.6
NDP	18.1	3.4
REFORM	–	30.7
NAT	–	1.5
NLP	–	0.5
ABOLITION	–	0.1
TOTAL	*49,597*	*56,923*

ONTARIO

	1988	1993
	%	%
STORMONT-DUNDAS		
PC	29.3	17.6
LIBERAL	46.0	63.4
NDP	12.7	2.7
REFORM	–	13.8
CONFED RWP	12.0	–
NAT	–	1.4
NLP	–	1.0
COMMONWEALTH	–	0.2
TOTAL	*42,853*	*42,714*
SUDBURY		
PC	22.0	8.7
LIBERAL	42.0	66.1
NDP	27.8	8.7
REFORM	–	13.7
CONFED RWP	8.0	–
NAT	–	1.2
NO AFFILIATION	–	0.7
NLP	–	0.5
INDEPENDENT	–	0.3
OTHER	0.2	0.2
TOTAL	*42,538*	*42,298*
THUNDER BAY-ATIKOKAN		
PC	31.2	8.2
LIBERAL	32.7	57.3
NDP	35.9	19.0
REFORM	–	15.6
COMMUNIST	0.2	–
TOTAL	*36,629*	*39,580*
THUNDER BAY-NIPIGON		
PC	25.6	9.6
LIBERAL	40.2	65.1
NDP	34.1	9.0
REFORM	–	14.9
NAT	–	1.2
COMMONWEALTH	–	0.2
TOTAL	*38,147*	*37,319*

ONTARIO

	1988	1993
	%	%
TIMISKAMING-FRENCH RIVER		
PC	36.6	15.5
LIBERAL	33.5	59.8
NDP	25.5	8.8
REFORM	–	13.3
CONFED RWP	3.9	–
NO AFFILIATION	–	1.7
NLP	–	1.0
INDEPENDENT	0.5	–
TOTAL	*30,712*	*29,198*
TIMMINS-CHAPLEAU		
PC	30.8	14.2
LIBERAL	32.5	55.5
NDP	36.6	26.7
NAT	–	1.4
NLP	–	1.3
INDEPENDENT	–	0.9
TOTAL	*31,751*	*30,800*
VICTORIA-HALIBURTON		
PC	46.8	22.2
LIBERAL	34.8	36.7
NDP	17.2	3.7
REFORM	–	28.5
INDEPENDENT	–	6.4
NAT	–	1.1
CHP	–	0.7
LIBERTARIAN	0.6	–
NLP	–	0.4
SC	0.4	0.4
CP	–	0.3
COMMONWEALTH	0.2	0.2
TOTAL	*47,568*	*55,832*
WATERLOO		
PC	45.1	24.2
LIBERAL	36.3	42.1
NDP	17.4	4.5
REFORM	–	25.5
CHP	–	1.5
LIBERTARIAN	1.1	0.8
NLP	–	0.7
INDEPENDENT	–	0.5
TOTAL	*59,745*	*62,332*

ONTARIO

	1988	1993
	%	%
WELLAND-ST. CATHARINES-THOROLD		
PC	34.6	11.6
LIBERAL	37.8	54.0
NDP	26.7	7.9
REFORM	–	25.2
NLP	–	0.7
GREEN	0.6	0.6
OTHER	0.3	0.1
TOTAL	*47,212*	*47,304*
WELLINGTON-GREY-DUFFERIN-SIMCOE		
PC	50.9	32.7
LIBERAL	30.2	35.8
NDP	15.1	3.5
REFORM	–	27.0
CHP	3.4	–
GREEN	–	1.0
LIBERTARIAN	0.3	–
TOTAL	*51,224*	*57,023*
WINDSOR-ST. CLAIR		
PC	19.4	11.1
LIBERAL	37.2	55.6
NDP	43.4	21.9
REFORM	–	10.1
GREEN	–	0.7
NLP	–	0.4
OTHER	–	0.3
TOTAL	*43,560*	*41,294*
WINDSOR WEST		
PC	14.3	4.6
LIBERAL	56.2	72.8
NDP	28.9	9.2
REFORM	–	11.4
GREEN	–	1.0
NLP	–	0.4
INDEPENDENT	–	0.4
NO AFFILIATION	0.3	–
COMMUNIST	0.3	–
M-L	–	0.3
ABOLITION	–	0.1
TOTAL	*42,398*	*38,954*

ONTARIO

	1988	1993
	%	%
YORK NORTH		
PC	42.6	13.7
LIBERAL	42.7	63.3
NDP	13.2	2.7
REFORM	–	17.8
LIBERTARIAN	1.5	0.8
NAT	–	1.1
NLP	–	0.6
TOTAL	*87,825*	*113,012*
YORK-SIMCOE		
PC	47.2	23.3
LIBERAL	35.1	38.9
NDP	13.2	2.5
REFORM	–	32.2
CHP	3.9	1.4
NAT	–	1.0
NLP	–	0.6
LIBERTARIAN	0.6	–
ABOLITION	–	0.1
TOTAL	*56,664*	*69,192*

ONTARIO (Metropolitan Toronto)

	1988	1993
	%	%
BEACHES-WOODBINE		
PC	29.2	10.0
LIBERAL	33.2	40.7
NDP	35.2	18.6
REFORM	–	15.8
NAT	–	2.6
LIBERTARIAN	0.8	–
INDEPENDENT	0.8	10.7
GREEN	0.7	0.8
NLP	–	0.6
M-L	–	0.2
OTHER	0.1	0.1
TOTAL	*44,813*	*43,306*
BROADVIEW-GREENWOOD		
PC	22.4	9.3
LIBERAL	38.9	61.1
NDP	36.0	14.0
REFORM	–	11.3
NAT	–	2.5
NLP	–	1.0
LIBERTARIAN	1.1	–
GREEN	0.7	–
RHINO	0.6	–
INDEPENDENT	–	0.4
OTHER	0.1	0.4
TOTAL	*40,643*	*38,575*
DAVENPORT		
PC	18.6	4.6
LIBERAL	58.9	73.8
NDP	18.8	9.2
REFORM	–	7.8
NAT	–	1.7
LIBERTARIAN	1.7	0.7
NLP	–	1.0
GREEN	–	0.9
RHINO	0.8	–
COMMUNIST	0.7	–
NO AFFILIATION	0.5	–
OTHER	–	0.3
TOTAL	*27,913*	*27,402*

ONTARIO (Metropolitan Toronto)

	1988	1993
	%	%
DON VALLEY EAST		
PC	44.7	23.2
LIBERAL	37.9	53.7
NDP	15.1	3.8
REFORM	–	16.9
LIBERTARIAN	1.3	0.6
NAT	–	1.0
NLP	–	0.5
INDEPENDENT	0.6	–
COMMUNIST	0.4	–
OTHER	–	0.3
TOTAL	*41,874*	*40,281*
DON VALLEY NORTH		
PC	43.4	19.3
LIBERAL	41.9	59.9
NDP	11.8	3.7
REFORM	–	16.1
INDEPENDENT	1.4	–
LIBERTARIAN	1.4	–
NLP	–	0.9
ABOLITION	–	0.2
TOTAL	*40,412*	*37,593*
DON VALLEY WEST		
PC	53.3	29.1
LIBERAL	36.8	49.8
NDP	8.3	2.7
REFORM	–	15.2
NAT	–	1.9
LIBERTARIAN	0.8	–
GREEN	–	0.6
INDEPENDENT	0.6	–
NLP	–	0.5
NO AFFILIATION	–	0.2
OTHER	0.2	0.1
TOTAL	*51,896*	*51,982*

ONTARIO (Metropolitan Toronto)

	1988	1993
	%	%
EGLINTON-LAWRENCE		
PC	30.9	10.7
LIBERAL	51.0	71.6
NDP	15.6	5.2
REFORM	–	10.9
LIBERTARIAN	1.3	–
COMMUNIST	0.5	–
NLP	–	1.0
NO AFFILIATION	0.3	–
COMMONWEALTH	0.3	–
M-L	–	0.4
ABOLITION	–	0.3
TOTAL	*40,078*	*39,980*
ETOBICOKE CENTRE		
PC	48.4	19.5
LIBERAL	40.5	54.4
NDP	9.6	2.2
REFORM	–	22.1
NAT	–	1.1
LIBERTARIAN	0.7	–
NLP	–	0.4
GREEN	0.4	–
COMMUNIST	0.2	–
ABOLITION	–	0.2
OTHER	0.2	0.2
TOTAL	*50,268*	*47,360*
ETOBICOKE-LAKESHORE		
PC	47.1	31.0
LIBERAL	–	42.1
NDP	43.4	5.0
REFORM	–	18.8
LIBERTARIAN	6.8	0.4
NAT	–	1.9
GREEN	1.5	–
NO AFFILIATION	0.9	–
NLP	–	0.6
COMMUNIST	0.3	–
M-L	–	0.2
ABOLITION	–	0.1
TOTAL	*45,217*	*46,211*

ONTARIO (Metropolitan Toronto)

	1988	1993
	%	%
ETOBICOKE-NORTH		
PC	34.6	10.8
LIBERAL	45.3	61.2
NDP	17.3	4.0
REFORM	–	20.8
CHP	1.7	–
NAT	–	1.4
LIBERTARIAN	0.9	0.7
NLP	–	0.6
M-L	–	0.2
NO AFFILIATION	0.1	0.2
TOTAL	*49,889*	*45,919*
PARKDALE-HIGHPARK		
PC	36.4	13.8
LIBERAL	43.5	54.4
NDP	17.7	9.4
REFORM	–	16.2
NAT	–	3.2
GREEN	–	1.1
LIBERTARIAN	1.0	0.6
NLP	–	0.9
RHINO	0.6	–
INDEPENDENT	0.5	0.3
COMMUNIST	0.4	–
ABOLITION	–	0.2
M-L	–	0.1
TOTAL	*45,136*	*41,131*
ROSEDALE		
PC	41.4	21.7
LIBERAL	41.2	50.0
NDP	15.1	10.7
REFORM	–	12.7
LIBERTARIAN	0.7	–
GREEN	0.7	0.9
RHINO	0.5	–
COMMUNIST	0.2	–
INDEPENDENT	0.2	0.4
NAT	–	2.0
NLP	–	1.5
OTHER	0.1	0.2
TOTAL	*54,887*	*55,437*

ONTARIO (Metropolitan Toronto)

	1988	1993
	%	%
ST.PAUL'S		
PC	47.5	24.4
LIBERAL	40.8	54.3
NDP	10.0	5.2
REFORM	–	11.2
NAT	–	2.5
GREEN	0.7	0.9
LIBERTARIAN	0.7	0.2
NLP	–	0.6
INDEPENDENT	–	0.5
COMMUNIST	0.3	–
M-L	–	0.2
TOTAL	*53,029*	*51,151*
SCARBOROUGH-AGINCOURT		
PC	42.4	21.3
LIBERAL	44.3	59.7
NDP	11.6	2.3
REFORM	–	14.6
LIBERTARIAN	0.7	–
NAT	–	0.7
INDEPENDENT	1.0	0.8
NLP	–	0.5
ABOLITION	–	0.2
TOTAL	*43,906*	*41,373*
SCARBOROUGH CENTRE		
PC	40.6	20.3
LIBERAL	39.7	52.5
NDP	18.9	4.0
REFORM	–	21.0
NAT	–	0.8
LIBERTARIAN	0.8	0.4
NLP	–	0.5
INDEPENDENT	–	0.5
OTHER	–	0.2
TOTAL	*42,440*	*40,158*

ONTARIO (Metropolitan Toronto)

	1988	1993
	%	%
SCARBOROUGH EAST		
PC	43.3	16.6
LIBERAL	39.0	50.5
NDP	16.4	3.8
REFORM	–	25.9
NAT	–	0.9
LIBERTARIAN	0.7	0.9
GREEN	0.5	0.6
NLP	–	0.5
COMMUNIST	0.2	–
ABOLITION	–	0.2
TOTAL	*41,929*	*39,704*
SCARBOROUGH-ROUGE RIVER		
PC	37.6	11.7
LIBERAL	47.1	66.1
NDP	13.6	2.8
REFORM	–	16.8
LIBERTARIAN	1.1	0.7
INDEPENDENT	–	0.7
NAT	–	0.6
GREEN	0.6	–
NLP	–	0.5
ABOLITION	–	0.1
TOTAL	*48,341*	*51,208*
SCARBOROUGH WEST		
PC	35.7	14.5
LIBERAL	36.8	54.4
NDP	26.4	7.1
REFORM	–	21.2
NAT	–	1.5
LIBERTARIAN	1.1	–
GREEN	–	0.7
NLP	–	0.5
ABOLITION	–	0.1
TOTAL	*41,745*	*39,190*

ONTARIO (Metropolitan Toronto)

	1988	1993
	%	%
TRINITY-SPADINA		
PC	21.3	8.1
LIBERAL	37.4	51.0
NDP	38.5	27.3
REFORM	–	7.8
NAT	–	2.3
GREEN	–	1.5
LIBERTARIAN	1.2	0.7
RHINO	1.1	–
NLP	–	1.0
INDEPENDENT	0.3	–
M-L	–	0.2
OTHER	0.1	0.1
TOTAL	*40,379*	*40,177*
WILLOWDALE		
PC	43.4	16.8
LIBERAL	47.0	61.3
NDP	8.8	3.6
REFORM	–	15.2
NAT	–	1.5
GREEN	–	0.6
NLP	–	0.5
RHINO	0.5	–
INDEPENDENT	–	0.4
LIBERTARIAN	0.3	–
ABOLITION	–	0.1
TOTAL	*51,510*	*46,720*
YORK CENTRE		
PC	22.4	6.9
LIBERAL	60.5	69.7
NDP	15.3	4.0
REFORM	–	5.5
INDEPENDENT	–	10.2
NAT	–	1.9
LIBERTARIAN	1.8	0.5
NLP	–	0.6
GREEN	–	0.5
M-L	–	0.2
ABOLITION	–	0.1
TOTAL	*41,243*	*38,951*

ONTARIO (Metropolitan Toronto)

	1988	1993
	%	%
YORK SOUTH-WESTON		
PC	21.6	7.0
LIBERAL	53.7	70.1
NDP	23.1	5.5
REFORM	–	14.8
LIBERTARIAN	0.8	0.8
NLP	–	0.8
COMMUNIST	0.5	–
COMWEALTH	0.3	0.2
ABOLITION	–	0.3
INDEPENDENT	–	0.4
M-L	–	0.2
TOTAL	*39,304*	*35,867*
YORK WEST		
PC	19.1	4.7
LIBERAL	59.6	79.8
NDP	18.2	3.4
REFORM	–	10.6
LIBERTARIAN	1.5	–
NO AFFILIATION	0.8	–
NLP	–	0.7
M-L	–	0.5
INDEPENDENT	0.4	–
COMMUNIST	0.4	–
ABOLITION	–	0.3
TOTAL	*33,424*	*31,813*

MANITOBA

	1988	1993
	%	%
BRANDON-SOURIS		
PC	46.7	22.4
LIBERAL	30.7	33.0
NDP	13.5	11.9
REFORM	4.2	30.4
CHP	3.6	0.9
CONFED RWP	0.9	–
NAT	–	0.9
NLP	–	0.3
INDEPENDENT	0.3	–
CP	0.3	0.2
TOTAL	*37,137*	*36,757*
CHURCHILL		
PC	20.5	10.3
LIBERAL	23.0	40.7
NDP	56.4	36.9
REFORM	–	9.6
NAT	–	2.5
TOTAL	*25,132*	*23,712*
DAUPHIN-SWAN RIVER		
PC	41.4	15.8
LIBERAL	19.6	31.7
NDP	33.4	22.2
REFORM	3.4	29.5
CONFED RWP	1.1	–
NO AFFILIATION	1.1	–
CP	–	0.8
TOTAL	*35,581*	*33,404*
LISGAR-MARQUETTE		
PC	53.9	24.0
LIBERAL	22.1	26.8
NDP	6.8	5.5
REFORM	8.7	41.0
CHP	5.6	1.2
CONFED RWP	1.5	–
RHINO	1.3	–
NAT	–	1.1
CP	–	0.4
TOTAL	*32,420*	*32,627*

MANITOBA

	1988	1993
	%	%
PORTAGE-INTERLAKE		
PC	38.7	19.7
LIBERAL	30.2	40.7
NDP	18.6	8.5
REFORM	11.8	27.5
NAT	–	2.6
LIBERTARIAN	0.7	0.3
NLP	–	0.5
CP	–	0.2
TOTAL	*34,343*	*35,661*
PROVENCHER		
PC	55.5	10.3
LIBERAL	32.5	44.0
NDP	7.3	5.0
REFORM	3.6	36.8
NAT	–	3.3
CONFED RWP	1.0	–
NLP	–	0.4
CP	–	0.2
TOTAL	*34,214*	*36,608*
ST.BONIFACE		
PC	33.5	7.2
LIBERAL	51.6	63.4
NDP	10.7	7.1
REFORM	2.7	16.8
NAT	–	4.2
LIBERTARIAN	0.9	–
CP	–	0.7
NLP	–	0.5
INDEPENDENT	0.4	–
NO AFFILIATION	0.1	–
M-L	–	0.1
TOTAL	*46,815*	*47,417*

MANITOBA

	1988	1993
	%	%
SELKIRK-RED RIVER		
PC	38.2	11.7
LIBERAL	26.7	32.9
NDP	29.8	25.7
REFORM	1.3	25.5
NAT	–	2.9
CHP	2.5	0.8
CONFED RWP	0.8	–
RHINO	0.7	–
NLP	–	0.4
CP	–	0.2
NO AFFILIATION	0.1	–
TOTAL	*46,687*	*48,677*
WINNIPEG NORTH		
PC	24.6	4.6
LIBERAL	38.3	51.3
NDP	34.1	31.7
REFORM	1.9	9.6
NAT	–	1.8
INDEPENDENT	0.5	0.3
COMMUNIST	0.5	–
NLP	–	0.5
CP	–	0.3
NO AFFILIATION	0.2	–
TOTAL	*42,750*	*43,340*
WINNIPEG NORTH CENTRE		
PC	18.3	4.7
LIBERAL	41.3	50.2
NDP	35.8	32.2
REFORM	1.4	8.2
LIBERTARIAN	1.4	–
NAT	–	3.3
INDEPENDENT	0.8	0.4
NLP	–	0.6
COMMUNIST	0.6	–
CP	–	0.4
NO AFFILIATION	0.3	–
TOTAL	*29,210*	*27,718*

MANITOBA

	1988	1993
	%	%
WINNIPEG-ST.JAMES		
PC	40.8	13.0
LIBERAL	44.8	55.0
NDP	10.2	6.6
REFORM	3.7	21.0
CONFED RWP	2.8	–
NAT	–	3.8
LIBERTARIAN	0.6	–
NLP	–	0.4
COMMUNIST	0.2	0.2
INDEPENDENT	–	0.2
M-L	–	0.1
CP	–	0.1
TOTAL	*41,693*	*39,332*
WINNIPEG SOUTH		
PC	45.9	12.3
LIBERAL	44.5	49.6
NDP	6.3	4.2
REFORM	2.9	12.6
LIBERTARIAN	0.5	–
NLP	–	0.4
INDEPENDENT	–	0.2
M-L	–	0.1
CP	–	0.1
TOTAL	*49,762*	*52,318*
WINNIPEG SOUTH CENTRE		
PC	28.6	9.3
LIBERAL	58.5	61.4
NDP	10.5	8.3
REFORM	1.8	12.6
NAT	–	7.4
NLP	–	0.5
LIBERTARIAN	0.3	0.2
NO AFFILIATION	0.3	0.2
CP	–	0.1
TOTAL	*42,140*	*42,127*

MANITOBA

	1988	1993
	%	%
WINNIPEG-TRANSCONA		
PC	25.6	5.1
LIBERAL	31.9	38.3
NDP	41.1	38.9
REFORM	–	14.1
NAT	–	2.2
INDEPENDENT	1.1	–
CHP	–	0.9
NO AFFILIATION	0.3	–
M-L	–	0.1
CP	–	0.1
TOTAL	*42,206*	*41,363*

SASKATCHEWAN

	1988	1993
	%	%
KINDERSLEY-LLOYDMINSTER		
PC	45.0	13.6
LIBERAL	15.0	27.8
NDP	33.4	16.4
REFORM	6.6	40.5
NAT	–	1.3
CP	–	0.4
TOTAL	*33,543*	*30,389*
MACKENZIE		
PC	36.9	12.8
LIBERAL	14.6	26.7
NDP	46.5	31.1
REFORM	2.0	27.1
CHP	–	2.0
CP	–	0.4
TOTAL	*34,257*	*30,309*
MOOSEJAW-LAKE CENTRE		
PC	41.1	12.2
LIBERAL	15.9	27.2
NDP	42.2	29.4
REFORM	–	30.3
CONFED RWP	0.8	–
NLP	–	0.5
CP	–	0.3
TOTAL	*37,691*	*34,387*
PRINCE ALBERT-CHURCHILL RIVER		
PC	25.9	4.7
LIBERAL	15.8	38.6
NDP	56.4	30.3
REFORM	1.6	19.0
INDEPENDENT	–	5.5
NAT	–	1.5
CP	–	0.4
CONFED RWP	0.3	–
TOTAL	*31,755*	*30,047*

SASKATCHEWAN

	1988	1993
	%	%
REGINA-LUMSDEN		
PC	26.5	7.4
LIBERAL	15.6	33.0
NDP	57.6	35.9
REFORM	–	21.3
NAT	–	2.2
NO AFFILIATION	0.4	–
CP	–	0.2
TOTAL	*37,506*	*35,925*
REGINA-QU'APPELLE		
PC	31.5	10.1
LIBERAL	14.6	31.1
NDP	54.0	34.4
REFORM	–	22.6
NAT	–	1.2
CP	–	0.6
TOTAL	*34,490*	*32,432*
REGINA-WASCANA		
PC	34.0	15.7
LIBERAL	32.8	44.2
NDP	32.9	21.2
REFORM	–	15.7
NAT	–	1.7
NLP	–	0.5
CHP	–	0.4
INDEPENDENT	–	0.4
COMMUNIST	0.2	–
LIBERTARIAN	0.1	–
CP	–	0.1
TOTAL	*45,113*	*44,233*
SASKATOON-CLARK'S CROSSING		
PC	35.8	10.4
LIBERAL	15.8	28.2
NDP	47.9	30.9
REFORM	–	28.0
NAT	–	1.6
GREEN	0.5	–
NLP	–	0.5
INDEPENDENT	–	0.3
CP	–	0.2
TOTAL	*41,077*	*39,760*

SASKATCHEWAN

	1988	1993
	%	%
SASKATOON-DUNDURN		
PC	31.8	8.9
LIBERAL	19.3	35.3
NDP	47.9	27.6
REFORM	–	24.7
NAT	–	1.9
CONFED RWP	0.9	–
INDEPENDENT	–	0.7
NLP	–	0.5
CP	–	0.2
NO AFFILIATION	–	0.1
COMMONWEALTH	0.1	–
TOTAL	*43,569*	*41,677*
SASKATOON-HUMBOLDT		
PC	36.1	9.4
LIBERAL	34.3	34.3
NDP	22.9	22.9
REFORM	–	29.8
NAT	–	2.4
NLP	–	0.7
INDEPENDENT	–	0.4
TOTAL	*40,938*	*37,386*
SOURIS-MOOSE MOUNTAIN		
PC	46.8	15.0
LIBERAL	19.0	32.4
NDP	32.4	16.5
REFORM	–	30.7
INDEPENDENT	–	2.7
NO AFFILIATION	–	2.0
CONFED RWP	1.7	–
CP	–	0.8
TOTAL	*36,723*	*33,660*
SWIFT CURRENT-MAPLE CREEK-ASSINIBOIA		
PC	44.1	15.6
LIBERAL	22.0	32.4
NDP	32.7	16.5
REFORM	–	34.9
CONFED RWP	1.3	–
NLP	–	0.7
TOTAL	*36,221*	*32,930*

SASKATCHEWAN

	1988	1993
	%	%
THE BATTLEFORDS-MEADOWLAKE		
PC	40.4	13.7
LIBERAL	15.1	23.5
NDP	42.5	31.2
REFORM	1.4	28.9
INDEPENDENT	–	2.0
CP	–	0.7
CONFED RWP	0.6	–
TOTAL	*34,130*	*31,289*
YORKTON-MELVILLE		
PC	34.6	8.7
LIBERAL	14.2	29.4
NDP	51.1	29.2
REFORM	–	32.7
TOTAL	*36,215*	*32,448*

ALBERTA

	1988	1993
	%	%
ATHABASKA		
PC	52.8	19.2
LIBERAL	12.3	24.6
NDP	27.3	7.6
REFORM	5.5	47.1
CHP	1.8	–
GREEN	–	1.0
NLP	–	0.6
COMMUNIST	0.3	–
TOTAL	*32,660*	*32,614*
BEAVER RIVER		
PC	44.3	12.6
LIBERAL	21.0	24.7
NDP	20.9	3.4
REFORM	13.4	58.0
NLP	–	1.0
CONFED RWP	1.0	–
INDEPENDENT	–	0.3
TOTAL	*31,077*	*30,559*
CALGARY CENTRE		
PC	53.7	14.9
LIBERAL	11.7	30.2
NDP	20.0	4.3
REFORM	12.4	45.1
NAT	–	3.5
GREEN	1.3	1.0
LIBERTARIAN	0.7	–
NLP	–	0.7
NO AFFILIATION	0.2	–
CP	–	0.2
M-L	–	0.2
TOTAL	*53,601*	*50,137*
CALGARY NORTH		
PC	57.7	15.4
LIBERAL	13.0	26.4
NDP	12.5	2.4
REFORM	16.2	52.5
NAT	–	2.0
GREEN	–	0.5
NLP	–	0.5
INDEPENDENT	–	0.4
LIBERTARIAN	0.4	–
CONFED RWP	0.2	–
TOTAL	*60,984*	*67,703*

ALBERTA

	1988	1993
	%	%
CALGARY NORTHEAST		
PC	54.7	11.3
LIBERAL	16.2	32.3
NDP	15.5	2.8
REFORM	13.0	44.4
NAT	–	1.8
INDEPENDENT	0.6	6.8
NLP	–	0.4
GREEN	–	0.3
TOTAL	*47,323*	*46,450*
CALGARY SOUTHEAST		
PC	62.7	20.1
LIBERAL	10.2	13.6
NDP	13.2	3.4
REFORM	12.8	59.9
NAT	–	2.0
NLP	–	0.8
RHINO	0.6	–
CP	–	0.3
NO AFFILIATION	0.3	–
CONFED RWP	0.1	–
COMMONWEALTH	0.1	–
TOTAL	*51,825*	*56,083*
CALGARY SOUTHWEST		
PC	65.2	18.6
LIBERAL	11.5	16.3
NDP	8.1	1.6
REFORM	13.4	61.2
NAT	–	1.3
INDEPENDENT	1.1	0.1
RHINO	0.6	–
GREEN	–	0.4
NLP	–	0.4
CONFED RWP	0.1	–
TOTAL	*61,993*	*48,003*

ALBERTA

	1988	1993
	%	%
CALGARY WEST		
PC	58.5	15.7
LIBERAL	12.6	26.5
NDP	11.6	2.1
REFORM	16.6	52.3
NAT	–	1.9
NLP	–	0.8
GREEN	–	0.6
LIBERTARIAN	0.4	–
CONFED RWP	0.3	–
CHP	–	0.2
TOTAL	*54,729*	*57,821*
CROWFOOT		
PC	53.7	18.0
LIBERAL	6.6	12.6
NDP	7.7	2.4
REFORM	32.1	66.0
NLP	–	0.7
INDEPENDENT	–	0.3
TOTAL	*35,540*	*35,785*
EDMONTON EAST		
PC	36.5	7.4
LIBERAL	18.2	33.0
NDP	38.2	22.1
REFORM	4.4	32.6
NAT	–	2.9
CHP	2.0	0.6
NLP	–	0.6
GREEN	–	0.5
COMMUNIST	0.3	–
NO AFFILIATION	0.1	0.1
CP	–	0.2
TOTAL	*39,403*	*36,171*

ALBERTA

	1988	1993
	%	%
EDMONTON NORTH		
PC	39.9	9.3
LIBERAL	19.5	39.5
NDP	32.9	6.9
REFORM	5.5	39.1
NAT	–	4.4
CHP	1.5	–
NLP	–	0.5
NO AFFILIATION	0.3	–
CP	–	0.2
INDEPENDENT	–	0.2
COMMUNIST	0.1	–
COMMONWEALTH	0.1	–
CONFED RWP	0.1	–
TOTAL	*45,257*	*49,499*
EDMONTON NORTHWEST		
PC	40.1	9.9
LIBERAL	17.3	35.8
NDP	34.0	4.8
REFORM	7.6	35.8
NAT	–	12.8
NLP	–	0.5
NO AFFILIATION	0.5	0.1
CONFED RWP	0.3	–
GREEN	–	0.3
COMMONWEALTH	0.2	–
TOTAL	*38,827*	*35,195*
EDMONTON SOUTHEAST		
PC	48.7	6.4
LIBERAL	20.8	46.2
NDP	18.9	4.0
REFORM	10.7	39.7
NAT	–	2.9
NLP	–	0.4
GREEN	0.4	0.3
CP	–	0.2
CONFED RWP	0.2	–
COMMONWEALTH	0.2	–
NO AFFILIATION	0.1	–
TOTAL	*48,481*	*50,108*

ALBERTA

	1988	1993
	%	%
EDMONTON SOUTHWEST		
PC	53.6	16.1
LIBERAL	19.2	33.5
NDP	15.9	3.7
REFORM	10.5	45.5
NLP	–	0.8
LIBERTARIAN	0.7	–
INDEPENDENT	–	0.5
CONFED RWP	0.2	–
M-L	–	0.1
TOTAL	*53,987*	*58,482*
EDMONTON-STRATHCONA		
PC	33.5	11.3
LIBERAL	17.9	38.5
NDP	25.3	5.1
REFORM	22.2	39.3
NAT	–	4.3
GREEN	0.3	0.6
NLP	–	0.6
RHINO	0.4	–
INDEPENDENT	0.2	0.2
CP	–	0.2
NO AFFILIATION	0.2	–
CONFED RWP	0.1	–
TOTAL	*54,054*	*49,682*
ELK ISLAND		
PC	48.2	12.5
LIBERAL	9.0	25.3
NDP	22.4	2.8
REFORM	20.1	56.0
NAT	–	2.7
NLP	–	0.5
CP	–	0.3
CONFED RWP	0.3	–
TOTAL	*40,360*	*45,906*
LETHBRIDGE		
PC	58.4	15.2
LIBERAL	18.6	25.5
NDP	9.8	2.8
REFORM	6.8	52.6
CHP	6.4	–
NAT	–	3.4
NLP	–	0.5
TOTAL	*45,790*	*46,608*

ALBERTA

	1988	1993
	%	%
MACLEOD		
PC	50.5	17.3
LIBERAL	9.4	16.5
NDP	8.8	1.9
REFORM	31.2	63.3
GREEN	–	0.6
NLP	–	0.5
COMMONWEALTH	0.2	–
TOTAL	*33,630*	*37,661*
MEDICINE HAT		
PC	59.2	16.9
LIBERAL	12.1	20.9
NDP	15.2	4.5
REFORM	10.8	54.7
CHP	2.7	2.4
CP	–	0.6
TOTAL	*42,520*	*41,011*
PEACE RIVER		
PC	54.3	14.4
LIBERAL	13.4	15.5
NDP	17.2	5.5
REFORM	15.2	60.2
NAT	–	3.9
NLP	–	0.6
TOTAL	*43,035*	*42,775*
RED DEER		
PC	52.7	16.3
LIBERAL	10.4	13.5
NDP	12.6	2.7
REFORM	20.8	64.8
CHP	2.9	–
NAT	–	2.2
CONFED RWP	0.6	–
NLP	–	0.6
TOTAL	*45,440*	*49,180*

ALBERTA

	1988	1993
	%	%
ST.ALBERT		
PC	46.7	12.0
LIBERAL	16.7	28.3
NDP	19.6	2.9
REFORM	13.9	50.9
NAT	–	4.5
CHP	2.1	0.6
NLP	–	0.5
RHINO	0.5	–
NO AFFILIATION	0.3	0.2
CONFED RWP	0.1	–
TOTAL	*42,695*	*49,003*
VEGREVILLE		
PC	65.3	22.7
LIBERAL	7.8	15.6
NDP	16.1	3.3
REFORM	9.9	54.7
NAT	–	1.6
INDEPENDENT	0.4	1.3
NLP	–	0.5
NO AFFILIATION	0.5	0.4
CONFED RWP	0.1	–
TOTAL	*37,596*	*36,047*
WETASKIWIN		
PC	50.2	14.8
LIBERAL	8.4	16.7
NDP	14.3	3.6
REFORM	18.5	63.4
CHP	7.7	–
CP	–	0.8
CONFED RWP	0.6	–
NLP	–	0.7
NO AFFILIATION	0.3	–
TOTAL	*40,022*	*41,332*

ALBERTA

	1988	1993
	%	%
WILDROSE		
PC	48.2	15.5
LIBERAL	10.1	14.2
NDP	7.8	2.2
REFORM	33.4	63.8
NAT	–	1.7
INDEPENDENT	–	1.2
GREEN	–	0.9
CONFED RWP	0.5	–
NO AFFILIATION	–	0.2
TOTAL	*41,621*	*48,609*
YELLOWHEAD		
PC	44.6	14.0
LIBERAL	10.0	21.7
NDP	15.4	4.4
REFORM	27.8	55.0
NAT	–	2.8
CHP	1.8	1.1
NLP	–	0.6
INDEPENDENT	0.2	0.5
CONFED RWP	0.2	–
TOTAL	*40,034*	*41,405*

BRITISH COLUMBIA

	1988	1993
	%	%
BURNABY-KINGSWAY		
PC	30.0	10.0
LIBERAL	22.2	26.3
NDP	43.2	34.2
REFORM	2.7	25.0
NAT	–	2.8
LIBERTARIAN	1.0	0.7
NLP	–	0.5
GREEN	0.4	–
INDEPENDENT	0.5	0.2
COMMONWEALTH	–	0.2
NO AFFILIATION	–	0.1
M-L	–	0.1
TOTAL	*58,193*	*53,962*
CAPILANO-HOWE SOUND		
PC	47.0	17.7
LIBERAL	29.6	31.8
NDP	14.2	3.3
REFORM	8.1	42.0
NAT	–	3.2
GREEN	–	1.0
RHINO	0.7	–
NLP	–	0.6
INDEPENDENT	–	0.2
LIBERTARIAN	0.4	0.2
TOTAL	*43,217*	*45,910*
CARIBOO-CHILCOTIN		
PC	36.7	22.3
LIBERAL	25.1	26.8
NDP	35.8	10.4
REFORM	1.7	36.4
RHINO	0.7	–
NAT	–	1.7
CP	–	1.0
NLP	–	0.7
GREEN	–	0.7
TOTAL	*31,421*	*31,587*

BRITISH COLUMBIA

	1988	1993
	%	%
COMOX-ALBERNI		
PC	28.3	9.7
LIBERAL	16.6	20.4
NDP	42.8	16.6
REFORM	9.9	44.2
NAT	–	5.8
GREEN	1.1	2.3
CHP	1.0	–
COMMUNIST	0.3	–
NLP	–	0.5
INDEPENDENT	–	0.5
CP	–	0.1
TOTAL	*49,331*	*56,603*
DELTA		
PC	44.3	21.0
LIBERAL	19.9	30.5
NDP	29.3	5.7
REFORM	4.5	38.2
CHP	1.6	0.7
NAT	–	2.6
NLP	–	0.4
GREEN	–	0.4
INDEPENDENT	0.3	0.2
LIBERTARIAN	0.2	–
NO AFFILIATION	–	0.2
TOTAL	*44,640*	*47,872*
ESQUIMALT-JUAN-DE-FUCA		
PC	25.1	9.9
LIBERAL	12.0	21.5
NDP	50.9	27.2
REFORM	10.4	35.3
GREEN	1.0	–
NAT	–	4.8
NLP	–	0.9
INDEPENDENT	0.3	–
NO AFFILIATION	0.2	–
CONFED RWP	0.1	–
CP	–	0.2
TOTAL	*44,469*	*46,339*

BRITISH COLUMBIA

	1988	1993
	%	%
FRASER VALLEY EAST		
PC	38.8	13.0
LIBERAL	21.2	30.8
NDP	28.0	5.3
REFORM	3.1	45.9
CHP	8.3	2.3
NAT	–	1.7
RHINO	0.6	–
GREEN	–	0.5
NLP	–	0.4
CP	–	0.1
TOTAL	*42,874*	*51,172*
FRASER VALLEY WEST		
PC	45.8	11.4
LIBERAL	19.6	29.5
NDP	25.6	5.2
REFORM	3.5	49.1
CHP	4.7	1.7
NAT	–	2.1
LIBERTARIAN	0.7	0.4
NLP	–	0.5
INDEPENDENT	–	0.1
TOTAL	*51,412*	*62,463*
KAMLOOPS		
PC	32.4	8.7
LIBERAL	13.2	24.3
NDP	52.3	36.3
REFORM	1.1	26.8
NAT	–	3.2
GREEN	0.6	–
NLP	–	0.3
LIBERTARIAN	–	0.3
COMMUNIST	0.2	–
NO AFFILIATION	0.2	0.1
CP	–	0.1
TOTAL	*41,155*	*44,270*

BRITISH COLUMBIA

	1988	1993
	%	%
KOOTENAY EAST		
PC	38.5	10.9
LIBERAL	12.1	22.5
NDP	43.2	14.5
REFORM	4.1	48.4
CHP	2.2	0.6
NAT	–	1.7
GREEN	–	0.8
NLP	–	0.5
CP	–	0.2
TOTAL	*34,487*	*35,210*
KOOTENAY WEST-REVELSTOKE		
PC	36.0	8.9
LIBERAL	15.6	30.4
NDP	46.5	15.7
REFORM	–	32.5
NAT	–	8.5
GREEN	1.9	2.3
CHP	–	1.0
NLP	–	0.6
CP	–	0.2
TOTAL	*35,201*	*34,960*
MISSION-COQUITLAM		
PC	–	11.7
LIBERAL	–	26.9
NDP	–	16.8
REFORM	–	36.7
NAT	–	5.0
CHP	–	0.9
GREEN	–	0.7
NLP	–	0.5
LIBERTARIAN	–	0.4
INDEPENDENT	–	0.3
NO AFFILIATION	–	0.1
TOTAL	–	*54,936*

BRITISH COLUMBIA

	1988	1993
	%	%
NANAIMO-COWICHAN		
PC	9.6	9.1
LIBERAL	34.0	22.5
NDP	49.3	19.6
REFORM	–	41.2
NAT	–	5.6
GREEN	0.9	–
NLP	–	0.8
LIBERTARIAN	–	0.4
INDEPENDENT	–	0.6
COMMUNIST	0.3	–
CP	–	0.2
TOTAL	*55,377*	*61,472*
NEW WESTMINSTER-BURNABY		
PC	31.5	11.6
LIBERAL	19.3	27.9
NDP	43.6	26.1
REFORM	3.0	29.3
NAT	–	3.2
SC	1.3	–
NLP	–	0.7
GREEN	0.6	0.6
LIBERTARIAN	0.6	0.5
COMMUNIST	0.2	–
INDEPENDENT	–	0.1
COMMONWEALTH	–	0.1
TOTAL	*57,157*	*55,438*
NORTH ISLAND-POWELL RIVER		
PC	24.4	7.9
LIBERAL	16.2	25.6
NDP	51.8	16.8
REFORM	1.8	39.3
NAT	–	7.4
CHP	3.5	–
GREEN	1.2	2.2
NLP	–	0.6
RHINO	0.7	–
CP	–	0.3
COMMUNIST	0.3	–
TOTAL	*45,188*	*46,477*

BRITISH COLUMBIA

	1988	1993
	%	%
NORTH VANCOUVER		
PC	37.6	15.4
LIBERAL	27.2	31.5
NDP	23.9	6.4
REFORM	8.9	40.0
NAT	–	4.4
GREEN	0.9	1.0
NLP	–	0.9
RHINO	0.7	–
LIBERTARIAN	0.5	0.2
COMMUNIST	0.2	–
NO AFFILIATION	0.2	0.3
TOTAL	*49,186*	*50,574*
OKANAGAN CENTRE		
PC	37.3	19.2
LIBERAL	17.1	23.8
NDP	30.2	6.9
REFORM	14.5	46.6
NAT	–	1.6
GREEN	0.9	1.0
NLP	–	0.3
CP	–	0.3
NO AFFILIATION	–	0.2
TOTAL	*52,302*	*65,854*
OKANAGAN-SHUSWAP		
PC	36.2	9.9
LIBERAL	15.9	18.4
NDP	43.5	23.7
REFORM	3.1	42.4
NAT	–	4.1
GREEN	1.2	0.6
NLP	–	0.3
CP	–	0.2
NO AFFILIATION	0.2	0.4
TOTAL	*42,551*	*49,322*

BRITISH COLUMBIA

	1988	1993
	%	%
OKANAGAN-SIMILKAMEEN-MERRITT		
PC	35.5	12.7
LIBERAL	17.4	24.5
NDP	38.6	14.8
REFORM	5.8	43.6
NAT	–	2.4
GREEN	1.6	1.0
SC	1.0	–
NLP	–	0.6
CP	–	0.5
TOTAL	*43,195*	*48,522*
PORT MOODY-COQUITLAM		
PC	36.2	12.8
LIBERAL	15.5	27.8
NDP	44.2	21.2
REFORM	3.0	34.0
NAT	–	2.6
GREEN	0.7	0.6
NLP	–	0.6
LIBERTARIAN	0.5	0.4
INDEPENDENT	–	0.1
COMMONWEALTH	–	0.1
TOTAL	*53,983*	*59,625*
PRINCE GEORGE- **BULKLEY VALLEY**		
PC	31.7	12.2
LIBERAL	24.9	22.3
NDP	38.2	23.3
REFORM	1.6	40.3
CHP	3.2	1.0
GREEN	–	0.6
NLP	–	0.5
INDEPENDENT	0.5	–
TOTAL	*37,335*	*36,623*

BRITISH COLUMBIA

	1988	1993
	%	%
PRINCE GEORGE-PEACE RIVER		
PC	39.6	11.3
LIBERAL	11.9	19.5
NDP	33.3	11.0
REFORM	14.5	56.4
NLP	–	0.8
INDEPENDENT	0.5	0.2
CHP	–	0.5
CONFED RWP	0.3	–
COMMONWEALTH	–	0.3
TOTAL	*35,115*	*36,843*
RICHMOND		
PC	44.0	19.1
LIBERAL	22.8	37.1
NDP	27.2	6.3
REFORM	3.3	30.9
NAT	–	3.9
CHP	1.2	0.5
LIBERTARIAN	0.8	0.3
GREEN	0.4	0.6
NLP	–	0.6
NO AFFILIATION	–	0.6
INDEPENDENT	–	0.3
COMMUNIST	0.2	–
TOTAL	*58,025*	*57,912*
SAANICH-GULF ISLANDS		
PC	33.5	11.6
LIBERAL	17.6	25.9
NDP	35.4	18.9
REFORM	12.5	37.2
NAT	–	5.4
NLP	–	0.7
LIBERTARIAN	0.3	–
INDEPENDENT	0.6	0.3
COMMUNIST	0.1	0.1
CP	–	0.1
TOTAL	*65,447*	*71,169*

BRITISH COLUMBIA

	1988	1993
	%	%
SKEENA		
PC	28.3	6.8
LIBERAL	14.6	24.0
NDP	52.7	20.7
REFORM	0.9	37.9
NAT	–	7.7
CHP	3.6	2.0
GREEN	–	0.6
NLP	–	0.5
TOTAL	*31,910*	*31,647*
SURREY NORTH		
PC	32.8	13.8
LIBERAL	24.9	26.4
NDP	37.0	17.1
REFORM	2.3	36.9
NAT	–	3.3
CHP	1.6	1.5
NLP	–	0.6
LIBERTARIAN	0.5	–
RHINO	0.4	–
GREEN	0.3	–
NO AFFILIATION	0.2	0.2
COMMONWEALTH	–	0.1
TOTAL	*53,881*	*60,612*
SURREY-WHITEROCK-SOUTH LANGLEY		
PC	43.5	12.2
LIBERAL	23.5	33.8
NDP	24.3	4.2
REFORM	6.3	44.1
NAT	–	3.3
CHP	1.4	1.2
GREEN	0.4	0.6
NLP	–	0.3
LIBERTARIAN	0.2	–
NO AFFILIATION	0.2	0.1
COMMUNIST	0.2	–
M-L	–	0.1
CP	–	0.1
COMMONWEALTH	–	0.1
TOTAL	*60,531*	*72,991*

BRITISH COLUMBIA

	1988	1993
	%	%
VANCOUVER CENTRE		
PC	37.2	25.2
LIBERAL	22.8	31.1
NDP	36.8	15.2
REFORM	1.4	17.4
NAT	–	8.0
NLP	–	1.0
GREEN	0.8	1.0
RHINO	0.4	–
CHP	–	0.4
LIBERTARIAN	0.2	0.4
INDEPENDENT	0.2	0.2
NO AFFILIATION	0.1	0.2
TOTAL	*63,409*	*64,629*
VANCOUVER EAST		
PC	15.6	8.8
LIBERAL	29.8	36.0
NDP	51.1	31.2
REFORM	–	11.8
NAT	–	6.1
LIBERTARIAN	0.7	2.0
GREEN	1.4	1.4
NLP	–	1.0
RHINO	0.7	–
COMMUNIST	0.5	–
M-L	–	0.2
NO AFFILIATION	0.2	1.6
TOTAL	*39,201*	*39,565*
VANCOUVER QUADRA		
PC	30.5	17.4
LIBERAL	44.0	39.5
NDP	21.4	10.8
REFORM	2.0	22.2
NAT	–	6.5
RHINO	1.4	–
GREEN	–	1.2
LIBERTARIAN	0.2	0.8
NLP	–	0.7
CHP	–	0.4
M-L	–	0.2
INDEPENDENT	–	0.2
COMMONWEALTH	0.0	0.1
NO AFFILIATION	0.1	0.2
TOTAL	*54,654*	*51,611*

BRITISH COLUMBIA

	1988	1993
	%	%
VANCOUVER SOUTH		
PC	42.2	23.5
LIBERAL	28.8	35.6
NDP	23.7	7.5
REFORM	2.1	25.4
NAT	–	4.4
LIBERTARIAN	1.9	1.2
GREEN	0.7	0.9
NLP	–	0.6
INDEPENDENT	–	0.6
RHINO	0.3	–
M-L	–	0.1
COMMUNIST	0.1	–
NO AFFILIATION	0.1	0.2
TOTAL	*50,294*	*48,337*
VICTORIA		
PC	29.9	10.4
LIBERAL	21.4	37.2
NDP	38.0	14.1
REFORM	8.4	27.6
NAT	–	7.0
GREEN	1.8	2.0
NLP	–	0.9
RHINO	0.4	–
LIBERTARIAN	–	0.3
INDEPENDENT	0.2	0.2
CP	–	0.1
NO AFFILIATION	–	0.2
TOTAL	*58,999*	*57,937*

NORTHWEST TERRITORIES

	1988	1993
	%	%
NUNATSIAQ		
PC	22.9	20.6
LIBERAL	39.9	69.8
NDP	33.2	9.7
INDEPENDENT	4.0	–
TOTAL	*8,403*	*9,579*
WESTERN ARCTIC		
PC	28.6	13.3
LIBERAL	42.4	62.5
NDP	25.1	6.3
REFORM	–	14.1
INDEPENDENT	3.9	–
GREEN	–	2.3
NLP	–	1.5
TOTAL	*12,779*	*14,194*

YUKON TERRITORY

	1988	1993
	%	%
YUKON		
PC	35.3	17.8
LIBERAL	11.3	23.3
NDP	51.4	43.3
REFORM	–	13.1
CHP	2.0	0.4
NAT	–	2.1
TOTAL	*12,823*	*14,425*